PANTANAL
WILDLIFE

A VISITOR'S GUIDE TO
SOUTH AMERICA'S GREAT WETLAND

JAMES LOWEN

T0343683

www.bradtguides.com

Bradt Guides Ltd, UK
The Globe Pequot Press Inc, USA

Bradt GUIDES
TRAVEL TAKEN SERIOUSLY

Second edition published March 2025
First published 2010
Bradt Travel Guides Ltd
31a High Street, Chesham, Buckinghamshire, HP5 1BW, England
www.bradtguides.com
Print edition published in the USA by The Globe Pequot Press Inc,
PO Box 480, Guilford, Connecticut 06437-0480

Text copyright © 2025 James Lowen
Maps copyright © 2025 Bradt Travel Guides Ltd
Photographs copyright © individual photographers (see below)
Project manager: James Lowen
Cover research and design: Pepi Bluck, Perfect Picture

ISBN: 978 1 78477 713 5

British Library Cataloguing in Publication Data
A catalogue record for this book is available from the British Library

Photographs
Pousada Aguapé (PA); Elspeth Beidas & Matt Coates; André Bittar/Fazenda Barranco Alto (AB/
FBA); Jo Dale (JD); Kit Day/w kitday.smugmug.com (KD); Matt Eade (ME); Stefan Grol/Fazenda
Barranco Alto (SG/FBA); Rob Jansen/w robjansenphotography.com (RJ); Aymara Lodge (AL);
James Lowen/w jameslowen.com (JL); Lourdes Matazo/Guyra Paraguay (LM/GP); Luiz Felipe
Mendes/Pousada Aguapé (LFM/PA); Yoav Perlman/w yoavperlman.com (YP); Ashley Saunders/
Oriole Birding (AS/OB); Chris Townend/Wise Birding (CT/WB); Howard Vaughan/Blue Eyed
Birder (HV/BEB). *Dreamstime* (D): Vladimir Cech/Dreamstime (VC/D); David Havel/Dreamstime
(DH/D); Ondřej Prosický/Dreamstime (OP/D). *Shutterstock* (SS): Gudkov Andrey (GA/SS);
Vinicius Bacarin (VB/SS); Uwe Bergwitz (UB/SS); Bildargentur Zoonar GmbH (BZG/SS); Henk
Bogaard (HB/SS); Reto Buehler (RB/SS); Cavan-Images (CI/SS); Danita Delimont (DD/SS); Joel
Delpanque (JD/SS); André Dib (AD/SS); Ilan Ejzykowicz (IE/SS); Elléon (E/SS); Foto 4440 (F/SS);
Ao.Garcia (AG/SS); Jay Gao (JG/SS); Diego Grandi (DG/SS); Gabriel Gabino/Shutterstock (GG/SS);
Gilbert S. Grant (GSG/SS); R A U H A U S Horizons/Shutterstock (RH/SS); Laurent Jamin (LJ/SS);
GTW (GTW/SS); Rob Jansen (RJ/SS); RHJPhotos (RHJP/SS); Rini Kools (RK/SS); Hugh Lansdown
(HL/SS); Lucas Leuzinger (LL/SS); Mariamalaya (MM/SS); Celso Margraf (CM/SS); Rafael Martos
Martins (RMM/SS); Martin Mecnarowski (MMe/SS); Leonardo Mercon (LM/SS); Geraldo Morais
(GM/SS); NoDrama_llama (N/SS); Dan Olsen (DO/SS); Paralaxis/Shutterstock (P/SS); Ondřej
Prosický/Shutterstock (OP/SS); Rogerio Rondon (RR/SS); Galina Savina (GSa/SS); Giedrius
Stakauskas (GS/SS); Roberto Tetsuo Okamura (RTO/SS); Sergey Uryadnikov (SU/SS).

Author photo by Sharon Lowen

Front cover jaguar (Bildargentur Zoonar GmbH/Alamy)
Back cover (*clockwise from right*) hyacinth macaw (OP/SS); yacaré caiman (OP/D);
giant anteater (OP/SS)
Title page (*clockwise from right*) hyacinth macaw (JL); giant otter (JL); yacaré caiman (UB/SS)

Maps
Malcolm Barnes, amended by David McCutcheon
Source material kindly supplied by ITMB, Conservation International and Guyra Paraguay

Typeset by Ian Spick, Bradt Travel Guides and by Chris Lane, Artinfusion
Digital conversion by www.dataworks.co.in
Production managed by Gutenberg Press; printed in Malta

Paper used for this product comes from sustainably managed
forests, and recycled and controlled sources.

CONTENTS

Author	iv
Acknowledgments	iv
Introduction	**2**
Introduction 2, About this book 4, What's in a name? 5	
The Pantanal environment	**7**
Geography and geology 8, Climate and seasonality 9, The human connection 10, Conservation 13, Habitats 14	
Mammals	**19**
Anteaters and armadillos 20, Primates 24, Carnivores 27, Ungulates 39, Bats 43, Rodents and rabbits 46, Marsupials 49	
Birds	**51**
Ground birds 52, Waterbirds 54, Raptors 62, Guans 65, Parrots and their allies 66, Near-passerines 69, Passerines 78	
Reptiles, amphibians and fish	**89**
Reptiles 90, Amphibians 99, Fish 102	
Invertebrates	**105**
Insects 106, Arachnids 114, Centipedes, snails and crustaceans 117	
Where to go	**119**
Mato Grosso (Brazil) 122, Mato Grosso do Sul (Brazil) 143, Paraguay 154, Bolivia 158	
Top tips	**161**
Finding wildlife 162, Practicalities 170, Wildlife photography 172	
Further information	**173**
Index	**175**

AUTHOR

James Lowen (w jameslowen.com) is an award-winning wildlife and travel writer. He has spent five years in Latin America – living, exploring, surveying and leading nature tours. He is the longstanding editor of *Neotropical Birding* magazine and deputy editor of the ornithological journal *Cotinga*, both of which are dedicated to South and Central America. James's four books for Bradt include two winners of Travel Guidebook of the Year awards (*A Summer of British Wildlife* and *52 European Wildlife Weekends*); his 11 other books include *Much Ado About Mothing*, a travel narrative longlisted for the 2022 James Cropper Wainwright Prize. He leads tours for Wildlife Travel (see advert, page 182).

ACKNOWLEDGMENTS

The many people who helped with the first edition of this book are credited in that guide: I extend my heartfelt gratitude again to them here. For this second version, in addition to owners and managers at a number of Pantanal lodges and tour companies, I am particularly grateful to the following for kindly providing information, responding to my queries, checking draft text or serving as sounding boards: Giuliano Bernardon (Aymara Lodge/Birding Pantanal); Elspeth Beidas; David Bromham (Abercrombie & Kent); Rob Clay; Jo Dale; Kit Day (w kitday.smugmug. com); Matt Eade; Peter Gasson; Jon Hall (w mammalwatching.com); Gill Hollamby; Ashley Howe; Rebeca Irala Melgarejo; Rob Jansen (w robjansenphotography.com); Nick McPhee (Nick's Adventures Bolivia); Andrew Mercer (w pantanalescapes. com); Yoav Perlman (w yoavperlman.com); Ashley Saunders (Oriole Birding); Tom Schulenberg; Rob Siegel (Stanford University); Paul Smith (Fauna Paraguay); Fernando Tortaro (Panthera); Chris Townend (Wise Birding); Howard Vaughan (Blue Eyed Birder); David Walker; Mike Watson (Wild Images) and Rodrigo Zárate (Guyra Paraguay).

I also thank, generically, the many authors of Pantanal trip reports covering birds, mammals and reptiles. I am grateful to my photographer friends listed in the photographic credits opposite the Contents page, plus individuals and lodges who generously offered photographs that were not, in the end, used. Finally, and as ever, the Bradt Travel Guides team was magnificent, so I thank: Pepi Bluck (Perfect Picture); Hugh Brune; Sue Cooper; David McCutcheon; Anna Moores; Claire Strange; Ian Spick and Marianne Taylor.

N

Bradt

0 ————————————————— 160km

BRAZIL
BOLIVIA The Pantanal
PARAGUAY

SOUTH
AMERICA

Cuiabá

Cáceres

Poconé

Rondonópolis

MATO GROSSO

Porto Jofre

Transpantaneira

BOLIVIA

PANTANAL

BRAZIL

MATO GROSSO DO SUL

Puerto Suárez

Corumbá

Puerto Quijarro

Bahía Negra

Miranda

Aquidauana

Campo
Grande

PARAGUAY

KEY to maps on pages 120, 143 & 154

Pantanal

National boundary — · — · —

State boundary — — — — —

Road

Airport (international) ✈

Urban Area

Town ●

Village ○

Lodge ■

KEY for this map

Approximate area
of the Pantanal

Major road

Major urban area ●

National boundary — · — · —

State boundary — — — — —

INTRODUCTION

In some ways, the Pantanal is to the Americas what the Serengeti is to Africa. The world's largest wetland showcases some of the most breathtaking gatherings of birds, reptiles and mammals that you could ever hope to see. As the dry season peaks, the density of wildlife can challenge credulity, with the smallest of lakes often so crowded with fur, feather and scale that you'll be pushed to spot unoccupied water. And all of this at mesmerisingly close range. The Pantanal, in short, is a wildlife-watcher's paradise.

And it's not just any old bird or mammal that joins the throng. The aquatic heart of South America oozes quality as well as quantity. Record breakers of the natural world stalk, swim, slither, soar and skulk across the region. Every visitor wants to spot the largest cat in the New World (the jaguar), which is very reliably seen in fortunate parts of the Pantanal. Here this hulking feline feasts on an abundance of the world's largest rodent (the pig-sized greater capybara) and the world's largest gathering of crocodilians (yacaré caiman). Also on display are the world's largest parrot (the electric-blue hyacinth macaw), the continent's heaviest land mammal (lowland tapir) and one of the ten heftiest snakes on the planet (yellow anaconda).

This swarm of superlatives is matched by diversity. At least 475 species of bird and 150 mammals have been recorded on the Pantanal plains, along with 80 reptiles,

The Pantanal is the best place in the world to watch jaguars. (AS/OB)

50 amphibians and perhaps 325 fish. And the voyages of biological discovery are far from over. In a famous survey of Pantanal fish, one-quarter of the 200 species found were new to science. Similarly, botanists surmise that the current ballpark of 1,700 plant species likely represents half of the actual total.

Whatever your particular wildlife interest, there is masses to see. Much is out in the open – almost within touching distance and easily within reach of a camera. And the longer you stay, the deeper you can delve. If you like birds, seek out the chestnut-bellied guan – a pheasant-like creature on the road to extinction that occurs almost exclusively within the northern Pantanal. If smaller flying creatures are your thing, look for a butterfly with wings bearing the eyes of an owl, the Illioneus giant owl, or drop to your knees and get a buzz from the emergence of thousands of winged termites at the tip of your nose.

If mammals tickle your fancy, look to the trees for five species of monkey or wander grasslands for two types of anteater and several armadillos. And if it's life in cold blood that excites, try to keep up with fleet-footed spiny lizards then catch your breath by enjoying the orchestrations of the nightly frog chorus.

This fantastic diversity derives from the region's position as a biogeographical melting pot. The Pantanal laps up influences as diverse as Amazonia, Atlantic forest, Chaco and Cerrado. It then swirls them together with highly seasonal rainfall to create a perpetually dynamic environment. Water – its presence or absence, its ebb or flow – is fundamental to all Pantanal life. After the summer rains, rivers burst their banks, spreading nutrient-bearing liquid over parched grasslands. A giant sponge, the Pantanal holds water for months, gradually releasing it towards the Atlantic Ocean. If the Amazon forests provide South America's lungs, then the Pantanal is the continent's kidneys. As waters subside and winter materialises, so a once abundant commodity becomes a prized resource. Fish become trapped in shrinking lakes, attracting an abundance of sharp-eyed and long-billed storks, ibises, herons and egrets. Capybaras try to keep cool by immersing themselves in any semblance of muddy puddle. Caimans jostle for space in the shallows to avoid dehydration. The dry season is show time and we visitors are the Pantanal's privileged audience.

As recently as the 1960s, Pantanal wildlife was cherished in a different way: as a resource to be exploited. Poachers killed vast numbers of otters and ocelots to provide fur for fashion. Egrets and caimans suffered the same fate for their feathers and skins. Trappers plundered populations of hyacinth macaws and other parrots to supply the cage-bird trade with its living trophies, forlornly incarcerated. There was money in wildlife – as long as it could be removed from the Pantanal and sold on national and international markets.

Against this background, it is remarkable that wildlife-based tourism ever took off. But taken off it has. Unknown in the Pantanal until the 1980s, wildlife-watching has become a very big business. New lodges open regularly, wildlife-viewing facilities constantly improve and access becomes easier. Increasingly, landowners recognise that wildlife is an asset to maintain not exploit. One 2017 study showed that jaguar-watching alone generated $6.8 million annual income in just one part of the Pantanal. We have finally learnt to place value on the wild and living animal, rather than the captive or dead one. Our reward for this realisation? The finest wildlife experience in South America.

Yacaré caimans abound in the Pantanal's wetlands. (OP/SS)

ABOUT THIS BOOK

This book aims to be a handy, wide-ranging guide for wildlife-watchers visiting the Pantanal (and the Pantanal alone: it does not cover nearby areas often visited together, such as Bonito, Chapada dos Guimarães or the Amazon). It is designed to address visitors' principal needs: to understand where they should go and what they are seeing. It has no pretensions to be a specialised field guide that enables you to identify every animal you encounter. Instead, this guidebook looks across the wildlife spectrum, aiming to sate your curiosity about a critter you have just seen – or want to see – without filling your luggage with weighty tomes. Chapters

The enormous, lofty nest of a pair of jabirus is a quintessential Pantanal sight. (UB/SS)

cover the most visible wildlife groups: *Mammals* (page 19); *Birds* (page 51); *Reptiles, amphibians and fish* (page 89); and *Invertebrates* (page 105). Engaging vignettes encompass ecology, behaviour and conservation as well as identification, bringing to life the Pantanal's characteristic and charismatic creatures.

Shorter chapters contextualise the wildlife experience. The *Pantanal environment* (page 7) explains what makes the Pantanal a wildlife haven and discusses its key habitats, the pressures they face and the conservation projects seeking to safeguard the region. *Top tips* (page 161) offers suggestions as to how to find Pantanal wildlife, when to travel and what to bring. A *Further information* section (page 173) identifies some specialised resources to help you plan and enjoy your trip.

A true traveller's companion needs to go beyond the 'what', and to encompass the 'where' and 'how'. Treating the Pantanal in its three-country entirety, *Where to go* (page 119) details excellent areas in which to search for the region's wildlife specialities. With helpful synopses of major lodges and advice on how to get around, this section provides the key information you need to arrange your trip. In sum, this guide intends to make Pantanal animals real and to make your wildlife-watching life easier.

What's in a name?

Ascribing names is a fundamental trait of human behaviour, reflecting our need to communicate and also, perhaps, our desire to order (and thereby 'own') confusing external entities. Biologists are no different from the rest of us, and have developed a honed system for naming organisms and defining their place in the natural world. This is called taxonomy or classification, and a grasp of its basic principles will help you understand the flow of this book.

The highest tier in nature's hierarchy of complex life is called a kingdom. Kingdoms are very broadly delineated, for example into animals, plants or fungi. The subsequent two layers – phyla (phylum in the singular) and subphyla – remain high-order divisions. All creatures with a backbone (commonly known as vertebrates),

The rufous-tailed jacamar is a confiding bird of Pantanal forests. (JL)

for instance, are housed in the animal kingdom, phylum Chordata and subphylum Vertebrata.

Within the vertebrates, conventional taxonomy recognises five classes, and these constitute the bulk of this book: mammals, birds, reptiles, amphibians and fish. Each subsequent taxonomic division is progressively more tightly defined, through orders, families and genera (singular: genus) until the organism is identified as a species. For complex groups, taxonomists sometimes use intermediate ranks such as suborders, subfamilies and subgenera. To take a Pantanal example, the black-tailed marmoset belongs to the class Mammalia, order Primates, suborder Haplorhini ('dry-nosed' primates), the superfamily Ceboidea (New World monkeys), family Callitrichidae (marmosets and tamarins) and ultimately to the genus *Mico* (one of nine marmoset and tamarin genera).

This hierarchy can seem confusing. To make things easier, each species has a scientific name, which consists of just two elements: the genus and species. These are written in italics, with the genus capitalised. The black-tailed marmoset referred to in the previous paragraph is thus known as *Mico melanurus*. The advantage of scientific names is that they constitute a universal language that transcends international borders – unlike common names, which vary between and sometimes within countries.

Travelling by boat is a key part of the Pantanal experience. (AG/SS)

The scientific name often derives from some aspect of the animal's appearance or habitat, from its geographical range or even from its human discoverer. In the Pantanal, for example, a common sight in forest is the rufous-tailed jacamar *Galbula ruficauda*, a bird whose specific name divides into *rufi* (meaning rufous) and *cauda* (meaning tail). Walking the trails, we may be startled by a Mato Grosso lancehead *Bothrops mattogrossensis*, a snake with a range centred on the eponymous Brazilian state. At night, we might conceivably chance upon an Azara's night monkey *Aotus azarae*, named after Félix de Azara, a Spanish military officer who catalogued central South American wildlife during the 18th century.

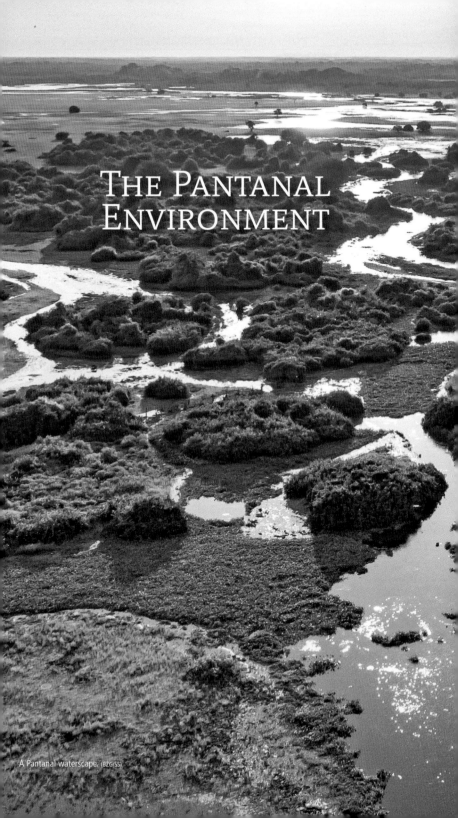

THE PANTANAL
ENVIRONMENT

A Pantanal waterscape. (BZG/SS)

GEOGRAPHY AND GEOLOGY

The Pantanal is the world's largest contiguous wetland. Estimates of its size vary, but most fall in the range of 140,000–230,000km² – somewhere between that of Greece and Guyana, with a midpoint over half the size of Germany. Around three-quarters of the Pantanal lies in west-central Brazil, divided between the states of Mato Grosso (40%) and Mato Grosso do Sul (60%). Of the remainder, two-thirds are in Bolivia and a third in Paraguay.

This whole vast expanse lies in a sedimentary basin surrounded by uplands: the Serras do Bodoquena and Maracajú to the south; the Brazilian *planalto* (plateau) to the east; the Matogrossense equivalent to the north; and the Serra do Amolar and Maçico do Urucum to the west. It is tempting to think of the Pantanal – from *pântano*, Portuguese for swamp – as one big wetland, but the region is far from homogeneous, and comprises ten or so large rivers and their deltas, plus thousands of lakes, interspersed with different types of grassland and forest.

The principal river is the Paraguay; this joins the Paraná 2,500km to the south before both emerge into the La Plata and reach the Atlantic Ocean in Argentina. Other major rivers include the Taquari, Miranda, Negro, Cuiabá and Aquidauana. All are slow-flowing and, during the rainy season (see *Climate and seasonality*, page 9), burst their banks to flood large areas of low-lying plains. Only higher areas – formed by ancient dunes and now often covered with forest – remain dry. Altitude varies only from 80–150m throughout the upper Paraguay basin. The barely perceptible gradient rarely exceeds a 20cm drop in altitude per kilometre, slopes falling westwards and southwards.

The Transpantaneira highway of Mato Grosso, Brazil, provides access to fabulous wildlife-watching. (BZG/SS)

The Pantanal is the world's largest contiguous wetland. (BZG/SS)

CLIMATE AND SEASONALITY

The nature of a visitor's wildlife experience depends hugely on the season. A dry-season visit differs so greatly from a wet-season trip – in landscape, species and numbers – that you might imagine you were in an entirely different place. The key is rainfall distribution and timing. The Pantanal typically receives 1,000–1,600mm of rain per year, predominantly between November and March, although the global climate crisis is causing longer, more intense droughts and decreasing, less predictable rainfall. There are differences across the region – the south tending to receive less precipitation – and between years.

During the rainy season, rivers overflow and disperse across the plain to inundate 25–75% of the Pantanal, carrying fish and other aquatic wildlife with them. The flooded area can be ten times larger than the world's most famous wetland, Florida's Everglades, and 15 times the size of the best-known wetland for watching wildlife, Botswana's Okavango Delta. Water levels rise by up to 5m, soil nutrient levels increase and aquatic vegetation blooms. Dry land is at a premium, and higher areas (in Brazil, called *caapões* if small or *cordilheiras* if sizeable) hold concentrations of terrestrial mammals. Humidity rises from a winter mean of 62% (June) to a sticky summer figure of 80% (February). As the months pass, temperatures rise to 40°C from their mean of 25°C. Gradually, the tables turn.

As temperatures drop – falling to 7°C during winter cold snaps, when Antarctic air races north – terrestrial animals spread out and water becomes the precious commodity. Fish and other aquatic creatures are trapped in a dwindling number of shrinking water bodies, which become magnets for piscivores such as caimans and herons.

When floodwaters recede, they often leave a 'tidemark' on trees. (JL)

The pulse of the flood (called *cheia* in Brazil) affects the Pantanal at different times. As rivers move from north to south, water levels peak four months earlier in the north than the south. By the time the south is fully flooded, the north has started its dry season. In the north, water levels respond quickly to rainfall, but flood retention smooths the peaks and troughs in the south. Flood intensity is also subject to multi-year cycles, with periods of extensive flooding alternating with more meagre periods.

THE HUMAN CONNECTION

People have inhabited the Pantanal for 5,500 years, but we know most about the indigenous residents of the last millennium. Some lived on the Cerrado plateau but made hunting forays to the plains. Others, such as the Payaguá, Mbayá-Guaicurú and Guató, resided on islands within what was then an enormous lake, the Sea of Xaraes, subsisting by fishing. During the 16th and 17th centuries, Spanish and Portuguese colonialists traversed the region in their quest for El Dorado and initiated a long decline in native cultures. Today, few Guató remain, although the Mbayá-Guaicurú (represented by their descendants, the Kadiwéu) retain title to a reserve granted by the Portuguese in gratitude for their help in ousting the Spanish.

The discovery of alluvial gold accelerated colonisation. Towns such as Corumbá, Cuiabá and Cáceres sprang up to meet the need for secure trading bases. To satisfy their taste for meat, the colonialists imported cattle during the 18th century. The bovines thrived and, by the early 20th century, beef exports – corned and dried – boomed. The same period marked the heyday of the trade in wildlife commodities: peccary skin for gloves, otter fur for coats and egret feathers for hats. *Pantaneiros* (residents of the Pantanal) were making a considerable living by plundering the land.

But all good things come to an end. While descendants of the ranchers plumped for the bright lights of coastal cities, their parents' cattle suffered a double whammy of drought and disease. By the 1980s, the frangible equilibrium between nature and nourishment developed by the *pantaneiros* was out of kilter. Outsiders moved in, bringing disharmonious land management techniques. They cleared forest to create additional pasture – 500,000ha in the final quarter of the 20th century – and

In the dry season, cattle are driven up the Transpantaneira highway in search of water. (LJSS)

cultivated exotic grasses laced with herbicides. Not content with the well-established Nelore cattle (*Bos indicus*), incomers introduced water buffalo (*Bubalus bubalis*) as an alternative.

Despite subsequent economic diversification (to include mining, horticulture and tourism), cattle-ranching remains the bedrock of the *pantaneiro* lifestyle, with 3,000 such ranches occupying 90% of the Brazilian Pantanal. Some 3.8 million cattle are accompanied by the traditional *peão* or *boiadeiro* (cowboy), whose way of life fascinates many visitors and forms an integral part of any Pantanal trip.

Estimates of the Pantanal's human population vary as widely as approximations of its area or wildlife species totals. A rough estimate for the Brazilian sector is 3 million, almost double what it was in 1991. This

No *pantaneiro* is ever without a machete. (JL)

burgeoning population is inevitably placing ever-greater demands on the Pantanal's natural resources. Dams disrupt headwater flows and interrupt annual flooding patterns. Agriculture-driven deforestation not only reduces forest cover but causes erosion and sedimentation. Pesticides (including for industrial soybean cultivation) pollute rivers. Two of the world's most destructive invasive alien species (a snail and a mussel) lurk in Pantanal wetlands. Since 2019, massive, uncontrolled wildfires – exacerbated by climate dysfunction – have become a terrifying new normal and

In the dry season, fires burn swathes of vegetation, leaving only termite mounds standing. (JL)

caused unparalleled wildlife mortality. In 2022–23, the Brazilian government issued preliminary licences to construct port facilities on the River Paraguay – potentially the precursor of a commercial waterway (*hidrovia*) through the Pantanal that would permanently alter natural cycles and shrink the wetland.

PANTANAL MYTHS

As people developed their relationship with the Pantanal over centuries of living there, many myths and legends emerged. The mermaid-like *mãe d'água* ('mother of the waters') combs her hair atop a river rock. She protects river fish, so luckless fishermen ascribe their barren days to having hooked her blessing rather than any fish. Pantanal rivers are also reputedly

Fishing is a key subsistence and sport activity. (VB/SS)

inhabited by the *minhocão* or *minhocuçu*, a giant earthworm-like monster. So protective is the *minhocão* of its tranquil environment that, when disturbed by noisy fishermen, it emerges from its watery lair, destroying riverside huts, capsizing fishermen's canoes and even changing river courses. As if this were not enough for poor fishermen, they are also susceptible to pranks played by *negrinhos d'água*, mysterious 'Indians of the waters', who trawl the waterways in groups, looking for fishers to drag down to the river bottom and tickle.

Landowners are keen to conserve hyacinth macaws, in part as a tourist attraction. (KD)

CONSERVATION

It is not only wildlife and the *pantaneiro* way of life that run the combined gauntlet of these anthropogenic pressures. The stakes are higher and the vested interests more wide-reaching. At its peak, the Pantanal comprises 3% of the world's freshwater wetland area. For 8 million people living downstream, it purifies water, recharges groundwater supplies, abates floods, provides arteries for commercial transportation, generates ecotourism income, irrigates crops and soaks up carbon dioxide, doing its bit in the battle against climate change – ecosystem services that have been valued collectively at $112 billion per year.

Accordingly, it is reassuring that some of the Pantanal has legal protection. But not enough. According to the IUCN, under 5% of the Brazilian share is protected. Pantanal reserves form just 4% of the country's total protected area – meaning that only the Brazilian Pampa protects a lower proportion of its species. Perhaps 600,000 hectares of the Bolivian Pantanal is ostensibly safeguarded through reserves, plus a third that in Paraguay. Meanwhile, various non-governmental organisations help conserve the Pantanal. The Worldwide Fund for Nature (WWF) runs a large-scale plan that targets social and economic issues associated with water use. In Brazil, Onçasafari studies jaguar behaviour, seeking to improve conservation strategies, while Panthera aims to mitigate human–jaguar conflict, support Pantanal riverside communities and develop best practice for jaguar-oriented tourism. Other non-profit organisations survey and conserve giant otter, lowland tapir and hyacinth macaw. In Paraguay, Guyra Paraguay, WWF-Paraguay and local organisations are seeking to conserve the country's Pantanal.

HABITATS

Extending across four major South American biomes, the Pantanal displays a mosaic of distinct habitat types – including forests, seasonally flooded grasslands and permanent lakes – whose distribution follows topography and soil type. Forests tend to lie atop raised areas (*capões* or *cordilheiras*) with calcium- and magnesium-enriched soils. Grasslands and cerrado usually dominate low-lying areas with poor soils. A basic understanding of Pantanal habitats will help you decide where to look for specific animals. There is little point in looking for a capybara in deciduous forest, nor much chance of finding a woodpecker in a swamp. At a more subtle level, certain species of bird favour, say, tracts of shrubby cerrado in Mato Grosso do Sul rather than the Chaco-influenced scrub of Paraguay. Botanists identify 16 vegetation classes, at least 1,700 flowering plant species and 530 aquatic plant species (flowering or not) in the Pantanal; here we home in on the most important and easily recognisable.

WETLANDS

Water is as innate to the Pantanal's identity as it is to that of the sea. The seasonal rhythm of the Pantanal's ebbing and flowing waters governs the distribution, reproduction and growth of all manner of flora and fauna, as well as the movements and behaviour of humans – residents and visitors alike. A mosaic of aquatic habitats, the Pantanal has several types of watercourse, each with its own vegetation and wildlife community.

Permanent rivers and streams form the basis of aquatic life. Sandbanks along wide rivers provide nest sites for terns and skimmers, and resting points for lolling capybaras and dozing jaguars. On the tributaries, otters and kingfishers make their home amidst free-floating plants, such as the lilac-flowered common water hyacinth or *aguapé* (*Pontederia crassipes*), and carnivorous bladderworts (*Utricularia*) that float below the surface, feeding on small aquatic insects.

As water bodies dry up, they attract hundreds of egrets and storks. (RT/SS)

Treading lightly across aquatic vegetation, the wattled jacana is nicknamed the 'lily-trotter'. (RJ)

In permanent freshwater lakes – *baías* or *corixos* in Brazil – water hyacinth congregates into huge floating islands of vegetation (*camalotes*) that are home to wattled jacana and conceal yacaré caiman. Although locally destroyed by fires since 2020, still waters in the western Pantanal harbour that Goliath of plants, the giant waterlily (*Victoria cruziana*). Its circular leaves, strong enough to support a capybara, may reach 2m in diameter, and its flower 30cm. The bloom lasts but two nights and changes colour from white to pink during its short life. The flowers of a smaller, closely related waterlily (*Nymphaea*) open only at night, exuding a pungent scent.

Marshes and swamps are seasonal, expanding or contracting with floods and droughts. They are typically fringed with burheads (*Echinodorus paniculatus*), aquatic ferns (*Ceratopteris pterioides*) and bulrushes (*Typha domingensis*), the stems (rhizomes) of the last creeping under the mud before growing upwards. In the muddy margins, the purple flower spikes of pickerel weeds (*Pontederia cordata*) provide colour until nibbled by ducks. Yacaré caiman and yellow anaconda skulk in these vegetated shallows; a variety of herons and ibises stalk pointedly through the water; and marsh deer graze along the edge. As the dry season progresses, these waters become ever more precious and ever more densely populated, hosting the quintessential northern Pantanal spectacle of teeming mammals, birds and crocodilians jostling for space and food.

In Nhecolândia in Mato Grosso do Sul, including at Fazenda Barranco Alto (page 144), brackish lakes or *salinas* exist alongside rounded freshwater lakes. The salinity was formerly considered a residue from an arid period in the Pleistocene. However, it transpires that the same water table links saline and fresh lakes, suggesting that the saltiness results from a more recent concentration process. These lakes often heave with wildfowl, waders (shorebirds) and capybara, concentrations that frequently attract the attention of jaguars.

The Pantanal's dry grassland is characterised by termite mounds – and red legged seriemas. (AS/OB)

SAVANNAHS

Savannahs encompass almost one-third of the Pantanal, the highest proportion of any habitat type. Most are open grasslands dominated by native grasses (*Andropogon*, *Paspalum* and *Setaria*) in the family Poaceae; these lack shrubs or trees, hence their Brazilian name *campo limpo*, which literally means 'clean field'. In low-lying areas (*vazantes* in Brazil), grasslands are seasonally flooded and termed *campo alagado* (wet savannah); sedges (*Cyperus giganteus*) are common. Grassland with occasional shrubs and trees is called *campo sujo* (literally, dirty field). Typical shrubs include fruit-bearing plants such as *Annona* and guava (*Psidium guineense*). Grasslands are the battlefield for an incessant struggle between herbs and woody plants. In wetter areas or seasons, herbs and grasses have the upper hand. In drier areas or periods, cerrado trees such as the sandpaper tree (*Curatella americana*) encroach, along with short palms (*Bactris*). In areas that are dry in winter yet flooded in summer, stands of caranday wax-palms (*Copernicia alba*), known locally as *carandá*, form the palm savannah that are such a characteristic Pantanal sight.

Although they may look relatively uninteresting, grasslands are excellent places for watching wildlife. Greater rhea and red-legged seriema stride on long legs, while common brown brocket (and, in Mato Grosso do Sul, pampas deer) graze open fields. Giant anteater, southern tamandua and various armadillos trawl the termite mounds on raised areas with *Elionurus muticus* grass, passing groups of long-tailed ground-doves scuttling across the open ground.

CERRADO

Some biogeographers consider the Pantanal to be a seasonally flooded extension of the Cerrado, the wooded savannah that formerly dominated the plateau of central Brazil. This habitat typically comprises slim, twisted trees that grow 5–10m above herbaceous vegetation and grasses, and tends to occur on elevated areas on well-drained, sandy soils with few nutrients and high aluminium levels. Dominant cerrado trees include the pequi (*Caryocar brasiliense*) – the nuts and fruit of which are popular human foods – and hardwoods such as *Qualea grandiflora* and *Pouteria ramiflora*, used for timber and firewood. Most are adapted to withstand regular dry-season fires. Denser, taller woodland is called *cerrado*, and often contains *algarrobo* or *jatobá* (*Hymenaea stigonocarpa*) and *capitão* (*Terminalia argentea*). *Pantaneiros* harvest *jatobá* sap on a waning moon, as its minerals and proteins are thought to stimulate kidneys and ovaries. Trunks of the congeneric anami gum (*Hymenaea courbaril*) are fashioned into kayaks. Cerrado wildlife is similar to that in savannahs, but also sometimes includes the maned wolf and scarce birds such as the white-rumped tanager.

FORESTS

Cerrado is not the Pantanal's only wooded habitat. The variety of floristic influences results in a batch of closed-canopy formations.

Rivers and streams are usually lined with a thin strip of gallery forest, the canopy topping 20m and the flora demonstrating affinities with Amazonian or Atlantic forests. Common trees include a palm (*Bactris glaucescens*), *churimo* (*Inga vera*), with its long seedpods, figs (*Ficus*) and *cambará* (*Vochysia divergens*). The last disperses its seeds via floodwater and so the tree's distribution expands during high-water years. *Pantaneiros* weave *cambará* leaves into brooms and hats, and use it to fight infections and asthma. The *novateiro* (*Triplaris americana*), easily recognised by bunches of red, tubular flowers, is inhabited and protected by red ants (*Comatogaster*). *Pantaneiros* with a twisted sense of humour initiate newcomers to Pantanal life by asking them to fell the *novateiro* for firewood; ants rush out and sting the lumberjack who swiftly abandons his mission, screaming in pain. It is perhaps little wonder that Bolivians call this species the *palo de diablo* (devil's tree).

Gallery forests along secluded, slow-flowing rivers are great for wildlife-watching. (AL)

Inside the forest, woody vines such as *Cissus spinosa* criss-cross above the sparse undergrowth. On damp ground nearby, *acuri* (*Scheelea phalerata*) and *bocaiúva* (*Acrocomia totai*) palm trees often dominate the understorey, their nuts a prized

Forest forms: a strangler fig's twisted roots and the spiky bromeliad, *Bromelia balansae*. (JL)

food for hyacinth macaws. Other prominent wildlife in gallery forests includes two monkeys – black-and-gold howler and hooded capuchin – plus bare-faced curassow, and small birds such as helmeted manakin and cinereous-breasted spinetail.

Mesophitic (semi-deciduous and deciduous) forests grow on drier ground. In semi-deciduous forests, figs and *acuri* palms are also common, the latter often so tightly packed that they shade out shrubs. There are also *manduvi* (*Stercula apetala*) – the nest-tree for 95% of hyacinth macaws – silk trees (*Pseudalbizzia niopioides*), *gonçalo alves* (*Astronium fraxinifolium*), *aroeira peta* (*Myracrudruon urundeuva*) and persimmon (*Diospyros*). Deciduous forests tend to be less dense, with large, spiky bromeliads (*Bromelia balansae*) often providing the only ground cover. In the southwest Pantanal, the Chacoan influence reveals itself with columnar cacti such as *Cereus hexagonus*, which often reaches tree-like proportions, and prickly pear (*Opuntia stenarthra*), a succulent shrub. In these forests, birdlife includes undulated tinamou on the ground, antbirds in the undergrowth, woodcreepers on the main branches and toucans in fruiting trees. Among mammals, look for lowland paca and Azara's agouti rooting in leaf litter, and Azara's night monkey and black-tailed marmoset among arboreal foliage.

Both mesophitic formations may be found as 'forest islands' or *capões* – isolated woodlots slightly elevated above a seasonally inundated grassy plain that provide valuable refuges for ground-dwelling wildlife during floods. From July to September the most obvious trees are *lapacho* or *ypê* (*Tabebuia* spp.). The glorious blooms of these imposing trees may be yellow, pink or purple – depending on the species – and are the Pantanal's best-known floral spectacle. All flowers open simultaneously, a strategy that prevents birds such as the orange-backed troupial from eating the lot before they have served their pollination purpose. The pink *ypê* or *piúva* is Paraguay's national tree; its bark has medicinal properties that have prompted its commercialisation as *pau d'arco* tea.

MAMMALS

Jaguar: the Americas' largest cat. (LL/SS)

Giant anteaters are a delightfully frequent Pantanal sight. (LL/SS)

South America, like Africa, has a mammal 'big five' that wildlife-watchers dream of seeing: jaguar, maned wolf, giant anteater, giant otter and lowland tapir. With effort, a judicious itinerary and a dose of luck, the Pantanal offers a good chance of clapping eyes on the entire quintet. There is no better place to see four of them, and there are a couple of plausible sites for the fifth (maned wolf). But even without these five biggies, the Pantanal provides the continent's best mammal-watching, with most visitors enjoying close views of a wide variety of species. In total, around 150 species occur.

ANTEATERS AND ARMADILLOS

Among the most bizarre mammals on the planet are undoubtedly those that make up the superorder Xenarthra. In a Pantanal context, these comprise two species of anteater (family Myrmecophagidae) and five armadillos (order Cingulata); the third group is sloths (suborder Folivora). Their evolutionary connection is based on shared features such as modified vertebrae, a small brain and few, if any, teeth. The first of these characteristics provides the basis for the superorder name, Xenarthra being derived from the Greek for 'strange joints'. The third explains the former superorder name of Edentata, which comes from the Latin for 'toothless'.

ANTEATERS

With a long snout, small eyes, strong front claws and an extendable, sticky tongue instead of teeth, anteaters are supremely adapted for eating ants and termites. But such useful adaptations have their cost. To protect the front claws, anteaters must walk on their wrists. To survive on their low nutrition diet, they need a low metabolic rate and must sleep extensively – the record non-stop snooze lasted three days. And as the small mouth and hooked claws are no use for carrying offspring, a youngster must travel aboard its mother's back until it is old enough to fend for itself. Seeing an anteater is an undoubted trip highlight. The good news is that both species are relatively common in the Pantanal and active by both day and night, so your chances of an encounter or two are good.

Giant anteater

Lumbering through grasslands on its daily trip to harvest termite mounds in its home range, a giant anteater (*Myrmecophaga tridactyla*) evokes awe and amusement in equal measure. Measuring up to 250cm from snout to tail and weighing more than 30kg, this is a big animal. But with its Pinocchio-like snout and shaggy tail, the 'ant bear' (as it is known in Spanish) has an undeniably comical demeanour.

A key use of the remarkable tail – which inspires the *pantaneiro* name of *tamandua-bandeira* (flag-anteater) – is to provide cover when the anteater is sleeping. On hot days, it provides shade; when cold (and the species is more diurnal on chilly days), it helps conserve body heat. The bold patterning is thought to serve as disruptive camouflage and possibly a warning to predators not to risk being slashed by sharp claws. With poor eyesight and

The giant anteater uses its elongated snout to sniff out ants and termites – and to drink. (RJ)

hearing, a giant anteater depends on smell to locate ant and termite colonies. Using powerful forelimbs and hooked claws, it hacks into the hardened mound then inserts its snout and extends a 60cm-long tongue coated with tiny spines and smeared with saliva. The tongue traps the colony occupants and, with a quick flickering motion, slurps them up the long vacuum cleaner-like snout. The meal ends with the arrival of the soldier ants or termites, which bite the intruder or release chemical secretions that force it to retreat – until the next day. By keeping its meals small rather than destroying the colony outright, the anteater maintains a sustainable resource.

Southern tamandua

In the Pantanal, an anteater up a tree is always a southern tamandua (*Tamandua tetradactyla*). An excellent climber, the tamandua uses its prehensile tail to improve balance as it reaches for arboreal termite mounds or bee nests, its fondness for the latter explaining the Spanish name *oso melero* (honey bear). The tamandua rips apart colonies or branches with its four sharp foreclaws, then inserts its elongated snout and long, sticky tongue to extract the tiny prey. If you hear ripping wood, you have probably chanced upon a tamandua. These animals are equally at home on the ground, however, where their two-tone pelage can be remarkably difficult to spot in the dappled light of an open woodland. Should a tamandua feel threatened, it may stand on its hind legs and sway its forelimbs from side to side, drawing attention to its sharp claws. The overall impression is of a punch-drunk boxer, but a single slash can inflict serious damage.

The extraordinarily long tongue of the southern tamandua helps it access termites inside their mounds. (OP/SS)

ARMADILLOS

Few mammals appear more off-putting to a predator than armadillos. With bony armour-plating covering head, back and sides, there is no entry point for any but the wiliest of carnivores. This body armour, however, is the last line of armadillo defence: when sensing danger they prefer either to flee (preferably into thorny vegetation that does them no harm but impedes predators), or burrow to safety using their muscular front legs. The overlapping 'bands' of plates are separated at the mid-body by soft skin, thus allowing the body to flex, permitting movement.

Six-banded Armadillo. (RJ)

The Pantanal is home to a handful of armadillo species, ranging in length from 0.3–1.5m and in weight from 1–60kg. Most are shy and nocturnal, in part a legacy of poaching pressure. Visitors are most likely to bump into a nine-banded armadillo (*Dasypus novemcinctus*), hearing snuffling in pathside vegetation before the animal bumbles onto the track and into your torchlight. Stay still and this myopic mammal may approach closely, even wandering over your toes. Such an encounter will reveal its long nose, tail and ears, and may enable you to count its movable bands – one way to distinguish it from other armadillos (though beware as it can also have eight or ten bands). This species is an excellent excavator and leaves telltale diggings around its territory. It uses its long claws to bore its own burrows then lines the hole with leaves for comfort and insulation; this last process makes for an amusing spectacle, as the armadillo clasps the foliage under its body with its front legs and hops back to the burrow on its hindquarters.

Typically seen by day and also common, the six-banded or yellow armadillo (*Euphractus sexcinctus*) is omnivorous and even scavenges carrion. Otherwise solitary, individuals will congregate to feast on a carcass and the maggots that seethe

The once-mythical giant armadillo can occasionally be seen in at a couple of Pantanal sites. (GM/SS)

over it. Southern naked-tailed armadillo (*Canassous unicinctus*) is widespread but rarely seen, being largely nocturnal and essentially living underground.

Giant armadillo (*Priodontes maximus*) is the nearest living relative of the glyptodonts – massive armadillos with a mace-like tail that died out during the last Ice Age. For decades, this armoured Goliath was considered near-mythical – known by local people but never seen by scientists or ecotourists. Pioneering conservation research in Mato Grosso do Sul's Pantanal (particularly at Baia das Pedras) has revealed many of its secrets.

At the bottom of the size spectrum is the southern three-banded armadillo (*Tolypeutes matacus*) that only just squeezes three armoured bands onto its stunted body. Like other armadillos, it flees when cornered, zigzagging away like a demented clockwork toy. Should it fail to escape, however, the armadillo has a unique defence. The front and back sections of its armour hang like a cloak, enabling it to roll into an impregnable armoured ball that denies predators access to its soft underbelly, now safely hidden inside the shell.

PRIMATES

The Pantanal is not overladen with primates, but this makes seeing one of its five species rather special. Within the superfamily Ceboidea (New World monkeys), each species sits in a separate family. Recent taxonomy has preferred to increase the number of species rather than consolidate them (see box on page 26, *Splits, lumps and shuffles*) – a tendency that enhances mammal-watchers' interest in Pantanal monkeys.

The range of the black-tailed marmoset (*Mico melanura*; family Callitrichidae) is centred on the Pantanal. Bird-like twittering and high whistles in the forest draw attention to a family of these diminutive monkeys busying themselves in the middle storey; several lodges offer the chance to enjoy watching this species. Diurnal, arboreal

Black-tailed marmoset is the Pantanal's smallest primate. (RJ)

and omnivorous, marmosets readily gouge tree bark to extract sap and gum. This species is the only Pantanal primate that gives birth to twins rather than the standard single offspring.

Another primate whose presence is usually betrayed by its voice is the black-and-gold howler (*Alouatta caraya*; Atelidae). An adult male's dawn roar, however, could not be less like the marmoset's demure chirping; easily carrying 3km, it is among the most distinctive Pantanal sounds. This is the region's largest monkey, about the size of a large house cat, but when silent it can be surprisingly unobtrusive. Families of up to ten munch quietly on leaves high in the forest canopy. Males are much larger than females, and young males take four years to attain the black pelage of adulthood.

The male black-and-gold howler's dawn roar carries up to 3km. (RJ)

Capuchins get their English name from an order of Catholic friars who wore robes that covered their heads – and if you squint, you might concur that the dark tuft of the Pantanal species – hooded (or Azara's) capuchin (*Sapajus cay*; Cebidae) – resembles a hood. In Pantanal forests, troops of up to 40 animals feed primarily on arboreal fruit and seeds, but also search through leaf litter for invertebrates. Unlike the larger howlers, capuchins move and feed noisily, crashing through trees, and clucking, whistling or whining as the mood takes them. At some lodges, groups have become habituated, allowing close approach and even taking fruit at bird tables.

Considerably smaller, but proportionately longer-tailed, is the white-coated titi (*Callicebus pallescens*; Pitheciidae), which just about reaches the Pantanal in Paraguay and Bolivia. Titis live in small groups, each comprising a pair and their offspring from various years. These arboreal herbivores forage particularly near rivers, and spend long periods inactive, digesting food and conserving energy.

Aotus night monkeys (Aotidae) are the New World's sole nocturnal primates. With luck, particularly in Mato Grosso you may come across Azara's night monkey (*A. azarae*) by day as it roosts quietly in the sub-canopy. This primate's big brown eyes are framed by white crescents. At night, the monkey is quick to turn its small, round head away from torchlight, so all that you may see is a long, black-tipped tail, hanging perpendicular to a branch. On moonlit nights, this species gives a triple hoot that explains its alternative English name of owl monkey.

A view of Azara's night monkey by day reveals the large eyes typical of nocturnal species. (JL)

25

Hooded (or Azara's) capuchin was long 'lumped' with other members of its genus. (RJ)

SPLITS, LUMPS AND SHUFFLES

For simplicity's sake, we present species names in this book as if they were set in stone. But taxonomic reality is not quite so immutable. When it comes to setting the limits for a particular species, biologists follow different schools of thought. In a process as ongoing as evolution itself, researchers propose 'splits' or 'lumps' whenever they consider species limits to be incorrect. Sometimes, evidence emerges that suggests that what were previously thought distinct species are actually so closely related as to be the same species ('lumping'). In the Pantanal, for instance, night monkeys (*Aotus* spp.) in Mato Grosso and Paraguay were formerly considered different species: now they are lumped together as Azara's night monkey (*A. azarae*). Alternatively, populations are sometimes adjudged to be sufficiently different that each merits elevation to the rank of full species ('splitting'). Sticking with primates, hooded capuchin (*Sapajus cay*) was one of several splits from what used to be known as 'brown capuchin' – and, in the first edition of this guide, had an entirely different scientific name: *Cebus libidinosus*! Biologists cannot even always agree at the level of genus – supposedly a less confusing grouping. It is clear that the only constant in taxonomy is that it is in permanent flux. In this book, we follow the most recent biological consensus wherever it exists, with the occasional exception to embrace user-friendly treatments.

CARNIVORES

Wherever one travels to watch wildlife, carnivores tend to top the wish list. The Pantanal is no different, with two of the most charismatic mammals in South America – the jaguar and giant otter – both being flesh-eaters. With a few exceptions, such as China's bamboo-munching giant panda (*Ailuropoda melanoleuca*), members of the order Carnivora survive primarily by catching, killing and consuming other vertebrates. Many hunt opportunistically, preying on whatever crosses their path. Five families occur in the Pantanal: dogs, cats, mustelids (such as otters and weasels), skunks and procyonids (raccoons and coatis).

Common and widespread, crab-eating fox is often seen on night drives. (VC/D)

DOGS

The Pantanal hosts only four species of dog (family Canidae) but these include the continent's smallest and largest. The crab-eating fox (*Cerdocyon thous*) is the region's most common canid. As the name suggests, it has a taste for crustaceans, with crabs monopolising its diet during the rainy season. But there would be obvious drawbacks in depending entirely on a food resource that effectively disappears during the dry season. Accordingly, these foxes also consume small mammals, reptiles and amphibians. Proper generalist omnivores, they will also eat fruit, seeds and other plant material, and scavenge scraps discarded by lodge kitchens. Such 'feeding times' are one way to get a good look at a crab-eating fox, with its distinctive

Seeing a maned wolf – a fox on stilts – is a red-letter day. (RJ)

short muzzle, black 'socks', truncated tail and black stripe along the spine. Pairs often forage in rough association, a few minutes apart. Readily seen on night drives, and not infrequently by day too, it is particularly common in the southern Pantanal. Genetic studies have shown that crab-eating fox, the sole member of its genus, is more closely related to maned wolf (see below) than it is to true South American foxes (*Lycalopex* spp.).

If you are lucky enough to spot a big-eared fox on stilts, you have struck gold. At almost 1m tall, the unmistakable maned wolf (*Chrysocyon brachyurus*) is South America's largest canid. Routinely omnivorous, its diet is as likely to include fruit as rodents; wolf's apple (*Solanum lycocarpum*) is a particular favourite. The chances of bumping into one in the Pantanal are slight, but it has recently become reliable along a river northeast of Porto Jofre and occurs in isolated cerrado patches in Mato Grosso do Sul. It can also be readily seen in Chapada dos Guimaraes, which many visitors combine with a Pantanal trip.

Last up are two even rarer canids that, realistically, only those fortunate enough to live in the Pantanal stand any chance of seeing. The bush dog (*Speothos venaticus*) is the only New World canid to live in packs, members keeping in contact with yelps as they hunt lowland paca in forest undergrowth. Pampas or Azara's fox (*Lycalopex gymnocerca*) scrapes into the Pantanal in Paraguay and Bolivia. It is essentially a species of the Chaco and of pampas grassland to the south and east. Gingery tones to the pelage and extensively white legs easily differentiate this canid from crab-eating fox.

CATS

Cats (Felidae) are consummate carnivores, eating nothing but flesh. Supreme predators, they grab prey with sharp, retractile claws, and dispatch it with a bite to the neck. The Pantanal hosts an outstanding selection of felids, with seven species recorded. Five have a spotted pelage, varying in size from the domestic cat-sized southern oncilla (*Leopardus guttulus*) to the jaguar (*Panthera onca*), king of South America's jungle. Two are unmarked, the heftier being the puma (*Puma concolor*). All are rare, solitary and largely nocturnal. Seeing any cat is normally a considerable challenge, but Pantanal researchers and guides have got to grips with the behaviour and movements of jaguar and ocelot. Accordingly, the Pantanal has become by far the best place anywhere in Latin America to encounter these two sought-after cats.

Jaguar

The jaguar is the largest cat in the Americas and the third largest worldwide, topped only by the tiger (*Panthera tigris*) and lion (*Panthera leo*). Deep-chested, large-headed and stocky, a male jaguar can measure 2.5m in length, including tail, and 130kg in weight – thus resembling a bodybuilding leopard. The Pantanal subspecies is the largest and heaviest – twice the size of those in Central America. It is hardly surprising that every visitor to the Pantanal wants to see one – and, joyously, most visitors to Mato Grosso, at least, do so (see box, *Jaguar-watching*, page 166).

Previously unthinkable, witnessing a mating pair of jaguars is now possible in the northern Pantanal. (JD)

Tributaries of the River Cuiabá in Brazil's Mato Grosso are prime jaguar terrain. (YP)

Jaguars are primarily forest animals with a fondness for riverbanks. They swim well, readily traversing rivers to move between forest tracts. Large carnivores need large prey populations that, in turn, require a large area of habitat. Jaguars thus have substantial home ranges, although those of several individuals may overlap. Estimates of Pantanal jaguar density vary from 4–12 individuals per 100km^2, with densities higher (or home ranges smaller) during the wet season. Every jaguar has different markings, enabling researchers to track individuals – and (near Porto Jofre, Mato Grosso) even construct family trees.

Jaguars are opportunistic and voracious predators, with 85 prey species recorded throughout Latin America and virtually no animal being too much to handle. A powerful bite through the back of the skull is sufficient to subdue a cow three times the cat's weight. Capybaras form much of the diet, but the jaguar's powerful bite can pierce even the protective armour of caimans, turtles and armadillos; it is the abundance of crocodilians that probably sustains such a large jaguar population near Porto Jofre. Using whatever cover is available, jaguars rely on their camouflaged pelage (in the interplay of light and shadow, the dark rosettes disrupt the cat's form) to disguise them as they stalk their target to within pouncing distance. If this involves chasing the victim into water and nabbing it before it dives to safety, so be it.

Like all Neotropical cats, jaguars are essentially solitary. Sightings of two animals together usually relate to a mother and offspring (which travel with one another until the youngster is 15–18 months old), to sub-adult siblings or to a female in oestrus with an attendant wandering male. Pair bonds are brief and intense: jaguars may mate 100 times per day during the female's one to two-week fertile period. During the mating season, both sexes roar to attract each other's attention, a series of deep grunts that carries for 400m.

Conservationists have no clear idea how many jaguars are left, but know that the species is declining and at potential future risk of extinction. Fortunately, the poaching heyday of the 1960s – when 15,000 spotty pelts were exported from Brazil each year – is long gone as a result of legislation banning international trade. Direct persecution remains a threat, however, with some ranchers killing cats where they are thought to predate livestock, something that is less likely in areas with ample quantity of wild prey. For a while, some landowners even went as far as to make money from shooting jaguars, charging sport hunters US$20,000 for a pop at a feline trophy. But the greatest threat to jaguars, as with so much of tropical biodiversity, is forest loss and fragmentation.

Nowadays there is hopefully a robust financial incentive to keep jaguars alive: even back in 2015, jaguar-watching around Porto Jofre generated $6.8 million for the local economy. With the growth in Pantanal tourism since then, this financial benefit is only likely to increase. Since the inaugural studies by famous mammologist George Schalling in the 1970, we now know a lot more about jaguar ecology and conservation. Organisations studying and conserving the species in the Pantanal include Panthera, Onçasafari and Instituto Onça-pintada: their activities variously include research, education, ecotourism, rewilding, advocacy and fire prevention.

Other spotted cats

Should you not be fortunate enough to enjoy a jaguar, do not despair. You have four additional opportunities for a spotted-cat experience, at a range of sizes. The ocelot (*Leopardus pardalis*) is roughly the size of a cocker spaniel. Relative to a jaguar, it also has a smaller head, larger ears and a more sprightly gait, and the spots on its neck and flanks coalesce into distinctive stripes. Ocelots are mainly nocturnal; an hour either side of dusk is the prime time to see one. Prey consists mostly of terrestrial rodents, which is why the rice fields of Fazenda São Francisco (Mato Grosso do Sul) are a good place to see one. In Mato Grosso, Southwild Pantanal Lodge provides viewing opportunites at a baited station.

The margay (*Leopardus wiedii*) is dainty and long-tailed, with large rosettes on its flanks. It is the only spotted cat that routinely climbs trees; flexible ankle joints enable it to descend vertical surfaces head first. Only the luckiest visitor will see a margay, as is also the case with southern oncilla. Built like a slim house cat, this felid has larger eyes and ears but a shorter tail than the margay. Of similar size, but stockier and with striped chest and legs, is the Pantanal cat (*L. braccatus*). As its English name suggests, the core of this cat's range is the Pantanal. Nevertheless, it would be an extremely fortunate visitor who came across one: night drives in Mato Grosso do Sul provide the best prospects.

The Pantanal offers good opportunities to see ocelot. (AS/OB)

Mato Grosso do Sul offers the Pantanal's best prospects of seeing puma (aka mountain lion). (LL/SS)

Plain cats

If spots are now dancing before your eyes, take a breather with the Pantanal's two monotone species of felid. Both are lithe creatures, with slim bodies and long tails, the jaguarundi (*Herpilaurus yagouaroundi*) being so long-bodied and short-legged as to recall a member of the weasel family (Mustelidae). Indeed, you might easily confuse it with one such animal – the tayra (page 36) – given that both are adept climbers, but the tayra has a shorter, bushier tail and a more undulating gait. The jaguarundi is unique among American felids in exhibiting a wide range of pelt colours, with chestnut, brown, grey and black all common. The much larger puma also varies in colour, but only between pale buff and tawny brown. In dimensions, it falls only slightly shy of the jaguar, but it is a rangier, more lithe animal with a noticeably lighter tread. This cat has one of the largest ranges of any land mammal, extending from the Arctic Circle south to Tierra del Fuego. It is scarce in the Pantanal – perhaps because it cannot compete with the stronger jaguar – but you are, however, more likely to see one in drier, open areas such as grasslands (particularly in Mato Grosso do Sul), where it hunts mainly by night for small and medium-sized mammals. Visitors from North America know the puma as the mountain lion, panther or cougar. Indeed, across its huge range, this species is known by some 40 English names, more than any other animal.

33

OTTERS AND WEASELS

Slinky of body and sinuous in movement, the Mustelidae family comprises otters, weasels and their allies. Though species vary in size, all share a similar general form: a long body with short legs and a comparatively short tail, and a broad head with small ears and eyes. Most species can hear and smell well, but see only poorly, which can be a boon if you observe them quietly from downwind. In the Pantanal, the family comprises two otters (subfamily Lutrinae) and two typical mustelids (subfamily Mustelinae).

Giant otter

While glimpsing a jaguar may be the Pantanal nirvana, another trip highlight is an hour spent in the company of a confiding family of giant otters (*Pteronura brasiliensis*) as they cavort and snort just a few metres away. Giant otters tick all the boxes required to be part of that exclusive club, South America's 'big five': they are undeniably big – up to 1.8m long and 34kg; they are impressive predators, all sleek muscularity underwater as they effortlessly catch their fishy prey; and they offer that irresistible blend of the elusive and the showy – hard to find (so raising the blood pressure) but consummate performers (so worth the effort). Finally, giant otters have rarity value, habitat destruction and persecution having caused populations to plummet so far that the species is classified as globally threatened. Nowhere in its range is it easier to see than the Pantanal.

Web-footed, dense-furred and with a broad, flattened tail that is encapsulated in its genus name (*Pteronura* deriving from the Greek for 'wing tail'), the giant otter is largely aquatic. Known in Spanish as *lobo del río* ('river wolf'), this species is a fan of slow-moving rivers with gently sloping banks and overhanging vegetation. If you whistle or gargle, an inquisitive otter may approach to check out the strange sounds. This should give you a good view of its pattern of cream blotches on the throat –

Giant otter are expert fishers, this one munching on a catfish. (HB/SS)

Highly social creatures, giant otters are usually seen in groups. (JL)

unique to each individual – and of the formidable canines that give fish no hope of escape. Giant otters have a particular taste for catfish (Siluriformes) and characins (Characiformes), which they consume noisily.

Giant otters are sociable creatures, living in cohesive families of up to eight individuals. Active by day, groups retreat to communal dens at dusk. These 'holts' are easy to spot: a wide hollow on the riverbank with a large landing beach cleared of vegetation but covered with webbed footprints. They are also highly audible animals, being the most vocal otter species and the one with the widest repertoire. Gruff barks alert pack members to danger, a growl serves as a warning and a soft coo soothes. Wider social interactions appear to be less harmonious: researchers are finding evidence of fractious conflicts between neighbours at territory boundaries. Such intraspecific aggression is rare among mustelids and is presumably the flip side of strong bonds within a group. The aggression is also directed towards potential predators: jaguars could plausibly kill otters, but are wary of taking them on.

Nevertheless, rival otters are less a source of danger than are humans. In the 1960s, more than 1,000 otters were killed each year in Amazonian Brazil alone. Fortunately, poaching for pelts has declined dramatically with the enforcement of new legislation. But current threats are more insidious. Loggers and fires destroy rainforest and farmers move in, removing riverside vegetation and degrading water quality. In turn, this reduces the viability of fragmented subpopulations. Despite such threats, there are signs that populations are recovering locally. In 2015, researchers estimated 1,100 breeding individuals (or 3,950 animals total) along 7,350 km of Pantanal rivers. Organisations such as Projeto Ariranhas are aiming to learn more: by mid-2024 its researchers had catalogued 412 individuals on the basis of unique throat patterns.

Neotropical otter

That the Neotropical otter (*Lontra longicaudis*) exists at all today is a relief. From the 1950s to the 1970s, extensive hunting nearly drove this aquatic mustelid to extinction: more than 30,000 otters were killed every year for their pelts. This shroud of historical exploitation increases the allure of this ostensibly less dramatic mustelid. Neotropical otters are less brawny than giant otters. They are also more catholic in their habitat requirements, inhabiting pretty much any watercourse. Such wide tastes help them avoid conflict with their larger cousin, as does their ability to fish at night. During the dry season, these solitary mammals disperse to find foraging grounds. Although less frequently seen than giant otter, lucky visitors may come across a Neotropical otter humping its way across land between far-flung water bodies, its head and tail distinctly drooped, or feeding under an awning of riverbank branches.

Our forefathers' desire for otter fur nearly drove the Neotropical otter to extinction. (JD)

Typical mustelids

At night, most carnivores' eyes glow orange when reflecting torchlight. Those of the tayra (*Eira barbara*) are the exception, facilitating identification by gleaming blue-green. However, you are more likely to see this active, powerful mammal by day. Tayras forage alone or in family groups, bounding through forests for up to 8km per day. They ascend trees to feast on fruit, snatch arboreal arthropods and rob bird nests, but are wary animals, fleeing at the first perception of a threat and growling aggressively as they leap away.

The final Pantanal mustelid, the lesser grison (*Galictis cuja*), is smaller and longer-necked than a tayra, with a distinctive black, white and grey coat. Primarily nocturnal, it is rarely seen – which perhaps explains why mammologists are not entirely sure whether or not the Pantanal additionally harbours the similar-looking greater grison (*G. vittata*).

The tayra is a lithe, agile and aggressive predator. (OP/SS)

SKUNK

Striped hog-nosed skunk (*Conepatus semistriatus*) has an isolated population in central Brazil, the western edge of which nominally extends into the Pantanal, although it is barely ever seen here. Like other skunks, this nocturnal animal has the dubious claim to fame of being known principally for its odour, used as a defensive weapon. When a skunk feels threatened, it squirts a fluid containing sulphuric liquid from anal scent glands; the spray can reach 5m and the scent can drift 1.5km downwind.

RACCOONS

The Pantanal's two members of the raccoon family (Procyonidae) split the 24-hour clock between them: the South American coati (*Nasua nasua*) is exclusively diurnal and the crab-eating raccoon (*Procyon cancrivorus*) mainly nocturnal.

With its bandit-like mask, short grey fur and faintly ringed tail, there is no mistaking a crab-eating raccoon. Individuals or pairs typically forage along the damp fringes of a watercourse, hunting any creature associated with wet habitats: from fish and amphibians to insects and, of course, crabs. During the dry

Night drives offer the best chance of connecting with crab-eating raccoon. (RJ/SS)

South American coati is an engaging and long-tailed mammal. (F/SS)

season, they also devour other foods such as fruits. As day breaks, raccoons scuttle back to their dens, snugly sited in hollow trees.

The coati has a comical appearance. Its long, narrow snout ends in an upturned nose that constantly sniffs the air for food or threat, while white crescents around the eye lend the animal a startled look. Females and youngsters form large groups that troop noisily through the forest, banded tails raised perpendicular to the body, tips swishing above the undergrowth. Coatis are opportunistic omnivores, climbing trees to harvest fruits or snuffling through leaf litter to unearth invertebrates. Groups signal danger with an abrupt bark, a cue for the members to scatter up trees from where they make a communal assessment of the threat.

South American coatis have eye-catching facial markings. (MM/SS)

UNGULATES

Ungulates (literally 'hoofed animals') comprise herbivores that walk on the tips of their hoofed toes. There are 'even-toed' ungulates (order Artiodactyla) and 'odd-toed' ungulates (order Perissodactyla). In even-toed ungulates, weight falls evenly between the third and fourth toes, which form a cloven hoof; a pair of smaller toes usually remain clear of the ground. Native families comprise peccaries (Tayassuidae) and deer (Cervidae). Odd-toed ungulates, by contrast, have a prominent third, central digit that bears the most weight. The best-known odd-toed ungulates are horses (Equidae), but their only native New World representatives are tapirs (Tapiridae).

The normally reclusive lowland tapir (here a mother and calf) is comparatively extrovert in the Pantanal. (LL/SS)

TAPIR

Only four species of tapir occur in the world, of which three are in the Neotropics (the other being in Indochina). By far the heaviest land mammal in South America, reaching 300kg, and impressively long (1.9–2.4m), the lowland (or Brazilian) tapir (*Tapirus terrestris*) would earn its place in the continent's 'big five' even without its rarity and bizarre looks. Due to hunting and habitat destruction, this species is globally threatened, and seeing one is a near-impossible task – except in the Pantanal, where it is a regular feature of safaris, particularly at night. As for looks, the pony-sized tapir is in a class of its own, with an elongated proboscis of an upper lip (useful for accessing fruit) and humped forehead that leads into a short, erect mane. Whereas adults are coloured a monotone grey, youngsters are striped chestnut and white, a resplendent garb that breaks up the animal's outline in shady forest, concealing it from the predatory gaze of large cats. This shy tapir is most frequent close to water. A common sign of its presence is a waterside pile of seed-filled droppings: this contribution to plant growth prompts the nickname 'gardener of the forest'.

PECCARIES

Scared of walking in the forest in case a jaguar pounces on you? Fair enough, but – perhaps surprisingly – a more likely source of danger is the white-lipped peccary (*Tayassu pecari*). Peccaries (Tayassidae) are the New World's answer to

White-lipped peccary. (RJ)

Old World pigs (Suidae), although they used to inhabit Eurasia before leaving it for South America three million years ago. While related, peccaries differ from pigs in terms of morphology and ecology. Pigs, for example, have large litters of helpless young, whereas peccaries usually have twins that are active from birth.

Peccaries are sizeable mammals, standing up to 60cm tall and 1.4m long, and weighing up to 40kg. They are front-loaded, with large heads and thick necks but a tiny tail. The head is tipped with a flexible snout that sniffs along the ground for fruit and seeds to supplement the main diet of foliage. The two Pantanal species are largely diurnal.

One reason for the fear invoked by white-lipped peccaries is that they gang up in herds that regularly exceed 100 animals. Should a herd feel threatened, members make a fearsome racket by collectively clattering their canines as well as releasing a pungent smell and raising their hackles. Should this not encourage the intruder to retreat, larger individuals may charge. Fortunately, peccaries see poorly, so they tend not to notice a silent, stationary human. Watching a hundred peccaries file past at close range is an exciting experience, but because white-lipped peccaries are semi-nomadic, seeing them requires either luck or up-to-date local knowledge.

In contrast, collared peccaries (*Dicotyles tajacu*) congregate only in single figures. Collared peccaries are wary, hiding in dense cover during the day, fleeing when sensing danger and leaving a strong cheese-like odour in their wake – the origin of their colloquial name of 'musk hog'.

Not every swine-like beast you may see in the Pantanal is a peccary, however. Large numbers of feral pigs (*Sus scrofa*) – identifiable, even at distance, by their dangling tails – also wander through forest and grassland. The head and jaw structure of these alien invaders enables them to root more efficiently, suggesting that, over time, they might outcompete the native peccaries.

40

A herd of white-lipped peccaries emerges from the forest. (LL/SS)

DEER

Originating in Eurasia, deer (Cervidae) reached South America during the late Pliocene (1.8–5 million years ago), whereupon different species evolved rapidly to fill different niches. Four species inhabit the Pantanal. All are large, graceful animals with long limbs. Males grow and shed antlers each year. Deer feed exclusively on vegetable matter: after eating, they must rest, regurgitate and ruminate – like cud-chewing cattle. All are best seen in early morning and late afternoon, when they emerge from cover to feed.

The largest is a comparative giant. Standing up to 1.3m tall and 1.8m long, male marsh deer (*Blastocerus dichotomus*) have thick, branching antlers 60cm in length. These deer inhabit long grassland or dense reeds near standing water. They have hooves that spread to maximise the area of contact in slippery or soft terrain – an adaptation for life in wet habitats. Inevitably, marsh deer distribution in the Pantanal shifts with the season: animals disperse widely during floods, but concentrate near water during the dry period. Habitat destruction, hunting and infection with cattle diseases have caused this deer to become very rare and localised, with densities no higher than 0.57 individuals/km². Nevertheless, this globally threatened cervid is fairly common in parts of the Pantanal, and most visitors should see it.

The marsh deer – here a young female – is in danger of extinction. (JL)

The pampas deer (*Ozotocerus bezoarticus*) is distinguished from the marsh deer by its smaller size, chestnut (not black) lower limbs and white eye-ring. The English names also convey the differing habitat preferences of the two species, pampas deer preferring dry grasslands. Populations have not yet recovered from massive hunting in the 19th century when, for example, more than 60,000 skins were exported from Buenos Aires (Argentina) in 1880. In consequence, conservationists consider this species at possible future risk of extinction. With Pantanal densities reaching 5.5– 9.8 deer/km², there is no better place to see this species.

The small size and short antlers of the Pantanal's two brocket deer (*Mazama* spp.) are probably adaptations for efficient movement through dense woody vegetation. Brocket deer are primarily shy and nocturnal, but may be diurnal and confiding where not hunted. Unlike the two larger deer, which often feed in small groups, the brockets live alone or in monogamous pairs. The common red brocket (*M. americana*) differs from the common brown brocket or grey brocket (*M. gouazoubira*) by coat colour and its preference for moister, denser forest.

The common brown brocket prefers dense, moist forest. (JL)

Common vampire bats are arguably responsible for bats' ghoulish reputation. (JL)

BATS

In the Western world, bats have a ghoulish image, largely because of their reputation as bloodsuckers. The reality is rather different, with most bats playing a critical ecosystem role as pollinators, seed dispersers and consumers of insects. Nevertheless, behind many a fear lies a smidgeon of justification, and so it is with New World bats, among which is the perpetrator of those bloodsucking phobias, the common vampire bat (*Desmodus rotundus*).

Bats are so evolutionarily distinct as to be allocated to their own order, Chiroptera. Their ability to fly has enabled them to exploit a large variety of food resources and thus to evolve into a significant variety and number of forms. The majority of Neotropical species are insectivores, but others consume fruit, fish, pollen, frogs, birds, crustaceans and, of course, mammalian blood. Bats are exclusively nocturnal. Hunting in darkness requires special skills, and all Neotropical bats home in on their target by using echolocation. A hunting bat uses its mouth or flaps of skin on its nose to amplify high-pitched clicks, and captures returning echoes with its large ears. From this information, it constructs an auditory 'picture' of its surroundings. Each bat family has its own echolocation system, with distinctive morphological structures that emit and gather aural data that only that family can interpret.

In the Pantanal, 73 bat species from seven families have been recorded. Distinguishing them is difficult, but, fortunately, some are distinctive. A dozen bats arranged in vertical lines on a sunlit riverside tree trunk, for example, with striped legs and pale squiggles either side of the spine will be proboscis bats (*Rhynchonycteris naso*). Named for its elongated nose, this species is part of the sheath-tailed bat family (Emballouridae). The pale markings help it to blend into lichen-covered trunks or become 'lost' in dappled light, thereby concealing it from predators. Unsurprisingly for a species that tolerates daylight, the proboscis bat is active early in the evening, hunting aerial insects low over water bodies.

The frosted pelage of proboscis bats offers camouflage. (RH/SS)

BULLDOG BATS

The family Noctilionidae has an even closer relationship with water. As night falls, skies above Pantanal rivers fill with two species of bulldog bat (*Noctilio* spp.), which soon descend on pointed wings to skim the water surface. These relatively big bats have long legs and sharp-clawed feet with which they snatch prey from the water. Of the two species, the lesser bulldog bat (*N. albiventris*) is smaller, emerges earlier and feeds on aquatic insects. The greater bulldog bat (*N. leporinus*) catches fish; hence its alternative English name of greater fishing bat. This species has such precise echolocation that it can pinpoint tiny fish from the slightest of ripples. It may catch 30 fish in a night, storing them in bulldog-like cheek pouches before returning to the colony.

LEAF-NOSED BATS

Leaf-nosed bats (Phyllostomidae) are named after the spear-shaped fold of skin that flares above their nostrils. Members of this diverse group differ so markedly in size, shape, feeding habits and sociality that the family is a microcosm for the order as a whole. The Pantanal hosts 40 species across five subfamilies. The most infamous is the common vampire bat, which is morphologically equipped for its specialised niche. Blade-shaped teeth make a painless incision in the skin of the bat's sleeping prey, while an anticoagulant in the saliva enables it to lap up the free-flowing blood. The Pantanal's main economic activity has been a boon for this bat, which targets cattle as more convenient blood banks than wild ungulates. *Pantaneiros* accuse vampires of being vectors for rabies, and tend to kill them. Another bat with a taste for flesh is the greater round-eared bat (*Tonatia bidens*), which grabs small birds while they roost. One of the New World's largest bats, the greater spear-nosed bat (*Phyllostomus hastatus*) uses its bulk to capture small rodents and even other bats before returning to its tiny colony.

White-lined broad-nosed bat is the Pantanal's most dramatically marked bat. (RJ)

Some members of this group differ markedly in social and foraging behaviour. One of several species that can sometimes be found roosting in abandoned buildings, Pallas's long-tongued bat (*Glossophaga soricina*) forms nurseries of several hundred females and their young. It routinely hovers by flowers, using its long muzzle and tongue to extract nectar and pollen, but also gleans insects from the underside of leaves. Sugar is a precious resource so bats defend nectar-producing *Agave* plants against rivals. Another valuable 'resource' is a mate – or several. Male Seba's short-tailed bats (*Carollia perspicillata*) guard harems of females. This frugivorous bat disperses seeds, helping regenerate the forest. Meanwhile, by day the great fruit-eating bat (*Artibeus lituratus*) roosts under 'tents' made from leaves nibbled into a protective shape.

INSECTIVOROUS BATS

Nectarivory and frugivory are actually rather rare in the bat world. The vast majority of bats eat insects. The family Vespertilionidae houses nine species, which typically fly rapidly and with agility around forest clearings, using their large tail membrane to scoop up tiny insects. The black myotis (*Myotis nigricans*) synchronises its breeding cycle with periods of insect abundance, with females able to store sperm until the time is right.

The Pantanal has a baker's dozen species of free-tailed or mastiff bat (Molossidae). These fly swiftly and erratically on narrow wings high in the sky, foraging for large insects. The alternative English names relate to the bats' appearance: a dog-like face (hence mastiff) and a long tail extending beyond its membrane (free-tailed). But these are not the family's only peculiarities: the flattened bodies of species such as the velvety mastiff bat (*Molossus molossus*) allow large numbers to roost packed together in confined spaces such as roofs.

RODENTS AND RABBITS

Rodents (order Rodentia) are a great mammalian paradox: they comprise nearly half the world's mammal species, yet most are very rarely seen. The reasons for this discrepancy lie in their basic ecology: rodents are generally shy, small, nocturnal creatures that frequently live

The Amazonian long-tailed porcupine is adapted for its arboreal life. (RJ)

underground or in dense vegetation. Whatever their size, however, all 27 Pantanal members of this order are united by their distinctive teeth – notably a pair of large, chisel-like incisors on each jaw that are constantly eroded to maintain a blade-like edge. These versatile tools can cut grass, pry open nuts, dig tunnels and gnaw anything worth gnawing; the word 'rodent' comes from the Latin *rodere*, which means 'to gnaw'. Rabbits and hares are not rodents but belong in the separate order Lagomorpha. The Pantanal is home to just one species.

LARGE ARBOREAL RODENTS

In the trees, keep an eye out for two large, arboreal rodents with long but very different tails. The generic bushy-tailed outline of the Guianan squirrel (*Sciurus aestuans*; family Sciuridae) will be familiar to visitors from North America and Europe. Active by day and a fan of palm nuts, its range only just reaches the Pantanal. The Amazonian long-tailed porcupine (*Coendou longicaudatus*; family Erethizontidae) is adapted for life among trees. Its feet have two modifications for grasping vines: a movable pad instead of a thumb, and a broad-soled hind foot. More noticeably, it has a muscular, prehensile tail that can spiral backwards to grip a branch. Porcupines are best known for the way in which they roll themselves into a ball as a defence strategy against predators, leaving only their barbed spines visible. One touch can leave these spines embedded in the aggressor's paw or muzzle, causing pain, at the very least, and sometimes more serious damage.

CAVY-LIKE RODENTS

Given their large size, hefty heads and tiny tails, you would be forgiven for thinking that the four rodents that make up this group were ungulates rather than rodents. Top of the list – in terms of size, abundance and entertainment value – is the greater capybara (*Hydrochaeris hydrochaeris*). This peccary-sized rodent is the world's largest, troubling the scales at a portly 50kg, and its squared-off muzzle and tiny eyes lend it a characteristic 'tough guy' demeanour. Capybaras are always in or near water, loafing on sandbanks or chomping on aquatic vegetation. They swim well, aided by partly webbed feet, and can hold their breath underwater for several minutes –

useful skills if a jaguar is patrolling the riverside. Active mainly by day, capybaras are sociable, living in family groups of up to six animals or in larger herds during the dry season.

The Brazilian guinea pig (*Cavia aperea*) resembles a small capybara – and for good reason, as both are housed in the family Caviidae. Unlike its

Greater capybara is the world's largest rodent. (KD)

larger cousin, the guinea pig (sometimes called a cavy) shuns water, grazing in short dry grassland but always within dashing distance of the dense vegetation that is criss-crossed with its runs.

A scuffling in the forest undergrowth may lead you to the region's sole representatives of the families Cuniculidae and Dasyproctidae. A nocturnal member of the first-named family, the lowland paca (*Cuniculus paca*) is easily identified by its distinctive lines of white spots on chestnut flanks. Pair members share a territory but forage and den separately; if necessary, they are capable of diving into water to escape predators. Azara's agouti (*Dasyprocta azarae*) belongs in Dasyproctidae and

Capybara litter size ranges from one to seven. (LL/SS)

Three superficially similar Pantanal rodents are Azara's agouti (*left, RJ*), Brazilian guinea pig (*right, JL*) and lowland paca (*below, RMM/SS*), but look for the paca's distinctive flank spots.

is, by contrast, a diurnal rodent with a grizzled grey-brown and ginger coat. It tends to favour forest patches within savannah. It is evidently a good planner, secreting fruit and nuts in subterranean caches to plunder during meagre times. It is also much easier to see than the paca, sometimes venturing close to lodge buildings.

MOUSE-LIKE RODENTS

Pity mammologists who specialise in the smaller end of the rodent spectrum. Theories on species limits and nomenclature among South American mice and rats (Cricetidae, subfamily Sigmodontinae) change every year, so rarely is there agreement on how many species are in the Pantanal – or even what they are called. Nevertheless, for the discerning visitor with an enquiring mind, these are fascinating mammals – not least for the variety of morphological adaptations with which evolutionary radiation has endowed the group.

Rice rats that live in trees, such as Robert's arboreal rice rat (*Oecomys roberti*), have broad feet with sharp curved claws, long tails and dense whiskers. Rodents that graze on the ground, such as the grass mice (*Akodon* spp.), have fine whiskers and short tails; these mice also have long claws for digging tunnels under leaf litter. Terrestrial omnivores such as the elegant oryzomys (*Euroryzomys nitidus*) have pointed snouts and large ears, so as to better detect insect prey. If disturbed, they often jump away to safety. A few species are aquatic, such as Amazonian marsh rat (*Holochilus sciureus*), which has partly webbed hind feet and dense, water-resistant fur. And if these diverse rodents don't tickle your fancy, there's always the roof or black rat (*Rattus rattus*), the ubiquitous scavenger transported to the New World on European ships several hundred years ago.

RABBIT

Bounding along with strong kicks of its long hind legs, the forest rabbit or tapeti (*Sylvilagus brasiliensis*) is a frequent nocturnal sight in the Pantanal. A small cottontail in the family Leporidae, this species has the long ears, large eyes and short, furred tail that visitors associate with 'their' rabbits in the northern hemisphere. It is most active shortly after dusk and before dawn, and has a taste for salt (including in dried human urine) as well as grass. If you succumbed to a call of nature during the day, it pays to return to the site shortly after nightfall!

Forest rabbit, sometimes called tapeti. (IE/SS)

MARSUPIALS

Opossums (family Didelphidae) are the sole Pantanal representatives of the marsupials, a group that has changed little since its evolution 65 million years ago. They are small to medium-sized mammals that recall rodents (order Rodentidae) with their pointed snouts, short legs, long tails and short fur.

Like other marsupials, opossums are famous for parental care. Opossum young are born tiny (1cm long and 0.5g in weight) and quickly ascend their mother's body to a nipple, where they remain attached for several weeks. Thereafter, some species (such as those in the genera *Didelphis* and *Philander*) protect their offspring in a pouch ('marsupium'); others carry young on their back or leave them in a nest

Look for Brazilian white-eared opossums on the forest edge or near water. (CM/SS)

while foraging elsewhere. Most opossums are nocturnal and arboreal omnivores, consuming anything they come across.

The number of species in the Pantanal varies with taxonomic ebb and flow; current thinking says six, but as many as 13 have been mooted by some authorities. *Didelphis* opossums are the largest New World marsupials, measuring up to 1m, including tail. The Brazilian white-eared opossum (*Didelphis albiventris*) has strikingly white ears and black stripes on a white head. It is most often seen on the forest edge or near water. This species is solitary, the sexes meeting only to mate.

The grey four-eyed opossum (*Philander opossum*) is slightly smaller than *Didelphis* and easy to identify, with a large pale spot above each eye (hence the name). A voracious breeder, it is sexually mature at seven months. The brown four-eyed opossum (*Metachirus nudicaudatus*) has dark ears and a largely hairless tail. Its stocky hind limbs are an adaptation to a terrestrial life. Seeing this marsupial requires stealth as, unlike other opossums, it flees at the slightest noise. As its name suggests, water opossum (*Chironectes minimus*) is semi-aquatic; it has strikingly bicolored pelage and swims with only its eyes and crown above the water.

Gracile opossums (*Gracilinanus* spp.) are small pouchless marsupials with a prehensile tail much longer than their body. Just one species – the agile gracile opossum (*G. agilis*) – occurs in the Pantanal, where it prefers the understorey of gallery forests. Dangling from a slender branch or vine by its prehensile-tipped tail, this mouse-sized animal freezes in the torchlight before resuming feeding. Black eye-rings accentuate its huge eyes, giving it an undeniably endearing appearance.

BIRDS

The poster bird of the Pantanal is the globally endangered hyacinth macaw. (GS/SS)

E ven if birds have not previously been your thing, they certainly will be after your Pantanal trip. Seasonally, the place heaves with them, particularly along the Transpantaneira – and many are large, colourful, entertaining and confiding. Each habitat holds a different bird community, so you should keep an eye out and an ear open wherever you are. At least 475 species, and probably around 550, have been recorded. An oft-cited figure of 650 refers to a wider area, but may not be far off the mark as much of the Pantanal remains surveyed. Attentive birders can rack up 130 species in a day and perhaps 200 across a typical four-night stay.

GROUND BIRDS

Three unrelated families stride or shuffle across the Pantanal's dry terrain. Two are entirely terrestrial, and one of these is even flightless.

Guarded by their father, greater rhea chicks stay together for four to six months until they become independent. (UB/SS)

RHEA

Standing taller than many *pantaneiros*, greater rheas (*Rhea americana*) are to Pantanal grasslands what ostriches (*Struthio* spp.) are to African savannahs. At 1.5m in height and 35kg in weight, this is South America's largest bird. Although long-legged, long-necked and flightless, dowdy plumage makes rheas remarkably tricky to spot. And once aware they have been detected, they use those lanky limbs to race for the horizon (and seemingly always run across water!). Males are promiscuous,

The normally retiring undulated tinamou can be rather showy in the Pantanal. (RJ)

mating with many females. Unlike most polygamous birds, however, females lay eggs in a single nest that is attended solely by the male. The huge eggs weigh 600g – the equivalent of 12 chicken eggs. The male takes full responsibility for incubating the clutch and raising up to 30 young.

TINAMOUS

As you walk through Pantanal forests in early morning or late afternoon, a haunting voice may stop you in your tracks as it pierces the background hum. The mournful three-note whistle emanates from an undulated tinamou (*Crypturellus undulatus*), a member of the terrestrial, partridge-like family Tinamidae. Tinamous are short-legged and short-tailed, but also long-necked and slender-billed. They lay arguably the world's most beautiful eggs: so shiny that they resemble porcelain. Tinamous' brown or beige plumage assists in concealment: in grasslands, you may nearly tread on a red-winged tinamou (*Rhynchotus rufescens*) or spotted nothura (*Nothura maculosa*), which freeze when nervous, before fleeing on whirring wings at the last second.

SERIEMA

The red-legged seriema (*Cariama cristata*) reinforces the impression of the African savannahs, recalling a secretarybird (*Sagittarius serpentarius*) as it strides majestically across grasslands. This tall, leggy bird can run at 60km/h and rarely takes to the air. *Pantaneiros* reportedly like seriemas because they eat snakes. Their faintly menacing air derives from a staring eye and stiff, forward-pointing crest – but this is also one of very few birds with prominent eyelashes.

Unexpectedly, the closest relatives of seriemas are now thought to be falcons (page 64). (KD)

WATERBIRDS

As the world's largest wetland, it is unsurprising that the Pantanal is famous for its waterbirds. Among familiar families are herons, ducks and assorted waders, while more exotic representatives include ibises and screamers. Dense congregations of feeding and nesting waterbirds provide unforgettable sights.

HERONS

Most herons (Ardeidae) saunter elegantly through the water before seizing a fish or frog with their dagger-shaped bill. More than a dozen species occur, many breeding in large, noisy treetop colonies. The compact striated heron (*Butorides striata*) calls stridently as it flies between riverbanks, where it adopts a rail-like crouch before pouncing on an unsuspecting fish. The rufescent tiger-heron (*Tigrisoma lineatum*) lives up to its name by starting life in tiger-striped plumage; juveniles take two years to assume the adult's distinguished rufous and grey garb. Alongside the lanky cocoi heron (*Ardea cocoi*) and suave little blue heron (*Egretta caerulea*), look for great egret (*A. alba*), snowy egret (*E. thula*) and cattle egret (*Bubuculus ibis*). The latter is a familiar Old World species that crossed the Atlantic of its own accord and subsequently colonised the Americas.

The extraordinary-looking boat-billed heron. (UB/SS)

The capped heron is elegance in avian form. (KD)

Three herons are primarily nocturnal. Of these, the black-crowned night-heron (*Nycticorax nycticorax*) is the most common but also frequently feeds by day. Amazingly similar in plumage – but only distantly related – is the boat-billed heron (*Cochlearius cochlearius*). Its bill shape is astonishing, being extremely wide and flat, with the upper mandible shaped like an inverted boat keel whose purpose may be to assist social signalling. The furtive zigzag heron (*Zebrilus undulatus*) is a predominantly Amazonian species that can sometimes be glimpsed in dense riparian vegetation in Mato Grosso.

The final trio of herons vie to be beauty queen. The whistling heron (*Syrigma sibilatrix*) is attired in pinkish-yellow and powder blue, with long head plumes and a bright pink bill-base. Its unique whistling call attracts attention when in flight. The capped heron (*Pilherodius pileatus*) has a subtler appearance, but its sublime cream plumage and cyan bill are breathtaking. Arguably the most stunning family member, however, and certainly the most fervently desired, is the agami heron (*Agamia agami*). Sticking to shady riverbanks, this shy heron shimmers chestnut and pale blue when it catches the light.

IBISES AND SPOONBILLS

Ibises (Threskiornithidae) represent an evolutionary link between herons and storks, and are a prominent feature of the Pantanal. Visitors are most likely to see the plumbeous ibis (*Theristicus caerulescens*), buff-necked ibis (*T. caudatus*) and green ibis (*Mesembrinibis cayennensis*). While most ibises breed in colonies, like herons, these three nest alone, like storks. The delicate plumbeous ibis sifts its downcurved bill through shallow water, neck ruffle rippling in the breeze. The buff-necked ibis

The green ibis is less secretive in the Pantanal than elsewhere. (JL)

is a noisier proposition, pairs broadcasting their arrival to all and sundry. Most intriguing is the green ibis. A secretive forest denizen elsewhere in its range, this small ibis loses its inhibitions here, feeding in the open, far from trees and apparently habituated to human proximity. In the sunlight, its wings and neck glint green and blue, bringing a superficially dowdy bird to life.

Extensively pink, with a spatulate bill, the roseate spoonbill is a spectacular creature. (F/SS)

Dowdy is not an adjective applicable to roseate spoonbills (*Platalea ajaja*). Even a hardened birder obsessed with plumage minutiae on little brown jobs cannot fail to be captivated by these flamingo-pink birds swishing their bills through the water, straining it for aquatic insects and small fish. Long, straight and flat, the spoonbill's beak broadens to a bulbous tip that gives the bird its name.

STORKS

Enormous nests – constructed from thick, metre-long branches – enthroning isolated tall trees can only mean one thing: we are in jabiru (*Jabiru mycteria*) territory. With a wingspan of 2.5m, the jabiru is the giant of the Pantanal skies, into which it rises on thermals before soaring to distant feeding grounds. When this enormous bird is excited or stressed, its inflatable throat sac fills with blood and turns vibrant scarlet. Jabirus differ from the two other Pantanal storks (Ciconiidae) in feeding behaviour; each species occupies its own niche in the wetland ecosystem. The jabiru bounces energetically, plunging its bill into the water to terrify hidden fish into the open. The bald-headed wood stork (*Mycteria americana*) forages more calmly, using its feet to stir up sediment and seizing any creature that brushes the sensitive tip of its immersed bill. The scarcer maguari stork (*Ciconia maguari*), red-faced and white-eyed, lurks in tall marshy vegetation, hunting by sight rather than touch.

The huge, prehistoric-looking jabiru stands 120–40cm tall. (top: KD; bottom: OP/D)

Anhinga swallowing a fish. (JL)

CORMORANT AND ANHINGA

An accomplished diver, the Neotropic cormorant (*Phalacrocorax brasilianus*) dries itself by extending its wings, allowing air to circulate and sun to warm. The anhinga (*Anhinga anhinga*) behaves identically, despite belonging in a separate family (Anhingidae). With its sinuous neck and long, fine bill, this attenuated bird resembles a cormorant that has been stretched on a rack. When swimming, with just its neck protruding above the surface, it resembles an altogether different creature, hence its colloquial name of 'snakebird'. The anhinga uses its bill to spear fish underwater. Then, raising head and fish above the surface, it tosses up the catch and swallows it in a single gulp.

WILDFOWL AND SCREAMERS

A first-time Pantanal visitor might expect the world's largest wetlands to be heaving with wildfowl (Anatidae). Yet the opposite is true: ducks can be relatively scarce. Only a dozen species occur – and patchily at that. Three species of whistling-duck (*Dendrocygna* spp.) consort in large, mixed flocks. Whistling-ducks are named after the sibilant calls of two of the trio. The other common duck may look vaguely familiar: muscovy ducks (*Cairina moschata*) have been domesticated for more than 2,000 years and their varied descendants waddle across farmyards worldwide.

Wildfowl, such as black-bellied whistling-duck, can be surprisingly few and far between. (RK/SS)

Given that their voice carries 3km, you will probably hear screamers (Anhimidae) before you see them. The deep, loud calls are alternately melodious and screechy, so the bird is well-named: indeed, the local name of *chajá* is an onomatopoeic rendition of the call itself. You may also discern two voices, for screamer pairs duet. The species involved is southern screamer (*Chauna torquata*), long-legged turkey-like birds on the ground that mutate into massive, eagle-like creatures in stately flight. Neither simile would lead you to believe that the screamers' nearest relatives are actually wildfowl, although the connection might become clearer should you see one swimming through water.

In flight, southern screamer appears massive, with long, broad wings. (JL)

RAILS, GALLINULES AND JACANA

Rails, crakes and gallinules (Rallidae) generally skulk in dense marshy vegetation. Nine species occur, ranging from the lark-sized grey-breasted crake (*Laterallus exilis*) to the duck-sized purple gallinule (*Porphyrio martinica*) and grey-cowled wood-rail (*Aramides cajanea*). The wood-rail and gallinule are the easiest to see: the former is lanky and loud-voiced; the latter lumbering and bright-coloured. Recalling gallinules but unrelated to them, the wattled jacana (*Jacana jacana*) is a firm favourite among visitors. The attraction lies in its gawky gait, riotous coloration and fascinating family life. Absurdly long legs and toes are adaptations to a life spent teetering on floating vegetation, a habit that prompts the colloquial name of 'lily-trotter'. Meanwhile, the adult's coppery sheen explodes into shockingly lemony wings when it takes flight. Jacanas are among just 1% of birds that practise polyandry, a breeding system where the female mates with several males that assume responsibility for parental care. A male's duties include fleeing danger with chicks lodged under his wings, only their dangling legs visible.

Crouched heron-like, the sunbittern is a mass of stripes. (KD)

SUNBITTERN, SUNGREBE AND LIMPKIN

This trio of striking, unrelated birds is taxonomically fascinating. The sungrebe (*Heliornis fulica*) is the sole New World representative of a frugal family (Heliornithidae) that also has single members in Africa and Asia. The other two – the sunbittern (*Eurypyga helias*) and limpkin (*Aramus guarauna*) – have an even greater claim to taxonomic uniqueness: each is the only member of its family.

Swimming furtively near a shady riverbank, a sungrebe resembles a flattened duck. This wary bird hides in vegetation or flees on long wings and drooping tail. Visitors often

In flight, the sunbittern exhibits astonishingly colourful and strikingly patterned wings. (BZG/SS)

see a sungrebe along the same stretch of river as a sunbittern. The Pantanal is the southernmost point of the sunbittern's range, but is also the easiest place to see it. Remarkably, its closest relative is New Caledonia's kagu (*Rhynochetos jubatus*). It resembles a stripy heron, with long legs, sinuous neck and sharply pointed bill. It even behaves like a hyperactive egret, striding along the shore before snatching at an unsuspecting crab. The sunbittern is simply dazzling when opening its wings in threat or flight. The flight feathers sport a startling pattern of chestnut, yellow and black, which suggests a pair of huge staring eyes and is enough to make any predator think twice. The limpkin is no less distinctive. Taking its name from its hobbling walk, this bird has a twisted windpipe that amplifies its call. Its distinctive flight – with deep, elastic wing beats – is unique. And its sharp, jinked bill-tip is the perfect tool for hammering open its principal prey, aquatic apple snails (*Pomacea lineata*).

WADERS

Of a score of waders spread across three families, four are resident while others migrate to South America from northern hemisphere breeding grounds. The resident quartet comprises three plovers and a stilt. The beautiful pied lapwing (*Hoploxypterus cayanus*), elegantly patterned with black, white and brown, breeds on sandy beaches flanking rivers.

Pied lapwing, a riverside treat. (KD)

This habitat, or a simple muddy shore, also attracts the collared plover (*Anarhynchus collaris*), which delights in sprinting long distances. The southern lapwing (*Vanellus chilensis*) is ubiquitous. Noisy and crested, it shrieks in alarm whenever it spots a potential predator, making it a favourite of *pantaneiros* guarding livestock. Black-necked stilts (*Himantopus mexicanus*) wade delicately through water on elongated limbs. Among visiting waders, white-rumped sandpipers (*Calidris fuscicollis*) swarm along lakeshores while groups of lesser yellowlegs (*Tringa flavipes*) loaf in knee-deep shallows. Unlike these sociable creatures, the aptly named solitary sandpiper (*T. solitaria*) prefers its own company on a secluded muddy pool.

The black skimmer furrows the water surface with its lower mandible. (OP/SS)

TERNS AND SKIMMERS

Terns (Laridae) are a feature of any river trip. South America's joint-smallest species – yellow-billed tern (*Sternula superciliaris*) – often sits alongside one of the biggest, the large-billed tern (*Phaetusa simplex*). Both breed on river beaches, often near black skimmers (*Rynchops niger*), a tern-like member of a different family (Rynchopidae). Skimmers have remarkable bills, the lower mandible being half as long again as the upper. They hunt by flying low over the water, lower mandible furrowing the surface. When one senses a small fish, it dips its head and scoops up the prize. Skimmers are a joy to watch.

Snail kites do not exclusively eat snails... (JL)

RAPTORS

Few birds evoke more immediate awe than raptors (or birds of prey). With sharp eyesight, powerful talons and malevolent hooked bills, these imposing predators sit regally atop the avian food chain. Around 40 species have been seen in the Pantanal, but many are rare, so a good haul would be a third of these.

KITES, HARRIER AND OSPREY

Floating languidly low over roadside wetlands, snail kites (*Rostrhamus sociabilis*) catch the eye. This raptor's narrow, sharply hooked bill provides a deft tool with which to prise apple snails and crabs from their shells. The species wanders in search of snails, so large agglomerations can occur seasonally. Other kites (Accipitridae) hunt higher above ground. About 30m up, a white-tailed kite (*Elanus leucurus*) hovers delicately on upraised wings, searching for an oblivious rodent. The pearl kite (*Gampsonyx swainsonii*) soars at great heights, its beauty apparent only when it descends. Plumbeous kites (*Ictinia plumbea*) and swallow-tailed kites (*Elanoides forficatus*) congregate in graceful flocks to hunt winged termites. Male and female long-winged harriers (*Circus buffoni*) differ markedly in plumage; they quarter grasslands, seeking frogs and

The savanna hawk captures small animals on the ground. (JL)

rodents. Ospreys (*Pandion haliaetus*), by contrast, dive at 80km/h to catch fish that venture too close to the surface. One of the front talons is reversible, so the osprey moves it backwards to help grab its prey.

HAWKS AND EAGLES

Pantanal hawks and eagles (also Accipitridae) are an eclectic bunch. They vary from true hawks (genus *Accipiter*) through buzzard-type birds (like *Geranoaetus* spp.) to the massive (and rare) harpy eagle (*Harpia harpyja*). Along the way are oddities such as the crane hawk (*Geranopsiza caerulescens*), which uses extremely long legs and short outer toes to reach into tree cavities, and the black-chested buzzard-eagle (*Geranoaetus melanoleucus*), whose short tail is barely visible beyond its immensely broad wings.

Black-collared hawks loiter on riversides before pouncing on discarded fish. (KD)

The commonest species are the black-collared hawk (*Busarellus nigricollis*) and savanna hawk (*Buteogallus meridionalis*). The latter waits near burning vegetation in order to capture small animals disorientated by smoke, and nabs subterranean creatures that emerge above ground during rain. Black-collared hawks are fixtures along rivers, their fish-catching abilities enhanced by long claws and spiny undersides to the toes. Some individuals have learnt to associate humans with fish; they loiter in riverside trees, waiting for discarded catches. Also seen along rivers, often seeking handouts, but particularly in marshy areas near forest, is the great black hawk (*Buteogallus urubitinga*), which has a taste for reptiles.

The roadside hawk (*Rupornis magnirostris*) is the smallest of three buzzard-like species. It scans for movement from a prominent vantage point, before flying with a distinctive action that alternates rapid flaps and long glides. The white-tailed hawk (*Buteo albicaudatus*) is one of several raptors that comes in two plumage varieties, including a confusing dark phase. The zone-tailed hawk (*Geranoaetus albonotatus*) is consistently dark-plumaged – and for good reason. This remarkable raptor imitates a vulture (*Cathartes* spp.) in coloration, wing shape and flight style. This lulls small birds and mammals into a false sense of security, as they believe it to be a vulture and thus incapable of attacking live prey.

Although they prefer snakes, great black hawks are also accomplished fishers. (JL)

The crested caracara both hunts live prey (like an eagle) and scavenges carrion (like a vulture). (DD/SS)

FALCONS AND CARACARAS

Members of Falconidae vary markedly in form and function. At the 'classic' end of the spectrum are four true falcons – dashing, aerodynamic hunters that pursue small birds and insects in rapid flight. The most common are the American kestrel (*Falco sparverius*) and bat falcon (*F. rufigularis*). The latter targets bats as they emerge from their roost at dusk – though during daylight it happily hunts dragonflies and other aerial insects. Forest-falcons are larger. The two species – collared (*Micrastur semitorquatus*) and barred (*M. ruficollis*) – are more often heard (at dawn) than seen. Known for its chortling call, the laughing falcon (*Herpetotheres cachinnans*) is admired by *pantaneiros* for its snake-catching abilities. Caracaras are generalist omnivores, nibbling fruit and digesting carrion. The dapper yellow-headed caracara (*Milvago chimachima*) perches on livestock, picking botflies off their backs and snatching insects disturbed by their hooves. The crested caracara (*Caracara plancus*) is a brute. With massive bill, shaggy crest and long legs, it bounds along the ground, chicken-like. Its bare face changes colour from red to yellow with excitement.

VULTURES

New World vultures (Cathartidae) are supremely adapted for an energy-efficient lifestyle, capable of travelling hundreds of kilometres without a single flap of their enormous wings. Vultures perform an essential ecological role by consuming decaying flesh and are immune to the botulism that would afflict a human scavenger. Bare heads render these birds ugly but perform a useful function, preventing

Black vultures scavenge dead flesh, even from a yacaré caiman. (JL)

decomposing animal matter from contaminating the plumage. The Pantanal's vulture quartet falls into two distinct groups, divided by whether they locate dead animals by sight or smell. The stunning king vulture (*Sacoramphus papa*) and reptilian black vulture (*Corygyps atrata*) soar high, using acute vision to spot their next meal: even 3,000m up, they can spot a corpse just 30cm long. In contrast, the turkey vulture (*Cathartes aura*) and lesser yellow-headed vulture (*C. burrovianus*) have exceptional olfactory powers so quarter low above trees, sniffing for a concealed carcass.

GUANS AND CURASSOWS

Guans, chachalacas and curassows (Cracidae) resemble pheasants that are at home both in trees and on the ground. All are very large birds with long legs, neck and tail sticking out from a bulky body. You have fine prospects of seeing five species in the Pantanal. Indeed, there is little chance of missing the Chaco chachalaca (*Ortalis canicollis*), an avian alarm clock with a pre-dawn song that reverberates for over 2km – far enough and at sufficient volume to incite a neighbouring group to respond.

Chaco chachalaca is abundant in the Pantanal. (GSG/SS)

Piping-guans display a fleshy dewlap of a throat sac that droops below the bill. The colour of this wattle helps birders distinguish between the (globally threatened) red-throated (*Pipile cujubi*) and blue-throated piping-guans (*P. cumanensis*) – although, confusingly, the dewlap of Pantanal blue-throated is often white! To further complicate matters, the Pantanal is a hybridisation zone, so it is tricky to draw taxonomic limits. Little wonder that some ornithologists lump the forms as a single species. Rather than struggle with identification challenges, then, far better simply to relax and enjoy the piping-guans' instrumental music. As the male display-glides between treetops, the movement of air through his outermost wing feathers – which narrow abruptly towards their tip – produces an explosive ripping sound rather like machine-gun fire.

The globally threatened bare-faced curassow (here, a male) suffers little hunting pressure in the Pantanal, so is easy to see. (KD)

The two other members of this family, both considered gloablly threatened, are no less remarkable. The chestnut-bellied guan (*Penelope ochrogaster*) has such a tiny distribution that the Transpantaneira is almost the only place to see it. Pressured by deforestation and by unsustainable hunting elsewhere in its range, bare-faced curassows (*Crax fasciolata*) top the cracid beauty stakes – doubly so because male and female differ so markedly in plumage that they could be thought separate species. The male's black garb fuses with forest shadows, so you may need binoculars to discern his curly crest feathers. The female has similar headgear but is tiger-striped above.

PARROTS AND THEIR ALLIES

Few bird families are as closely associated with humans as Psittacidae, which comprises macaws, parakeets, parrots and parrotlets. Their cultural importance needs little introduction, as parrots embed themselves in human life as pets, status symbols, meat and sartorial adornments. Nearly a score of parrots and their allies inhabit the Pantanal, of which the average visitor may easily see half.

HYACINTH MACAW

A raucous roar announces the arrival of a hyacinth macaw (*Anodorhynchus hyacinthinus*), the Pantanal bird that all visitors want to see. Measuring a full metre in length and hitting the scales at a hefty 1.5kg, this is the world's largest parrot. It is also among the rarest, its population having crashed as a result of habitat destruction and illegal trapping for the cage-bird trade. A frightening 10,000 birds were captured for trade during the 1980s alone. Despite conservation action, the latest estimate (from 2003!) suggests that just 6,500 birds remain, three-quarters in the Pantanal.

As if this combination of size and scarcity were not sufficient to whet the appetite of even the least bird-orientated of tourists, the hyacinth macaw is also breathtakingly beautiful. Rich cobalt-blue plumage is offset by bare yellow skin around eye and bill (page 51). The result is an engagingly clown-like grin, an impression exacerbated by the macaw's jaunty demeanour and clumsy movements as it waddles along the ground or uses its bill to clamber around a tree.

With their demonstrative behaviour, size and bright coloration, hyacinth macaws are crowd-pleasers. (JL)

The main function of the huge bill, however, is as a powerful nutcracker. The hyacinth macaw's diet largely comprises the hard fruit of a handful of palm trees, particularly the *acuri* and *bocaiúva*. Remarkably, macaws have learnt that Azara's agouti eats the outer layers of these nuts, but leaves the kernel – so some birds save themselves time and effort by dropping nuts to the ground for the mammals to do the hard work.

Conservation, including by the Instituto Arara Azul, has been motivated partly by the realisation that macaws are economic assets that draw tourists. Most tourist *fazendas* host breeding hyacinth macaws, often within metres of lodge buildings, years without human persecution leading Pantanal macaws to perceive man as friend rather than foe. Such a circle of trust benefits the visitor, who can enjoy scintillating views while sipping a beer. Like all Pantanal parrots bar one, the hyacinth macaw is a cavity-nester. While preferring natural holes in tall trees, particularly the *manduvi* (*Sterculia apetala*), it readily takes advantage of large nestboxes erected specifically for its use. Most pairs breed between July and December and are thus often incubating eggs or raising young during the main tourist season.

OTHER MACAWS

The other macaws are less easy to see. The smallest, and most common, is the yellow-collared macaw (*Primolius auricollis*). Mating for life, pairs mutually preen and canoodle. In reality it is a pseudo-macaw – in Portuguese, a *maracañã* rather than an *arara*. The true *araras* are large and gaudy. The blue-and-yellow macaw (*Ara ararauna*) reaches the southern limit of its range in the Pantanal and has predominantly cyan and yellow plumage. The red-and-green macaw (*A. chloropterus*) is similarly named after its principal colours, but also displays large blue patches on wings and tail. You are most likely to see these impressive birds as they fly between feeding grounds.

PARAKEETS

In a family that routinely nests alone in tree cavities, the monk parakeet (*Myiopsitta monachus*) is the proverbial sore thumb. It is the only New World parrot to breed colonially and the only one to build its own, stick nest – often enhancing the structure

Multiple pairs of monk parakeet share a communal nest (JG/SS)

Blue-and-yellow macaw is a feature of the southern Pantanal. (RJ)

of an active jabiru nest, providing early warning of predators by way of rent. The peach-fronted parakeet (*Psittacara aurea*) and nanday parakeet (*Aratinga nenday*) sometimes join monk parakeets in their unusual habit of foraging, dove-like, on the ground. The former is exquisite, with a subtle orange forehead, yellow eye-ring and blue flash on each wing. It is one of few members of this family to benefit from deforestation. Guttural cries from large flocks of nanday parakeet are a common sound of the southern Pantanal. Indeed, calls are the best way to identify parakeets as they zip overhead: large birds, such as white-eyed (*Psittacara leucophthalma*) and blue-crowned parakeets (*Thectocercus acuticaudata*), have deep, harsh vocalisations; flocks of the compact yellow-chevroned parakeet (*Brotogeris chiriri*) communicate with a shrill chirruping. The blaze-winged parakeet (*Pyrrhura devillei*) is a speciality of Mato Grosso do Sul.

PARROTS AND PARROTLETS

The most conspicuous of the Pantanal's six parrots is also the largest: the turquoise-fronted amazon (*Amazona aestiva*). It allows close approach, this trusting nature perhaps the cause of its frequent domestication; these heavily trapped parrots make excellent 'talkers'. Orange-winged amazons (*A. amazonica*) resemble their blue-fronted cousin, but have a yellow central crown stripe flanked with cyan. Scaly-headed parrots (*Pionus maximiliani*) are smaller and have a distinctive flight manner: whereas the heavy wingbeats of *Amazona* parrots recall ducks, and parakeets briefly close their wings between bouts of rapid flapping, the scaly-headed parrot's downstroke brings its wings vertically below the body.

Turquoise-fronted amazon. (JL)

TRAPPING AND TRADING

Humans have harvested and traded wild birds for thousands of years, whether for food, pets, culture or sport. In recent decades, however, the bird trade burgeoned into a billion-dollar industry. Increasing demand, improved access, enhanced capture techniques and expanding air travel are pushing the exploitation of many species beyond sustainable levels. More than one-quarter of the world's bird species have been recorded in international trade, with millions of individuals changing hands each year. Worse still, over one-third of birds threatened with global extinction are victims. Among Pantanal species – as in many parts of the world – parrots are the most susceptible, being prized for their beauty and their ability to mimic humans. A third more hyacinth macaws were snared in Brazil during the 1980s than remain in the whole of South America today. Trade is big business, but local benefits are small. A local farmer may sell a turquoise-fronted amazon to a local trader for a few dollars, just 1% of its final retail value. Songbirds are also prized: several seedeaters (*Sporophila*) that migrate through the Pantanal risk extinction due to intense trapping pressure.

NEAR-PASSERINES

The term 'near-passerine' is a convenient – if taxonomically controversial – catch-all for a disparate assemblage of bird groups that resemble the passerines (page 78) in general appearance and behaviour, but differ in toe morphology. Parrots fall into this group, but are treated separately (page 66).

Long-tailed ground dove is a speciality of central Brazil. (RJ)

PIGEONS AND DOVES

Most of the Pantanal's dozen members of this homogeneous family (Columbidae) feed on the ground, heads bobbing as they scuttle along, picking up seeds or fallen fruits. Ruddy ground doves (*Columbina talpacoti*) and eared doves (*Zenaida auriculata*) are regulars around bird tables and other human habitation. Less tame are the scaled dove (*C. squammata*), unique in its scaly appearance, and long-tailed ground dove (*Uropelia campestris*). The latter occurs only in the savannahs of central Brazil and east Bolivia, so the Pantanal is a great place to see it. With a surprisingly noisy take-off for such tiny birds, a skittish group of picui ground doves (*C. picui*) escape danger on whirring wings.

A handful of larger columbids are associated with wooded habitats. The otherwise dull plumage of picazuro pigeons (*Patagioenas picazuro*) is relieved by a glossy, reflective neck-patch. Pale-vented pigeons (*P. cayennensis*) sing from an exposed perch – like other columbids, with the bill apparently closed. Two stocky doves in the genus *Leptotila* are hard to differentiate, and even expert birders usually pass. Both offer interesting insights into columbid behaviour: a nervous white-tipped dove (*L. verreauxi*) bobs its tail, while a courting grey-fronted dove (*L. rufaxilla*) claps its wings while cooing softly.

With its beady eye, shaggy crest and baggy trousers, the guira cuckoo oozes personality. (JL)

CUCKOOS

Cuckoos (Cuculidae) are infamous for playing no part in parenthood other than laying their eggs in other species' nests. But this breeding strategy – brood parasitism – is actually deployed by only half of the world's cuckoos. The proportion in the New World tropics is even lower. Only two cuckoos breeding in the Pantanal do not raise their own

young: the striped cuckoo (*Tapera naevia*) and pheasant cuckoo (*Dromococcyx phasianellus*). These parasites lay noticeably petite eggs to match those of substantially smaller host species such as spinetails (*Synallaxis* spp.). Getting a good view of either cuckoo requires bags of patience: they typically sit motionless in dense vegetation, revealing their presence only through simple whistling calls, repeated indefatigably for hours. More visible – although far from tame – are the squirrel cuckoo (*Piaya cayana*) and little cuckoo (*Coccycua minuta*). The former is large and long-tailed, with chestnut upperparts and largely pink underparts. While foraging for caterpillars, it manoeuvres through vegetation with a nimbleness that belies its size. The little cuckoo is a pint-sized version of the squirrel cuckoo; the latter's 'Mini-Me', perhaps.

These four cuckoos are solitary and furtive birds. The remaining trio are the opposite – gregarious and showy. Flocks of the scruffy, punk-like guira cuckoo (*Guira guira*) play 'follow-my-leader', birds taking turns to flutter a short distance before crashing into vegetation, apparently exhausted. Anis recall guira cuckoos in behaviour and shape, but have iridescent black plumage and deep-based, steeply arched bills. The greater ani (*Crotophaga major*) is the size of a squirrel cuckoo, equipped with a menacing white eye and invariably found in waterside trees. The appreciably smaller smooth-billed ani (*C. ani*) has less restrictive habitat requirements; visitors frequently enjoy close views of groups sitting on *fazenda* fences.

Burrowing owls are active by day, perching prominently in open areas. (OP/D)

OWLS

Owls (Strigidae/Tytonidae) are among the most widely recognised of all bird groups, in part because of the fearful fascination that we have with these 'creatures of the night'. Thanks to excellent eyesight and superlative hearing, owls are to darkness what raptors are to day: consummate avian predators at the pinnacle of the food chain.

Great horned owl occurs widely in the Pantanal: listen for birds calling at dusk. (KD)

Their nocturnal habits mean that you should head out at night to see more than a couple of the Pantanal's ten species.

By day, the tropical screech-owl (*Megascops choliba*) and great horned owl (*Bubo virginianus*) avoid detection through their nondescript plumage and elongated ear tufts. The tufts have nothing to do with hearing, but assist camouflage by resembling the tip of a broken vertical branch. Despite such tricks, small birds often spot the owl and blow its cover. They mob the predator until the owl grudgingly accepts that it must find peace elsewhere.

You have a greater chance of seeing the two smallest owls, as both are predominantly diurnal. The burrowing owl (*Athene cunicularia*) shuns forests in favour of open grasslands. It breeds in armadillo burrows, termite mounds or other terrestrial holes. The nesting pair widens the entrance hole and excavates a horizontal gallery that they then line with manure or dry grass. The ferruginous pygmy-owl (*Glaucidium brasilianum*) is barely sparrow-sized, but has no qualms about tackling a victim as large as itself. Pygmy-owls fool prey with their false, 'occipital' face. On the back of the head, two black spots flanked by white lines give the impression of large eyes. An unsuspecting bird spots this 'face' and makes a beeline for the 'rear' of the owl, unwittingly entering the danger zone. Such is the fear that pygmy-owls generate among small birds that a whistled imitation of the owl's call may attract skulking passerines into view as they gang up on the perceived threat.

NIGHTJARS AND POTOOS

Nightjars (Caprimulgidae) are dove-sized birds that become active at dusk and characterise excursions on warm, dry nights. With narrow wings and long tails, they recall falcons as they hunt for aerial insects above forest, grassland or river. Huge eyes help them

The most frequently seen nightjar, common pauraques emerge onto roads at dusk. (JL)

spot their prey – and many species use bristles around the bill to funnel it into their wide mouths. By day, most nightjars roost on the ground or along horizontal branches, relying on complex plumage patterns to offer concealment from predators.

Of the ten species, you are most likely to see band-tailed nighthawks (*Nyctiprogne leucopyga*), large numbers of which hunt above rivers at dusk. Locally common around wetlands, nacunda nighthawks (*Chordeiles nacunda*) are the Pantanal's largest nightjar. They are easily identified in flight by their broad wings, short tail and white underparts, but less distinctive when roosting on the ground, when they resemble a cowpat! In wooded areas, you might spot a scissor-tailed nightjar (*Hydropsalis torquata*) enjoying the residual warmth of a road. The male is dramatically attired; elongated tail feathers account for two-thirds of his length. When caught in headlights, the common pauraque (*Nyctidromus albicollis*) makes a short vertical leap before returning to the ground. It has longer legs than other nightjars, enabling it to walk rapidly.

A great potoo at rest by day looks uncannily like part of a tree. (CI/SS)

Closely related to nightjars are potoos (Nyctibiidae). By day, both the great potoo (*Nyctibius grandis*) and common potoo (*N. griseus*) roost erect on tree stumps, mimicking a broken-off branch with their camouflaged plumage. These wonderful creatures have 'magic eyes': the upper eyelid has two incisions that enable the bird to keep a lookout even with its eyes closed. Never has an immobile bird been so interesting! Potoos come to life after dusk when they hawk insects from an exposed perch. At full moon, the common potoo's melancholic wail is a characteristic sound of the Pantanal.

HUMMINGBIRDS

The burst of glittering green is gone even quicker than it arrived, leaving the observer to wonder whether the mind is playing tricks. Such is a typical first encounter with a hummingbird, a beautiful and extravagant family (Trochilidae) exclusive to the Americas. Hummingbirds are jewels of the avian world, their names embodying precious stones such as amethyst, emerald, sapphire and topaz. They are also birds of extremes. One tiny species, the amethyst woodstar (*Calliphlox amethystina*), weighs just 2.5g, while even the black-throated mango (*Anthracothorax nigricollis*), one of the larger species, barely troubles the scales at 6.5g. A hummingbird's heart is relatively larger than that of any other bird, beating 1,000 times per minute to pump oxygen and nutrients around the body. A fast metabolism goes hand in hand with hyperactivity: hummingbirds fly at great speed, wings flapping up to 80 times per second.

'Hummers' are an enthralling part of the Pantanal experience. Sit quietly near a flowering plant and prepare to be entranced as hummingbirds hover by

Flying jewels: gilded hummingbird (left, RMM/SS) and male black-throated mango (right, JL).

the blooms, each inserting its bill to extract nectar. Common species around some fortunate lodge gardens include glittering-bellied emerald (*Chlorostilbon aureoventris*) and gilded hummingbird (*Hylocharis chrysura*). With luck, you may be graced with a visit from a larger species such as black-throated mango, the sumptuous male glittering with blue iridescence on his throat, or white-tailed goldenthroat (*Polytmus guainumbi*).

Alternatively, visit flowering trees in the forest – the domain of the fork-tailed woodnymph (*Thalurania furcata*), the male a shimmering blue. Males of some hummingbirds, such as the localised cinnamon-throated hermit (*Phaethornis nattereri*), congregate in a single place, called a 'lek', to sing and display to females. In the southern Pantanal, you may see the spectacular swallow-tailed hummingbird (*Eupetomena macroura*); pairs zigzag into the air in display.

Another gem of a bird: Amazonian motmot. (RMM/SS)

TROGONS, MOTMOTS AND JACAMARS

Amidst the forest gloom, the visitor's eye is drawn to a long-tailed bird sat serenely on a horizontal branch. It could equally be a trogon (family Trogonidae), jacamar (Gabulidae) or motmot (Momotidae), a distantly related suite of vibrantly coloured birds. A quick look at the bill clarifies the family: a trogon's is short and stubby; a jacamar's is long and fine-tipped (prompting its local name of 'needlebill'); and a motmot's lies in between, being downcurved and of moderate length. The sole trogon is the blue-crowned (*Trogon curucui*), the male of which has a blue-green sheen to the head and bright red underparts. Rufous-tailed jacamars (*Galbula ruficauda*) are common and allow close approach as they pose calmly between bouts of flycatching. These beautiful birds (page 6) shimmer green above and glow rufous below. The most distinctive feature of the Amazonian motmot (*Momotus momota*) is its tail, which it shows off by swinging sideways: the two elongated, central tail feathers have a bare shaft and terminate in a vivid blue spatula. Motmots excavate nest burrows in sandy banks – a habit shared with their nearest relatives, kingfishers.

KINGFISHERS

A sudden splash in the river and a jade bird zooms to an isolated branch, fish clamped in bill. The Pantanal is blessed with all of South America's five resident kingfishers (Alcedinidae), and many visitors are goggle-eyed at their hunting exploits.

Ringed Kingfisher is stunning both at rest (*above*, KD) and in flight (*below*, JL).

All employ an identical fishing strategy: sit, watch, wait and dive. But they are far from identical in size. The largest and most common species, the ringed kingfisher (*Megaceryle torquata*), is 20 times heavier than the tiniest and rarest, the American pygmy kingfisher (*Chloroceryle aenea*).

Erect-crested and conspicuous, the ringed kingfisher demands attention as it perches on roadside telegraph wires or other vantage points above a watercourse. Only the female exhibits the grey chest band encapsulated in the name. Two-thirds the size, the male Amazon kingfisher (*Chloroceryle amazona*) differs from the female in its chestnut breast band. Near-identical in plumage, but another degree smaller, is the green kingfisher (*C. americana*), which appears chequered in flight due to the white spots on its flight feathers. Roughly the same size is the reclusive green-and-rufous kingfisher (*C. inda*), which has dark green upperparts and warm cinnamon underparts. Together with the similar-plumaged but even smaller American pygmy kingfisher, this species favours dense riverine vegetation along small streams.

TOUCANS AND PUFFBIRDS

Sailing between forest canopy and fruiting tree on wings that alternately flap frantically and glide languorously, or even taking fruit from the bird tables of privileged lodges, the toco toucan (*Ramphastos toco*) would make an incongruous sight even without its outsized banana of a bill. This massive appendage provokes both astonishment and mirth in the first-time observer who may only know the bird from tourism adverts or television commercials. Remarkably, the bill helps the toucan regulate its body temperature by effectively sucking out excess heat from the body. Toco toucans regularly visit fruiting trees, where they move restlessly, tail cocked, before plucking a choice morsel with

Its huge bill poses no barrier to this toco toucan's dextrous consumption of tiny fruit. (KD)

surprising deftness. Tocos also have carnivorous tendencies, and groups ransack the hanging nests of yellow-rumped cacique colonies (page 88) or investigate tree holes to extract parrot eggs (page 76).

The other common member of the toucan family (Toucanidae) is the chestnut-eared aracari (*Pteroglossus castanotis*). Smaller and more gregarious than the toco, aracaris often bicker in a fruiting tree or buzz between feeding areas in fast, direct flight. This colourful species has a strongly patterned bill, yellow and chestnut

Chestnut-eared aracaris are gregarious toucans unafraid to venture close to human habitation. (KD)

underparts, and staring white eye. You may need a close look to pick out the brownish face sides that give this aracari its English name.

Perched motionless for long periods and cryptically garbed, puffbirds (family Bucconidae) can be hard to spot in dry, open-country vegetation as they wait for a lizard to break cover. At the end of their large heads, both white-eared puffbird (*Nystalus chacaru*) and spot-backed puffbird (*N. maculatus*) have powerful, hook-tipped red bills: the perfect tool for dismantling reptiles. Sun-worshipping puffbirds are absent from forest, where they are replaced by black-fronted nunbirds (*Monasa nigrifrons*). The shade-loving nunbird's bill and behaviour resemble those of the puffbirds, but its plumage is a uniform smoky-black. It is fearless and allows close approach.

A striking red bill relieves the sombre plumage of the black-fronted nunbird. (JL)

FRIEND OR FOE?

You might think it logical for birds to have an innate hatred of predators that steal their eggs or chicks. Yet there can be more to inter-species relationships than meets the eye. Toco toucans have a particular taste for hyacinth macaw eggs, accounting for more than half of losses. Yet tocos are also fond of the fruits of the *manduvi* tree (*Sterculia apetala*) and are responsible for more than four-fifths of seed dispersal. More than 90% of hyacinth macaw pairs nest in *manduvi*. Since the macaw population – as a whole and over time – depends on replenishment of the *manduvi* stock, it is best served by a large (if egg-thieving) toucan population. Some individual macaws take a hit – but for the greater good of their species. Conservationists must factor in such conflicting ecological pressures to their management decisions. Nature is never simple.

WOODPECKERS

Anyone who thinks the Pantanal is just about wetlands should pause to contemplate its woodpeckers (Picidae). No other bird family is so inextricably linked with trees – so the fact that visitors might see ten species in an average Pantanal trip suggests that the region must have plenty of woodland. Woodpeckers have evolved to cling to vertical trunks, with stiffened tail feathers offering support and strong feet – two toes pointing forwards and two backwards – to grip the trunk. Robust bills enable them to hammer into branches so that their long barb-tipped tongue can reach far into a cavity to extract insect larvae.

White woodpecker typically forages in noisy groups of 5–8 individuals. (JL)

Pantanal woodpeckers vary in weight from just 10g to nearly 200g. At the bottom end of the scale are piculets, miniature woodpeckers that creep along the slimmest of branches on the shortest of trees. White-barred piculets (*Picumnus cirratus*) inhabit the southern Pantanal whereas white-wedged piculets (*P. albosquammatus*) reside throughout. Campo flickers (*Colaptes campestris*) are open-country specialists – largely terrestrial woodpeckers that feast on ants and termites. They are gregarious – as are the white woodpecker (*Melanerpes candidus*) and, mainly in the far south, white-fronted woodpecker (*M. cactorum*). Both *Melanerpes* woodpeckers are noisy, striking and active species inhabiting forested savannahs.

In forest, there are woodpeckers at all levels. The little woodpecker (*Veniliornis passerinus*) forages mainly low down. In the mid-storey, look for two larger, verdent brethren: golden-green woodpecker (*Piculus chrysochloros*) and green-barred woodpecker (*Colaptes melanochloros*). The two *Celeus* woodpeckers are yellow and black with a long, erectile crest. This coiffure reaches punk proportions in the pale-crested woodpecker (*C. lugubris*) which is one of two species nicknamed the 'Billy Idol woodpecker', in homage to the shock-locked 1980s rocker. Meanwhile. the cream-coloured woodpecker (*C. flavus*) takes the genus's yellow pigmentation to the extreme, retaining just dark wings and tail. The largest woodpeckers are typically found at the top of the tallest trees. All are black-and-white with a mainly red head. To differentiate them, pay particular attention to the pale markings: the cream-backed woodpecker (*Campephilus leucopogon*) has an ivory mantle, while the crimson-crested (*C. melanoleucus*) has a whiter face than the lineated (*Dryocopus lineatus*).

Lineated woodpecker favours large trees in forest. (HL/SS)

77

PASSERINES

Around half the world's birds are classified as passerines. This order is characterised by having three forward-facing toes and one backward-pointing toe that meet the foot at the same level. This morphological adaptation enables passerines (or 'perching birds') to grasp a branch, toes locking into position even when the bird is asleep. All songbirds are passerines – although not all passerines are songbirds.

OVENBIRDS AND WOODCREEPERS

Ovenbirds and woodcreepers (collectively known as furnariids; family Furnariidae) constitute a large, diverse assemblage of insectivores whose dull plumage shrouds lives that are far from boring. Ovenbirds have radiated into almost every South American habitat, occupying finely separated ecological niches. The Pantanal's 20-odd species variously inhabit scrub, thickets, riverbanks, cerrado, marshes and forest. The family name derives from the horneros (*Furnarius* spp.), which build dome-shaped mud nests that resemble a traditional baker's oven (*horno* in Spanish).

Striding jauntily along the ground or duetting loudly from a tree with its partner, a rufous hornero (*Furnarius rufus*) – the best-known furnariid – demands attention. Its nest-building process is a labour of love, a pair needing three weeks to collect sufficient wet mud and straw to construct their two-chambered home. On shady riverbanks, look for a scarcer relative – the pale-legged hornero (*F. leucopus*) – strutting along, distinguished by a white stripe behind the eye.

Spinetails are predominantly arboreal ovenbirds with weedy bills and long tails. Members of the genus *Synallaxis* skulk in dense vegetation; obtusely, this obfuscatory habit endears these birds to birders, who are keen to see Pantanal specialities such as white-lored (*S. albilora*) and cinereous-breasted spinetails (*S. hypospodia*). A similar bird with an absurdly long tail will be a chotoy spinetail (*Schoeniophylax phryhanophilus*). During the breeding season, this yellow-chinned denizen of scrub and cerrado marks its presence with a large, spherical stick-nest. Prominent nests also alert birders to rufous-fronted thornbirds (*Phacellodomus rufifrons*), which weave sticks around a vertical branch, and to firewood-gatherers (*Anumbius annumbi*) and rufous (or grey-crested) cacholotes (*Pseudoseisura unirufa*), which both build large stick nests in a tree fork.

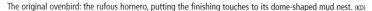

The original ovenbird: the rufous hornero, putting the finishing touches to its dome-shaped mud nest. (KD)

The red-billed scythebill is unmistakable. (LM/SS)

You might surmise that a large, brown, strong-billed bird spiralling up a tree would be a woodpecker. Not so. The bird is a woodcreeper, unrelated birds whose arboreal habits have converged with those of woodpeckers. Woodcreepers used to be afforded their own family (Dendrocolaptidae) but have lately been merged with the ovenbirds. The most common species is the narrow-billed woodcreeper (*Lepidocolaptes angustirostris*), which has a bold eyestripe and downcurved bill. The most impressive family members are great rufous woodcreeper (*Xiphocolaptes major*) and red-billed scythebill (*Campylorhamphus trochilirostris*). The former is a sturdy-billed giant, easily as big as the largest Pantanal woodpecker, usually adorning isolated trees in open terrain. As its name suggests, the scythebill has a remarkable bill that is very long, sharply downcurved and bright crimson.

ANTBIRDS

So named for their association with – rather than consumption of – ants, antbirds (Thamnophilidae) are a diverse collection of stocky passerines, some of which follow army ant (*Eciton*) swarms to feast on invertebrates forced to flee by the marching column. In order of increasing size, the Pantanal's 15 members comprise antvireos, antwrens, antbirds and antshrikes. The most attractive antwrens are the large-billed (*Herpsilochmus longirostris*), rusty-backed (*Formicivora rufa*) and black-bellied (*F. melanogaster*). The first-named inhabits gallery forest, and the startlingly cinnamon-coloured female is more eye-catching than the monochrome male. The reverse is true of the rusty-backed antwren: the

Mato Grosso antbird (here a male) is highly sought-after by visiting birders. (RJ)

striking male is rufous, black and white, but the female dowdy. The black-bellied occurs locally in scrub and the woodland understorey.

For birders, the most interesting antbirds are the band-tailed (*Hypocnemoides maculicauda*) and the Mato Grosso (*Cercomacra melanaria*). Both inhabit forest near water and typically forage in pairs. The latter is almost endemic to the Pantanal, and the region marks the southern limit of the range of the former, an Amazonian species. Mato Grosso antbird is judged to be particularly vulnerable to climate change, which is predicted to contract its floodplain-centric range; the bird has little potential for readjustment by moving its range uphill, for example.

Although they like to skulk, antshrikes are nevertheless the easiest members of the family to see, particularly the great antshrike (*Taraba major*) and the barred antshrike (*Thamnophilus doliatus*). In both cases, unless you saw a pair together, it would be easy to conclude that males and females belong to separate species. Only a flaming red eye connects the black-and-white male great antshrike to the rufous female. The female barred antshrike, unmarked and gingery, lacks the male's monochrome barring that gives the species its English name.

TYRANT FLYCATCHERS

The most speciose family in the New World, with 440 members, tyrant flycatchers (Tyrannidae) are also one of the most heterogeneous. The most widespread and familiar of the Pantanal's 60 species, the great kiskadee (*Pitangus sulphuratus*) is ten times heavier than the smallest, the common tody-flycatcher (*Todriostrum cinereum*). Almost all tyrannids have short tails, but the fork-tailed flycatcher (*Tyrannus savanna*) has dramatically long, forked appendages. Most tyrants are dowdy birds, clad in greys and greens, but several splash out on a flash of colour with a semi-concealed yellow or orange crown-stripe; two – the male vermilion flycatcher (*Pyrocephalus rubinus*) and both sexes of the cliff flycatcher (*Hirundinea ferruginea*) – break rank completely, being largely scarlet and terracotta respectively. But such variation is countered by incredible similarity between members of some genera: even experienced ornithologists struggle to distinguish species in the genera *Elaenia* (dull olive birds with white wingbars), *Myiozetetes* (like miniature

The great kiskadee is a familiar sight around Pantanal lodges. (JL)

kiskadees) and *Myiarchus* (brown flycatchers with yellow bellies).

Elaenia is one of several genera whose members sing exclusively at dawn, a habit so well known in Brazil that it has led to the colloquial name *Maria-já-é-dia* ('Maria, it's daytime!'). Smaller and longer tailed are the various tyrannulet genera, the most common species being the southern beardless-tyrannulet (*Camptostoma obsoletum*). Most male tyrant flycatchers advertise for females by singing, although others, such as the white-throated kingbird (*Tyrannus albogularis*), also have an impressive display flight, which helps communicate their availability over longer distances.

Should such courtship displays reap the desired prize of a mate, tyrant-flycatchers set about nest-building. Most Pantanal species construct simple cup-shaped or spherical nests, although a handful, such as the yellow-olive flycatcher (*Tolmomyias sulphurescens*), create a bag-shaped hanging nest. These structures attract the attention of piratic flycatchers (*Legatus leucophaius*). Uniquely among tyrannids, this stripy-headed insectivore bullies nest-owners into deserting, then steals the nest.

Tyrant-flycatchers occur in every

Shrubs offer the vermillion flycatcher convenient perches from which to hawk their insect prey. (RJ)

Cattle tyrants often use mammals, here a female greater capybara, as a base from which to hunt insects. (GS/SS)

habitat. In open country, look for the white monjita (*Xolmis irupero*) grey monjita (*X. cinereus*; occurs in the southern Pantanal only), vermilion flycatcher and cattle tyrant (*Machetornis rixosa*). The latter often hitches a ride on livestock or capybara (*Hydrochaeris hydrochaeris*), flitting to the ground to grab insects that the mammals disturb. In scrub, look for several small species with 'tody' in their name, particularly the rusty-fronted tody-flycatcher (*Poecilotriccus latirostris*) and stripe-necked tody-tyrant (*Hemitriccus striaticollis*). The black-backed water tyrant (*Fluvicola albiventer*) and white-headed marsh tyrant (*Arundinicola leucocephala*) specialise in foraging in wetlands. In forests, bran-coloured flycatchers (*Myiophobus fasciatus*) sally for arthropods while blending into low vegetation, their dull plumage helping them avoid the attention of both predators and prey.

ON THE BRINK

In life, we have neither the money nor the time to do everything we would like. Prioritisation is essential for every business and every organisation. And so it is for conservationists, self-appointed guardians of nature with the collective goal of preventing extinctions. Published by the World Conservation Union, the IUCN Red List of Threatened Species provides the global

The world population of chestnut-bellied guan may be as low as 1,700 birds, many around the Transpantaneira highway. (KD)

prioritisation, identifying species most in need of conservation attention if global extinction rates are to be reduced. The Red List has further in-built prioritisation. 'Critically Endangered' encompasses the species at extremely high risk of extinction, and is followed by 'Endangered' and 'Vulnerable'. Species that almost qualify are listed as 'Near Threatened' and those too poorly known to be assessed are 'Data Deficient'. BirdLife International manages the classification of the world's birds, nearly 1,500 of which are globally threatened. The Pantanal hosts at least nine – among them the near-endemic chestnut-bellied guan – plus a handful of Near Threatened species. Ecotourism helps protect the Pantanal, which helps save these birds from extinction.

The flaming crest of the male helmeted manakin catches the eye inside dark forest. (RMM/SS)

MANAKINS

In the gloom of the forest, two fireballs tremble and shake before zipping upwards with a mechanical buzz. These rival male band-tailed manakins (*Pipra fasciicauda*) are displaying at a traditional 'lek' site, each seeking to demonstrate its fitness to females. Males of this breathtaking species are bright red on the head, 'fading' to vivid yellow on the vent. Impressive displays are almost universal among manakins (Pipridae). Helmeted manakins (*Antilophia galeata*) display by making looping flights between canopy trees. Males are jet-black save for a flaming mantle stripe that culminates in a forward-pointing crest. But elaborate plumage is not a prerequisite for enticing displays. The localised pale-bellied tyrant-manakin (*Neopelma pallescens*), which scrapes into the eastern Pantanal, may not be much to look at but – should there be any chance of mating – it certainly performs, jumping vertically, beating its wings and calling loudly.

VIREOS AND ALLIES

The five members of Vireonidae are spread across three genera that inhabit the forest edge. The Pantanal's resident chivi vireo (*Vireo chivi*) population is complemented in summer by migrant red-eyed vireos (*V. olivaceus*) from North America. Formerly 'lumped' together, the two are now considered to be separate species, given their differences in wing structure and iris colour. Rufous-browed peppershrikes (*Cyclarhis gujanensis*) are robust with a notably hook-tipped bill designed to chop up caterpillars. Similar, but slender and slim billed is the ashy-headed greenlet (*Hylophilus pectoralis*), which picks delicately through foliage.

JAYS

Jays are the only Neotropical crows (family Corvidae). The two Pantanal species – large, charismatic birds with a sharp bill – belong in the same genus (*Cyanocorax*). In plumage and character, however, they have little in common. The purplish jay (*C. cyanomelas*) sits demurely, its ashy-lilac plumage merging with shadows. The brash, raucous plush-crested jay (*C. chrysops*) could not be more different, possessing startling electric-blue face patches and velvety head ruff. In the Pantanal, purplish jay has been recorded serving as a 'cleaner' for deer and lowland tapir, perching on the mammals' head or back to remove ticks.

Plush-crested jay sometimes visits feeding stations. (JL)

SWALLOWS AND MARTINS

Whether lining up on wires prior to migration or gracefully capturing aerial insects, swallows and martins (family Hirundinidae) are universally enjoyed. Fittingly, swallows are symbols of peace and happiness in Brazil. There are 11 species in the Pantanal, of which visitors should see four or more. Over wetlands, white-rumped (*Tachycineta leucorrhoa*) and white-winged swallows (*T. albiventer*) vie for the observer's attention. Given that both have white rumps, you should concentrate on the

White-winged swallows are a common sight around watercourses. (GTW/SS)

wings to distinguish one from the other. Along rivers, look for southern rough-winged swallows (*Stelgidopteryx ruficollis*): the common name derives from small serrations on the male's flight feathers, the purpose of which remains uncertain. Around human habitation, large hirundines that recall falcons are brown-chested martins (*Progne tapera*), one of the few family members with a dawn song.

WRENS AND ALLIES

With its sweet, melodious warble, the perky house wren (*Troglodytes aedon*) is one of South America's best-loved birds. The antics of this restless little brown job captivate visitors around lodge buildings. Another wren (family Troglodytidae) often found around lodge gardens – if they have palms, on which this species depends – is the thrush-like wren (*Campylorhynchus turdinus*). The comparison with a thrush (family Turdidae) enshrined in the wren's name reflects the latter's size, long bill and lengthy tail. Hardened birders may seek out two *Thrythorus* wrens that differ more in voice than plumage: buff-breasted (*T. leucotis*) in the northern Pantanal and fawn-breasted (*T. guarayanus*) farther south. Partners duet in perfect synchrony; each pair also develops its own particular phraseology or pace to differentiate itself from neighbours.

Black-capped donacobius is a taxonomically obscure bird whose pairs duet. (RB/SS)

Another bird that bonds through voice is the black-capped donacobius (*Donacobius atricapilla*). Pairs' vocal explosions are a characteristic sound of Pantanal swamps. Baffled scientists used to treat the donacobius as a wren, but now allocate it to its own family (Donacobiidae). Another group of uncertain evolutionary provenance is the gnatcatchers and gnatwrens, once classified as Old World warblers (Sylviidae), among other families, but now graciously accorded their own family (Polioptilidae). Gnatcatchers are dainty arboreal insectivores with slender physiques and long tails. Masked gnatcatchers (*Polioptila dumicola*) usually forage in pairs, the male recognisable by his black bandit mask.

THRUSHES, MOCKINGBIRDS AND PIPITS

One of Brazil's oft-cited literary quotations immortalises a thrush: 'My land has palms, where the thrush sings,' wrote Antônio Gonçalves Dias. The irony is that the 19th-century poet was thinking of a mockingbird (family Mimidae) – but this in itself suggests a degree of similarity that is reflected in the two groups' stocky, long-tailed appearance and vocal mastery. Of the Pantanal's four thrushes (Turdidae), two are relatively common. A garden bird over much of South America, the rufous-

Chalk-browed Mockingbird is resident in open areas and scrub. (JL)

bellied thrush (*Turdus rufiventris*), Brazil's national bird, is primarily a forest species here, as is the pale-breasted thrush (*T. leucomelas*). In the austral winter (May–August), warmth-loving creamy-bellied thrushes (*T. amaurochalinus*) migrate north to the Pantanal, swelling the thrush ranks.

Mockingbirds exhibit a similar pattern: white-banded mockingbirds (*Mimus triurus*) are an uncommon winter visitor, joining the resident chalk-browed mockingbirds (*M. saturninus*). More slender and longer necked than thrushes, these accomplished mimics jog along the ground as they forage for insects and seeds. A smaller streaked bird sprinting through long grass is usually a yellowish pipit (*Anthus lutescens*), the Pantanal's only representative of the family Motacillidae (which, in the Old World, also contains wagtails). This species sings exclusively in flight – a surprisingly rare habit among birds.

Silver-beaked tanager. (MMe/SS)

TANAGERS, CARDINALS AND ALLIES

Tanagers (family Thraupidae) are often a kaleidoscope of colour. In lodge gardens, look for palm tanagers (*Thraupis palmarum*) hogging palms as songposts, while closely related sayaca tanagers (*T. sayaca*) guzzle fruit nearby. In forests, common thraupids include two stocky birds with powerful bills: the grey-headed tanager (*Eucometis penicillata*) and silver-beaked tanager (*Ramphocelus carbo*). The latter would be hard to spot were it not for its swollen lower mandible gleaming in the gloom. The male white-lined tanager (*Tachyphonus rufus*) has a habit of flicking its wings. As it does, it flashes a white area on its armpit, which ensures that it quickly catches the eye. One thraupid oddity is a tiny bird with plumage recalling that

85

Yellow-billed cardinal is a common Pantanal bird, often seen around lodge buildings. (GTW/SS)

Double-collared seedeater. (F/SS)

of a greater kiskadee that sips nectar from forest flowers – a bananaquit (*Coereba flaveola*). This bird long baffled ornithologists, who argued about its taxonomic affinities: was it related to tanagers, grassquits (*Tiaris* spp.) or New World warblers (family Parulidae)?

Saltators (*Saltator* spp.) are noticeably thick-billed members of Thraupidae. Four species occur but you are most likely to encounter greyish (*S. coerulescens*) or green-winged (*S. similis*). The latter differs in its olive wings and strikingly white (rather than buff) throat. Given their wide habitat preferences and considerable abundance, you are likely to come across boisterous, crimson-headed cardinals. The red-crested cardinal (*Paroaria coronata*) is unmistakable with its long, erect crest; it is usually near water. The gregarious yellow-billed cardinal (*P. capitata*) hangs out in large flocks around stables, a habit that leads to its Brazilian name of *cavalaria* (cavalry).

Ornithologists with a taxonomical bent have strived to decipher where one seedeater species (*Sporophila* spp.) stops and another starts. This is pertinent because several are globally threatened or near threatened. Much comes down to male colour patterns and song. The situation is simpler, fortunately, with common species such as double-collared (*S. caerulescens*), rusty-collared (*S. collaris*) and white-bellied seedeaters (*S. leucoptera*). These often flock together to feed on grass seeds, bending a stem to the ground so as to feed in comfort.

FINCHES AND SPARROWS

Following taxonomic shuffling of the passerine pack, the Pantanal harbours one species of finch (family Fringillidae), three New World sparrows (Passerellidae) and a single introduced member of the Old World sparrows (Passeridae). The latter is a familiar bird, the house sparrow (*Passer domesticus*), although it proves rare away from the region's towns. Its native Latin American counterpart is the rufous-collared sparrow (*Zonotrichia capensis*), whose head features a raft of stripes that ends in a russet shawl. The second member of the New World sparrow family is the grassland sparrow (*Ammodramus humeralis*), a somewhat nondescript bird that often runs along the ground like a mouse. The final family representative is similarly reclusive: saffron-billed sparrow (*Arremon flavirostris*) feeds unobtrusively in the undergrowth of deciduous woodland and riverine forest. When encountered, however, it is seen to be attractive, with a bright orangey-yellow bill fronting a boldly patterned black and white head. The Pantanal's sole finch is purple-throated euphonia (*Euphonia chlorotica*), a colourful, stubby-billed fruit-eater.

A singing saffron-billed sparrow. (JL)

NEW WORLD WARBLERS

A flash of yellow in the undergrowth catches the eye. It is most likely a tropical parula (*Parula pitiayumi*) or flavescent warbler (*Basileuterus flaveolus*) – both vividly coloured residents of Pantanal forests. New World warblers are small, slim insectivores that hover or glean their prey from under leaves. They are restless birds, forever on the move, but often curious towards human observers. A close approach from a tropical parula is likely to be a memorable experience, as this gem has blue upperparts, bright yellow underparts and an orange wash to the breast. Masked yellowthroats (*Geothlypis aequinoctialis*) differ from other Pantanal warblers in having separate male and female plumages (only the male has a black eye-mask), and inhabiting damp scrub rather than forest.

Rufous-collared sparrow, a common sight in South America. (F/SS)

A male masked yellowthroat. (JL)

Orange-backed troupials are regular visitors to lodge gardens. (KD)

ICTERIDS

The combined life stories of icterids (family Icteridae) would make for a fantastic soap opera. All necessary elements are present: beauty, infidelity, deception and theft – and all conducted at top volume. Icterids comprise four distinct groups, each with specific roles in the show: oropendulas and caciques; orioles; blackbirds; and cowbirds.

Crested oropendulas (*Psarocolius decumanus*) and caciques, such as the yellow-rumped (*Cacicus cela*) and golden-winged (*C. chrysopterus*), have a swollen bill base that, in the oropendula, projects well up the forehead. The two genera have similar nests – hanging baskets of moss up to 2m long. With one exception – the well-named solitary black cacique (*C. solitarius*) – caciques are noisy colonial breeders. There are few more quintessentially Neotropical sights than a bevy of oropendula nests swinging from a tall palm.

The nuts of *buriti* palms are among the favoured foods of the orange-backed troupial (*Icterus croconotus*), a slender oriole attired in a heart-stopping combination of orange and black. The troupial shares with the promiscuous greyish baywing (*Agelaioides badius*), a cowbird, the disreputable tendency to take over other species' nests and use them as its own. This piratical behaviour is eclipsed by that of other cowbirds, which are true brood parasites. They lay eggs in other species' nests and play no further role in the parental process. Shiny cowbirds (*Molothrus bonariensis*) are known to parasitise 60 species.

The other two cowbirds are more selective, focusing their attentions, ironically, on fellow icterids: screaming cowbirds (*M. rufoaxillarius*) target greyish baywings; giant cowbirds (*M. oryzivorus*) focus on caciques and oropendulas.

The five species of blackbird are less scandalous in behaviour. Three are associated with wetlands and two with grasslands. One wetland species, the scarlet-headed blackbird (*Amblyramphus holosericeus*), is an expert at 'gaping', an extraordinary foraging behaviour unique to icterids. The bird inserts its pointed bill into a fruit then opens its mandibles to get at any food hidden within.

Shiny cowbirds may be associated with cattle, but are also seen around horses. (JL)

REPTILES, AMPHIBIANS AND FISH

Visitors to the Pantanal are guaranteed close encounters with yacaré caimans. (GS/SS)

REPTILES

No class of animals evokes more trepidation than reptiles (Reptilia). Even that most heinous of human crimes, murder 'in cold blood', invokes these ectothermic creatures, which are guilty of no more than an inability to generate their own body heat. Our fear has been enshrined in reptilian beasts of lore: dragons appear from the era of St George to that of Shrek, and basilisks slither from Greek mythology to Harry Potter's chamber of secrets. But few real reptiles are remotely as dangerous as their legendary counterparts, and the Pantanal is a fantastic place for herpetophobes to move from worry to wonder, with around 80 species to marvel at (although under a dozen are seen in a typical trip).

Traditional taxonomy recognises three orders of reptile in South America: Testudines (tortoises and turtles), Crocodylia (crocodilians) and Squamata (lizards, amphisbaenians and snakes). This approach unites animals that are covered with scaly skin and breathe through lungs rather than gills. The application of molecular biology briefly suggested a radically different treatment, positing that crocodilians were more closely related to birds than (other) reptiles. Sensibly, the conventional treatment prevailed! As reptiles are cold-blooded, their lives revolve around regulating temperature, moving between sun and shade (or water) as required, and – in the case of crocodilians – opening their jaws to offload excess heat.

TORTOISES AND TURTLES

The order Testudines is characterised by ostentatious in-house security. Hard shells cover all but head and limbs – and even these can be safely retracted under the carapace. With this almost impregnable fortress, unchanged for 200 million years, survival rates are high and lifespans long for those that make it to adulthood. Tortoises (family Testudinidae) have a domed shell and live on land. Side-necked turtles (Chelidae), with their flatter shell and slender limbs, are streamlined for a largely aquatic life.

Red-footed tortoise has red skin on its face as well as its feet. (RJ)

Of the 300-odd members of this order worldwide, the Pantanal has a miserly duo, divided one apiece between the two families. On the tortoise side of the taxonomic fence is red-footed tortoise (*Chelonoidis carbonaria*). Although nothing like as large, it is in the same genus as the famous Galapagos giant tortoise. Like that species, the red-footed tortoise is an herbivore that uses strong jawbones to chomp through terrestrial vegetation. When this tortoise senses that it is infested with ectoparasites, it heads for an ant nest and allows the inhabitants to forage over its skin.

As its name suggests, the big-headed Pantanal swamp turtle (*Acanthochelys macrocephala*) is a speciality of the world's largest wetland. This is a 'side-necked turtle', so-called because it retracts the neck sideways when withdrawing into its shell. It eluded discovery until 1984, perhaps because it slumbers through the dry season in soft mud, emerging only with subsequent rains. This turtle is scarce, with conservationists considering it at potential future risk of extinction.

The Pantanal's yacaré caiman form the world's largest gathering of any crocodilian. (JL)

CAIMAN

Crocodilians are among the most ancient of living reptiles, their form having scarcely changed in 100 million years. With a muscular tail, hefty jaws, superlative strength and razor-sharp teeth, these are the bruisers of the reptile school. Little wonder that the immense seasonal gatherings of their Pantanal representative – the yacaré caiman, or simply yacaré (*Caiman yacare*) – are among the biggest wildlife attractions in South America.

There are three species in the genus *Caiman* in the family Alligatoridae, all restricted to the Neotropics. Most taxonomic authorities consider the yacaré to be a species in its own right, although some lump it with the spectacled caiman (*C. crocodilus*), which occurs farther north. Like all crocodilians, yacaré are adapted for hunting by stealth. Their eyes and nostrils lie above the line of the body, enabling them to see and breathe while otherwise concealed by water or vegetation. Such features enable predator to approach victim without being detected. Should a caiman

Yacaré gather during the dry season in large groups around remaining waterbodies. (UB/SS)

submerge for the final attack, it lowers flaps over its throat, nostrils and ears to prevent water entering, and protects its eyes with transparent eyelids.

Although the yacaré is one of the world's smaller crocodilians, it nevertheless reaches lengths of 2–3m. Typical Pantanal prey comprises capybara, herons and fish. In the dry season, yacaré make a beeline for remaining ponds. Hundreds congregate en masse, lying parallel in the shallows. The gatherings have twin aims: to avoid drying out, and to indulge in the drought's fishy feast. Such gatherings allow for great photographic potential – whether an abstract image of serried ranks of armour plating or a portrait unexpectedly juxtaposing a delicate butterfly perching atop a crocodilian snout. And don't forget to head into the night with a torch and enjoy the reflections of scores of crocodilian eyes, gleaming like lacustrine stars. Then listen to caimans roar: to assert dominance, a male yacaré arches his back so that only head and tail are above the water, then 'bellows', making water above the animal dance into the air.

Seeing such hordes, you might think that yacaré are abundant. And you would be right – but only because of recent conservation efforts. For almost the entire 20th century, Pantanal caiman suffered catastrophic levels of hunting to supply the global demand for crocodile shoes. Even during the 1980s, a million yacaré were harvested annually. Only since 1990 has new trade legislation been sufficiently enforced for poaching to cease. Yacaré have recovered rapidly, and the current population may be around 10 million, with densities ten times higher than the 1970s. Nowadays, the yacaré is one reptile that you will see on even the briefest Pantanal visit. But for how long? Global heating means that more than half of the yacaré's habitat is calculated to become unsuitable by 2050, leaving just one-seventh of its range protected.

Green (or common) iguanas are often spied basking, and scratching, beside water. (JL)

LIZARDS

Lizards are the four-legged members of the order Squamata – allowing for a few that have only two legs or even none at all. The score of Pantanal species vary in size from geckos just 5cm long to iguanas that exceed 2m. Many lizards have a nifty, if rather dramatic, way of escaping danger. If a predator seizes their tail, they snap it off at a predetermined weak point. This leaves the predator with a wriggling tail tip – a decent, fatty meal in itself – while the lizard makes a getaway, regrowing its tail over time.

Iguana

The dragon of fables has its roots in a very real group of reptiles: the iguanas (Iguanidae). The Pantanal representative is the green or common iguana (*Iguana iguana*), a standard item in pet shops. With a spiny crest running the length of its back, this lizard has a fearsome appearance but is actually a placid vegetarian. Its beautiful lime-grey coloration provides excellent camouflage as it sprawls along a leafy branch above a river. Get too close to a resting animal, however, and it may plop into the water and swim to tranquillity.

Anoles and spiny lizards

Close relatives of iguanas, though much smaller, are anoles (Polychrotidae) and spiny lizards (Tropiduridae). Shared features include the fleshy throat fan that males erect in display. The Pantanal's only anole is the Brazilian bush anole or Brazilian monkey lizard (*Polychrus acutirostris*), whose eyes have a scaly appearance like those of a chameleon; indeed a further alternative vernacular name is point-nosed false chameleon. The Amazon lava lizard (*Tropidurus torquatus*) frequents dry areas such as grasslands, although it typically offers barely a glance as it scurries along branches or a fallen log, or ascends a tree.

Argentine black-and-white tegu – a New World equivalent of Old World monitor lizards. (JL)

Teiid lizards

A crashing in shrubbery is not always a mammal; tegus (family Teiidae) reach 1m in length and make a racket as they flee from danger on powerful legs. These are the New World equivalent of Old World monitors (*Varanus* spp.), with similar long claws for digging and forked tongue flicked out to 'taste' the air. The gold tegu (*Tupinambis teguixin*) occurs in gallery forests and the Argentine black-and-white tegu (*Salvator merianae*) in drier habitats. A third species, Matipu tegu (*Tupinambis matipu*), was described new for science in 2018. The semi-aquatic Paraguay caiman lizard (*Dracaena paraguayensis*) is tegu-sized; its genus name comes from the Greek *drakaina* (female dragon), while the English name is a reference to its spiny, crocodilian protrusions along back and tail. The imposing reptilian's range is centred on the Pantanal. Whereas caiman lizards and tegus exude power, smaller teiids such as the giant ameiva (*Ameiva ameiva*) embody speed – in name and nature. When not sprinting, the ameiva basks in sunny spots, its white flank spots and stripes gleaming.

Geckos, skinks and spectacled lizards

The Pantanal's remaining lizards fall into three families: geckos (Gekkonidae), skinks (Mabuyidae) and spectacled lizards (Gymnophthalmidae). Geckos have modified toe tips that enable them to scale even smooth vertical surfaces. Native to Asia, tropical house geckos

The Paraguay caiman lizard has crocodile-like spiny protrusions along its spine. (NL/SS)

(*Hemidactylus mabouia*) are invasive aliens, and their arrival may be adversely affecting two native geckos: South American dwarf gecko (*Lygodactylus wetzeli*) and Brazilian gecko (*Phyllopezus pollicaris*). Skinks are slender, smooth-skinned and small-eyed lizards that appear neckless. Uniquely among reptiles, some female skinks nourish their embryos via a placenta. Of the three Pantanal species, look for black-spotted skink (*Copeoglossum nigropunctata*) sunning itself on the forest edge, while Dunn's mabuya (*Manciola guaporicola*) is distinctively orange around its lips. The three species of spectacled lizard are not commonly encountered. Schreiber's spectacled lizard (*Cercosaura schreibersii*) can see with its eye closed, thanks to a transparent lower eyelid, while Maximilian's blue-tailed microteiid (*Micropblepharus maximiliani*) is named for its eyecatchingly blue tail.

AMPHISBAENIANS

Few Pantanal animals are as unearthly in appearance as amphisbaenians or worm lizards – legless cylinders with concentric rings of scales that move in concertina

The yellow anaconda is one of the world's biggest snakes. (KD)

fashion. Four species occur, including the red worm lizard (*Amphisbaena alba*). The group's fondness for lodging in ant nests, with their labyrinth of tunnels and ready supply of food, confused indigenous Brazilians, who named them 'ant kings'. Amphisbaenids' subterranean existence means that they are seen almost exclusively when heavy rain forces them to surface.

SNAKES

Snakes bear most blame for reptiles' poor public image. From the Garden of Eden onwards, snakes have been identified with evil, evoking fear and loathing in equal measure. Many would-be wildlife-watchers cite snakes as their reason for avoiding the tropics. Yet many societies worship snakes as symbols of health and rejuvenation. And the grounds for distress are slight: less than 10% of snakes are venomous, and even fewer pose any threat to humans. Moreover, seeing any snake is a challenge; most are secretive, nocturnal and far more scared of you than you are of them. The Pantanal hosts more than 50 species spread across five families: one lodge alone has 45 recorded species (Pouso Alegre in Mato Grosso). Ditch the dread and revel in a suite of animals as beautiful and diverse as any!

A battle to the end, but did the yacaré caiman target the yellow anaconda or vice versa? (GA/SS)

Snakes have much in common. With poor eyesight and hearing, almost all rely on their flickering tongue to gather olfactory information. All, moreover, are carnivores that swallow their prey whole. But there are differences that relate to ecological niches. A snake's shape fits its domain. Burrowing snakes are short and stout, arboreal serpents long and lithe. Snakes also move in different ways; not all slither. Those with thick bodies pull themselves forward in linear fashion. Small or arboreal snakes wriggle from side to side. And burrowing snakes move like a concertina through solid earth.

The beautiful patterning of the Brazilian redtail boa (or boa constrictor) assists camouflage. (LL/SS)

Blind snakes

Evolutionary biologists believe that snakes evolved from a group of limbless, burrowing reptiles. One group of serpents never even made it above ground: the blind snakes (family Typhlopidae), represented in the Pantanal by the South American striped blindsnake or Brongersma's worm snake (*Amerot brongersmianus*). Your best chance of seeing this sightless creature is after heavy rain, when its subterranean tunnels are flooded.

Anacondas and boas

One serpent both tops most visitors' Pantanal 'wish list' and scoops first prize for the world's biggest snake: the anaconda. There are two species in the region: the yellow anaconda (*Eunectes notaeus*, the genus name meaning 'good swimmer') and the green anaconda (*E. murinus*). The latter is larger (reaching 6m and 250kg), but also much rarer, being at the southern end of its range. In truth visitors can only hope to see yellow anaconda, but even its 4m length makes for a spectacle. Like caiman, anacondas are adapted for aquatic life. Elevated eyes and nostrils allow them to see and breathe while otherwise submerged. This enables them to stalk mammals as large as capybara, which they kill by asphyxiation, constricting the victim within their muscular coils. Good places to look for yellow anaconda are under bridges and inside holes in riverbanks, where they often slumber peacefully.

Two other members of the family Boidae, the Brazilian redtail boa or boa constrictor (*Boa constrictor*) and rainbow boa (*Epicrates cenchria*), also squeeze the life out of their prey. Both are beautifully patterned, although the markings aim to provide camouflage rather than appeal to aesthetic sensibility. Largely arboreal, boas wait motionless in trees, using pits running along the upper jaw to detect changes in heat distribution that indicate an approaching mammal. With such advanced perceptiveness, who needs sharp eyesight?

Vipers

Vipers (Viperidae) also use heat-sensing pits to track prey, but kill them by lunging with long, sharp fangs. Penetrating the victim's skin, the fangs release venom that causes internal haemorrhaging then death. Vipers can be aggressive if they feel threatened, so if you spot one, watch from a safe distance. The Mato Grosso lancehead (*Bothrops mattogrossensis*) is relatively common on warm nights near wetlands. Herpetologists think that its long tail helps it climb into trees during floods. This species is more densely patterned than the Brazilian lancehead (*B.*

The Neotropical rattlesnake rattles its warning only when it feels threatened. (LL/SS)

moojeni), a frequent road-kill victim. Neotropical rattlesnake (*Crotalus durissus*) bites can be very dangerous. However, it is in neither your interest nor the snake's for it to waste venom on a mammal it cannot eat, so if you get too close, a helpful rattling of the hard scales at its tail tip will sound a warning.

The Brazilian lancehead is more active by night than by day. (AD/SS)

Coral snakes – real and false

Elapids (Elapidae) eclipse even vipers in the venom stakes. Outside South America, this family includes cobras and mambas. The only Pantanal elapid (sneaking into the far south) is the Argentinian coralsnake (*Micrurus pyrrhocryptus*). Its black, white and red colouration is a warning to potential predators that it is venomous; get the message and stay away. Non-venomous snakes from another family (Colubridae), like the forest flame snake (*Oxyrhopus petolarius*), have cottoned onto this ruse, and have evolved to mimic the coral's colour pattern. But this strategy is not foolproof: a burrowing owl (*Athene cunicularia*) has been recorded killing *Oxyrhopus*, and laughing falcon (*Herpetotheres cachinnans*) eats both coral snakes and their mimics.

The forest flame snake may resemble a venomous coral snake, but is harmless to humans. (MR/SS)

A semi-aquatic snake, the false water cobra is often found in wetlands and near rivers. (BZG/SS)

Other colubrids

Most Pantanal serpents are also members of Colubridae. These 'typical snakes' come in many sizes and colours, and live in all manner of habitats. But they have some important similarities. Notably, they have relinquished their left lung to become more slender. A third are venomous, but most of these are back-fanged and thus harmless to humans.

Unsurprisingly in a wetland, several Pantanal colubrids are aquatic. The false water cobra (*Hydrodynastes gigas*) takes its name from the habit of raising a flattened neck prior to striking – like a true cobra (*Naja* sp.). This large reptile packs a vicious bite, so stay clear. If you see a swimming snake with black and orange-pink stripes on its sides, you are

The giant parrot snake is an agile, fast-moving serpent that glides with ease through trees and vegetation. (UB/SS)

probably watching a leopard keelback (*Helicops leopardinus*), a voracious consumer of Pantanal fish. Among arboreal serpents, the long but delicate, jade-coloured giant parrot snake (*Leptophis ahaetulla*) hunts tree-frogs (Hylidae) by stealth, sitting motionless then striking rapidly when the victim comes within range; when scared, it opens its mouth wide and mock-attacks.

Primarily terrestrial, the indigo snake or yellowtail cribo (*Drymarchon corais*) is an ambush expert that reaches 2m long. It is often seen hunting on the ground near water bodies, including rivers. Two often ill-tempered species to look out for include Chaco sepia snake (*Thamnodynastes chaquensis*) amid dry brush, and the tree-loving banded cat-eyed snake (*Leptodeira annulata*).

AMPHIBIANS

Amphibians (class Amphibia) were the first vertebrates to set foot on land, having evolved from fish roughly 375 million years ago. Their heyday was their first 100 million years, after which reptiles gradually ousted them from many terrestrial habitats thanks to their ability to lay eggs on land. Many amphibians became extinct – a process that, tragically, is being renewed today (page 101, *Frog fungus fears*). Amphibians never entirely abandoned their aquatic roots, however. Most depend on water to breed, with juveniles being aquatic (and breathing through gills, like fish) before transmogrifying into adults capable of respiration through their skin. This double life is embodied in the name 'amphibian', from the Greek for 'dual existence'. Two orders of amphibians occur in the Pantanal: frogs and toads – known collectively as anurans (Anura) – and caecilians (Gymnophiona), outlandish creatures that appear part-snake, part-earthworm.

The lesser snouted tree-frog is one of three species of 'bathroom frog' often seen inside Pantanal lodge buildings. (JL)

Although not visible here, Cuyaba dwarf frog has large fake eyes on its hindquarters, designed to scare would-be predators. (DO/SS)

A ground-dwelling amphibian, the whistling grass frog (*Leptodactylus fuscus*) is named after its distinctive call. (RMM/SS)

FROGS AND TOADS

Fifty anurans in six families inhabit the Pantanal, but others may remain to be discovered or have their taxonomic status realigned. All are broad-headed, fat-bodied animals with powerful hind legs that propel them on land and in water. On calm nights, particularly after rain, the Pantanal resounds with the calls of male frogs. Each species-specific vocalisation seeks to attract a female and deter rival males. Listen carefully to the chorus. To avoid being drowned out, individual frogs orchestrate their vocal interventions for the gaps between others' utterances. The result is a beautiful, incessant aural twinkling.

Adult anurans breathe through their skin, an adaptation that unfortunately increases their susceptibility to dehydration. To counter this, they must rest somewhere cool and moist during the day. To tell where that might be, examine a frog's feet: aquatic frogs have prominent webbing between toes to facilitate swimming; arboreal frogs have adhesive pads with which to grip vertical surfaces; and terrestrial frogs have protrusions on their soles to facilitate digging.

Tree-frogs (Hylidae) hog the bottom rung of the anuran size ladder and, in the Pantanal, comprise perhaps 15 delicate species. These include the first amphibians you are likely to see: one of three species collectively nicknamed 'bathroom treefrogs' (*pererecas de banheiro* in Brazilian Portuguese), which are frequently found inside buildings. Apparently entering via water pipes, they are typically seen around the shower, toilet and sink in lodge bedrooms. The smallest is the lesser snouted tree-frog (*Scinax nasicus*), which has stripes on its upper back. It lacks the bold yellow markings on the hindlegs that characterises the fuscous-blotched snouted tree-frog (*Scinax fuscovarius*). The third is the Mato Grosso snouted tree-frog (*Scinax acuminatus*), which – belying its name – occurs south as far as Buenos Aires, Argentina.

Other anurans are unusual in different ways. At the upper end of the tree-frog size spectrum, veined tree-frog (*Trachycephalus typhonius*) is literally a handful: it provides

Cururu toads often hunt around lodges. (JL)

anyone foolish enough to hold it with an unpleasant glob of mucus that resists washing off. Those in the genus *Leptodactylus* (Leptodactylidae), uniquely, pack their eggs in foam nests to protect them from predators. When threatened, dwarf frogs (subfamily Leiuperinae, currently housed within the family Leptodactylidae) such as Cuyaba dwarf frog (*Eupemphix nattereri*) and weeping dwarf frog (*Physalaemus biligonigerus*) face away from the predator and raise their legs to reveal an eye-like pattern in the groin that gives the impression of a larger animal. Microhylid frogs (Microhylidae) include the two-coloured oval frog (*Elachistocleis bicolor*), a fossorial species with a flattened body, a small pointed head and a taste for termites.

Finally, cururu toads (*Rhinella diptycha*; family Bufonidae) love foraging for flies around lodge buildings, where they astound visitors with their size (up to 20cm). If this toad's normal bulk, habit of voiding water and making angry clucking sounds do not deter a would-be predator, it inflates itself beyond the swallowing capabilities of most.

FROG FUNGUS FEARS
In the second half of the 1980s, reports began to emerge of dramatic declines in amphibian populations all over the world. Only recently has the true scale of the crisis become apparent. One-third of the world's amphibian species are now globally threatened or extinct, according to the World Conservation Union. Just 1% has increasing populations. Frogs and their allies are on the brink of disaster. Habitat loss poses the greatest threat, but a newcomer on the block is increasingly perturbing conservationists: fungal disease. First detected in Australia in 1993, herpetologists soon realised that the problem was global. Chytridiomycosis, caused by chytrid fungi *Batrachochytrium* spp., has so far affected 30% of species, often causing sudden and dramatic population declines that rapidly end in extinction. Although frog deaths due to the fungus have yet to be proven in the Pantanal, this is as likely due to sparse herpetological surveys as actual absence. If (when?) it arrives, there may be no holding back. No control measures are known, so conservationists will be powerless to stop its spread.

CAECILIANS
Caecilians live below ground and are rarely seen. If you dig into moist soil, you may unearth a slimy-skinned legless creature that moves by pushing the front part of its body forward into increasingly taut skin before allowing the hind part to catch up.

Once above the soil surface, however, it writhes like a serpent. Females take maternal care to a new level. Newborn caecilians feed by exfoliating their mother, eating her outer layer of skin – and do so every third day for up to 11 months. The species known from the Pantanal is Boettger's caecilian (*Siphonops paulensis*).

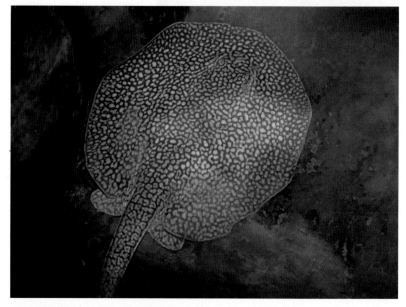

The largespot river stingray inhabits Pantanal rivers. (DG/SS)

FISH

Fish are the only animals in this book whose entire lifecycle is aquatic. They are adapted for underwater existence, with streamlined shapes, friction-reducing scales, fins for power-steering and gills for breathing. Seeing fish is problematic for the land-based wildlife-watcher. You are most likely to spy them in a predator's mouth or beak, splashing frantically in a dessicating pond, wriggling on a fishing line, or – identifiable by taste rather than morphology – laid out at your lunchtime buffet. Nevertheless, fish play an important role in Pantanal ecosystems and are integral to the local culture. An overview of the more prominent species is thus essential for this guide.

Between 260 and 325 species are thought to occur. Almost all are bony fish (superclass Osteichthyes) – characterised by their strong but light internal skeleton – with just a few cartilaginous fish (class Chondrichthyes). Among bony fish, characins (order Characiformes) and catfish (Siluriformes) each account for 40% of diversity. As with terrestrial animals, species composition depends on habitat. Small characids dominate in rapid rivers, small catfishes on sandy bottoms. Slow, deep waters have the highest diversity – and the most valuable fish for aquarium markets.

CARTILAGINOUS FISH

River stingrays

Cartilaginous fish include a few river stingrays (Potamotrygonidae). Related to sharks, flat-bodied stingrays swim sinuously just above the river bottom. Resting concealed in the mud, the largespot river (or Paraná freshwater) stingray (*Potamotrygon falkneri*) defends itself with a sharp spine on the tail: woe betide the shoeless fisherman!

Lungfish

The South American lungfish (*Lepidosiren paradoxa*) is a living fossil that inhabits stagnant waters. Usually considered only member of the family Lepidosirenidae, this eel-like creature has a dorsal fin running the length of its slender body and a long ventral fin. Whereas most fish succumb to dehydration or predation during the dry season, the lungfish hibernates in mud, leaving holes so that it can breathe.

The eel-like South American lungfish survives the dry season buried in a mucus cocoon beneath the mud. (GSa/SS)

BONY FISH

Characins

A diverse bunch, characins (Characiformes) include the Pantanal's most famous fish, the golden dorado (*Salminus brasiliensis*), and the most notorious, piranhas. If you have heard of only one South American fish, it is surely the piranha, renowned for its numerous, sharp teeth and reputedly voracious appetite. However,

Greatly prized by sport fishers, the golden dorado's sharp teeth enable it to catch small mammals. (DG/SS)

it is a myth that piranhas hunt in large packs; sizeable schools actually serve as defence against predators. Although piranhas occasionally nibble bathing humans, the infamous scene in the James Bond film *You Only Live Twice* bears no relation to reality.

A common Pantanal species is the red-bellied piranha (*Pygocentrus nattereri*), which is largely vegetarian. Growing up to 3.5kg and 35cm, it provides bounty for fishermen, with piranha soup being a typical Pantanal dish. Pirambebas (*Serrasalmus* spp.) may also be referred to as piranhas, and the red ruby piranha (*S. maculatus*) and spotted piranha (*S. marginatus*) both occur. A relative, pacu (*Piaractus mesopotamicus*), also often ends up on the menu.

Prized by sport fishers, the golden dorado is gold-coloured, up to 1m long and 10kg in weight. With powerful jaws replete with sharp teeth, this is a major river predator, consuming birds, small mammals and fish such as the streaked prochilod (*Prochilodus lineatus*). Another top predator that captivates sport fishers is the pike characin (*Acestrorhynchus pantaneiro*). The slender build and razor-edged teeth of this genus prompt aquarists to name it the 'freshwater barracuda'.

Catfish

Catfish are highly diverse and Pantanal members are spread across ten families. Although morphology varies considerably, many catfish have flattened heads with long snouts and sensory 'whiskers'. These barbels are taken to an extreme in long-whiskered catfish (Pimelodidae), such as the spotted sorubim or pintado (*Pseudoplatystoma corruscans*) and the barred sorubim (*P. fasciatum*). Having tasty, mostly boneless flesh and regularly measuring up to 90cm (the record is 1.6m and 100kg!), both are targeted by fishermen. In contrast, spiny dwarf catfish (Scoloplacidae) are just 2cm long and were formerly thought to be juveniles of other species. The skin of callichthyid armoured catfish (Callichthyidae) has overlapping bony plates; the cascarudo (*Callichthys callichthys*) is able to breathe intestinally, which enables it to move overland between water bodies during the dry season.

Red-bellied piranha is common in Pantanal rivers. (JL)

INVERTEBRATES

A postman butterfly in the genus *Heliconia*. (BZG/SS)

For most visitors, the stars of the Pantanal show are undeniably mammals, birds and reptiles. But there would be no spectacle without the backstage staff, a myriad of smaller creatures. The base of the animal food pyramid comprises a vast range of invertebrates that wriggle, bore, buzz and teem through earth, air and water. Worldwide, these spineless critters form 97% of all known animal species. There are probably more species in just one of the 30 phyla – arthropods (Arthropoda) – than in the rest of the animal kingdom combined. The qualifier 'probably' is pertinent. Pantanal invertebrates are poorly known, even for South America. From 2005–16, just six terrestrial arthropods new to science were described from the northern Pantanal – a negligible total for a biodiverse region. Here we sketch out some of the more visible invertebrate groups and their better-known members.

Male *Diastatops pullata*, abdomen a vibrant scarlet, are a common sight along rivers. (JL)

INSECTS

In evolutionary terms, no animals are more successful than insects. More than one million species have already been identified – and this may be just one-tenth of the final total. For every human, there are 160 *billion* insects. Insects owe their success to three main traits. Their small size enables them to occupy tiny niches. They can breed rapidly and thus make the most of temporary or local food abundance. And, critically, many can fly – enabling them both to disperse widely and escape predators.

DRAGONFLIES AND DAMSELFLIES

Of all arthropods, none repay close scrutiny more than dragonflies and damselflies (Odonata). These phenomenal aerial predators exhibit exceptional agility as they execute handbrake turns at up to 30km/h. When perched, they embody gracefulness. Through binoculars, their compound eyes are revealed as an iridescent feat of evolutionary engineering. Damselflies such as the cyan-and-black genus *Acanthagrion* are small and dainty, apparently capable only of weak flights interspersed with long rests. In contrast, dragonflies are robust creatures with powerful, dynamic flight. Although the Pantanal's total diversity is unknown, 41 species were found at just two ponds and 209 species are known from Mato Grosso do Sul overall. Amberwings (*Perithemis* spp.) flit repetitively round a small area, their burnt-yellow wings and orange thorax positively glowing. *Diastatops pullata* is common along rivers, the male resplendent with scarlet abdomen and wing bases.

Carmine skimmers (*Orthemis discolor*), here a female, favour isolated, prominent perches. (RJ)

CRICKETS AND GRASSHOPPERS, MANTIDS AND ANTLIONS

Crickets and grasshoppers (Orthoptera) are the string section of the insect world, rubbing wings against legs to produce impressively strident sounds for creatures just a few centimetres long. Their combined chirruping creates the Pantanal's background hum. Orthopterans have powerful hind legs, enabling them to leap from danger. Grasshoppers and locusts are diurnal and have short antennae, whereas crickets are nocturnal and long-horned. Some species have mass emergences that make quite the spectacle.

Two distantly related insect orders – mantids (Mantodea) and antlions (Neuroptera) – are patient hunters. The stealthy, camouflaged mantids bide time until a fly ventures within pouncing range. Some praying mantids (family Mantidae) are notorious

Up close, this species of unicorn mantis takes on an almost extraterrestrial air. (JL)

At the bottom of this conical pit, hidden under the sand, waits a hungry antlion larva. (JL)

A fight between two male rainbow scarab beetles. (RMM/SS)

for the female biting off the male's head during copulation. Amazingly, this cannibalistic act does not impede the male from disseminating his genes. Adult antlions of the family Myrmeleontidae catch insects on the wing and resemble damselflies but with club-headed antennae. The larvae, however, are terrestrial ambush-specialists. Excavating a conical sandpit, they lurk at the bottom and wait for an ant to approach the rim – at which point they flick up sand grains to knock down the unsuspecting victim within reach of their spiny mandibles.

BEETLES AND BUGS

Beetles

Few orders embody biological diversity quite like beetles (Coleoptera). Even accomplished entomologists only cautiously hazard a guess as to how many species exist worldwide: consensus is stuttering towards 370,000. Although beetles vary from tiny creatures best viewed with a magnifying glass to monsters bigger than your hand, all share a defining characteristic: hardened forewings (elytra) that protect soft hindwings.

Two Pantanal beetles attract attention by producing bioluminescence. Male fireflies (Lampyridae) attract females by flying slowly a metre above ground, pulsing green light from their abdomen. This light lacks ultraviolet rays so produces no heat – a highly energy-efficient process. Elaterid beetle larvae like *Pyrearinus termitiluminans* can produce light: abandoned termite mounds, as are common in the north Pantanal, often glow like Christmas trees when colonised.

Scarab beetles (part of the superfamily Scarabaeoidea) have been revered by many societies for shiny elytra that gleam like precious metals. In the Pantanal their number includes rainbow scarabs (*Phanaeus* spp.), which are among the region's 68 known species of dung beetle. By breaking down mammal excrement, dung beetles provide vital ecological roles such as nutrient cycling and seed dispersal.

Bugs

While many people refer to virtually any insect as a 'bug', true bugs are members of the order Hemiptera. Hugely diverse, they range from tiny aphids (Aphididae) to giant water bugs (Belostomatidae) that include 11cm-long 'toe-biters' (*Lethocerus maximus* that can be attracted to lodge lights as they fly between water bodies.). Portentously named assassin bugs (Reduviidae) – identified by flattened bodies and black, white and red colouration – feed on blood; some transmit Chagas' disease, which afflicts ten million people in the Americas and is frequently fatal. Cicadas (Cicadidae) evoke awe for different reasons. Larvae live underground for years before emerging for a brief fortnight of adult existence when their sole goal is procreation. Males attract mates by vibrating a membrane in their resonant abdomen to emit a wrenchingly loud screech. The cicada cacophony eclipses even the background hum of orthopterans as the omnipresent Pantanal sound.

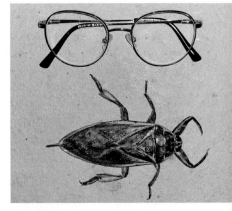

FLIES

Flies (Diptera) prop up a huge part of the Pantanal food chain, but many visitors may find it hard to appreciate their ecological value relative to their annoyance factor and role as disease vectors. Mosquitoes (Culicidae) are the greatest irritants, their incessant whine distracting even the most patient wildlife-watcher. Malaria, transmitted by nocturnal *Anopheles* mosquitoes, is not a particular problem in the Pantanal. However, beware the day-flying *Aedes aegypti*, the vector for yellow

Lethocerus maximus, a giant water bug, can reach 9cm in length. (HV/BEB)

and dengue fevers. Botflies (Oestridae) lay their eggs in live victims, either directly or via an intermediary such as a housefly (Muscidae). Body heat from the mammalian host prompts the egg to hatch, and the larva burrows under its host's skin where it remains until emergence. Most botflies parasitise cattle and deer (Cervidae), but the human botfly (*Dermatobia hominis*) prefers *Homo sapiens*. Forsaking the gross for the enjoyable, hoverflies (Syrphidae) are a delight to watch. These insect helicopters hover inquisitively a few centimetres from your face before buzzing off to investigate another intriguing sight. Striped in black and yellow, hoverflies resemble stinging bees, a disguise that deters predators.

Hoverflies are frequently inquisitive, venturing within a few centimetres of your face; who is watching who? (JL)

BUTTERFLIES AND MOTHS

Butterflies are aerial jewels, their flashes of colour provoking gasps of wonder. Alongside moths, they form the order Lepidoptera. By day you can readily see various butterflies and day-flying moths; at night, portable light sources (or lodge lights) additionally help attract nocturnal moths. Reproduction is a demanding process, with sperm production depleting the salt levels of many a male. Mammal urine, faeces and sweat provide opportunities for mineral replenishment, so many butterfly species congregate in areas frequented by capybara, for example.

Estimates of Pantanal butterfly diversity vary considerably, but some 900 are thought to occur in Mato Grosso overall, one-third of the national tally. Less clear is the Pantanal proportion of Brazil's 23,000-plus moths. And even the most assiduous lepidopterist has yet to venture estimates for Paraguay and Bolivia.

Grey crackers rest head-down on a tree, beautifully camouflaged. (JL)

The Nymphalidae are attractive butterflies: most have brightly coloured upperwings but dull underwings that offer camouflage. Gulf fritillaries (*Dione vanillae*) fly powerfully, crossing large rivers with ease. Tyrant-flycatchers only make the mistake of catching a banded orange heliconian (*Dryadula phaetusa*) once in their lives; this heliconiid is poisonous. When not perching upside down on a tree, superbly camouflaged, male grey crackers (*Hamadryas februa*) demarcate their territory with aggressive flights accompanied by a loud clicking (or 'cracking'). This sound is generated by the

Marcellina sulphur and other butterflies engage in 'mud-puddling' for mineral-rich water. (JL)

male striking together veins in its forewings – although entomologists once ascribed it to movement of the butterfly's genitalia! Larger nymphalids include two spectacular species. Concentric black and yellow circles stand out on the hind wing of the owl-butterflies (*Caligo* spp.) – the resemblance to a real owl's staring eye causing potential predators to backtrack. Equally stunning are morphos (*Morpho* spp.), huge creatures with iridescent blue patches on the upperwings that flap slowly through forest glades, each hefty wingbeat propelling the bearer upwards.

The Pieridae include several sociable butterflies. The great southern white (*Ascia monuste*) congregates in large numbers in midsummer, the effect recalling a snowstorm. The Marcellina sulphur (*Phoebis marcellina*) occurs in large lime-green flocks near rivers. Swallowtails (Papilionidae), such as *Hercalides* spp., are large and graceful, with long tail-like protrusions from their hindwings.

Julia Heliconian butterflies (*Dryas iulia*) often seem to tempt fate by resting on a caiman. (LL/SS)

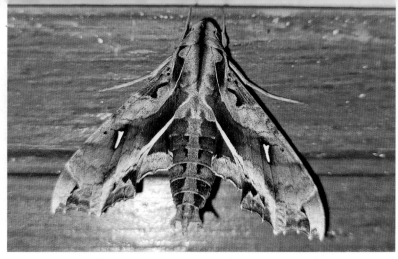

Look for moths, such as this *Hemeroplanes triptolemus* hawk-moth, around lodge lights. (HV/BEB)

Even experts can be flummoxed by moths, so most visitors content themselves with casual observations of obvious species, particularly those attracted to light. Hawk-moths or sphinx moths (Sphingidae) are capable of sustained flight of up to 50km/h. The banded sphinx (*Eumorpha fasciata*) – its wings an alarming blaze of black, brown and pink – is common. The hawk-moth *Hemeroplanes triptolemus* has a remarkable caterpillar whose abdomen mimics a parrot snake. Moths initiate the courtship process by secreting pheromones. Courting tiger moths (Arctiidae) go further, wooing prospective partners with a clicking sound. The closer the pair, the louder and more rapid the clicks.

Termites may build their citadels inside forest (even up trees) as well as in grasslands. (JL)

TERMITES

Tall cones of mud projecting above dry grasslands (a pronounced feature of the northern Pantanal); mud ovals adorning large forest trees. Welcome to the colonial world of termites (family Termitidae), the oldest social insects on Earth. Each termite mound can house a million individuals divided into 'castes' – each with a body adapted to its role in the colony. Tiny workers forage and care for larvae. With large heads and jaws, soldiers defend the colony from attacks by anteaters. Queens dwarf their bodyguards and lay the colony's eggs, sometimes thousands per day.

A termite colony is both an architectural masterpiece and the nirvana of social organisation. Builders 5mm long construct the metre-tall mound, the human equivalent of building a 3km-high skyscraper, even increasing its height to escape flooding. Below its sun-hardened surface, the mound contains numerous chambers, each with a specific purpose – food stores, egg nests, galleries replete with larvae and the queen's regal quarters. A remarkable ventilation system maintains constant temperature and humidity, expelling warm, stale air and admitting its cool, oxygen-rich replacement.

There are seven termite families and 2,750 species worldwide. Common Pantanal genera – *Cornitermes*, *Nasutitermes* and *Amitermes* – are most obvious during mass emergences, which are most frequent after the first spring rains. Winged individuals take to the air to disperse, mate and establish new colonies. Many never live to fulfil these functions, instead being snaffled by grateful swallows.

ANTS, BEES AND WASPS

If you're rudely awoken from your Pantanal reverie by a sharp sting, the chances are that you have inadvertently threatened a female hymenopteran (order Hymenoptera). But look beyond your mild, temporary discomfort and you will find the most ecologically valuable insects on Earth. Ants (Formicidae) disperse seeds, recycle nutrients and aerate soil; bees (Apoidea) pollinate plants; and wasps (which span several superfamilies) control biological pests.

A trap-jaw ant can snap its jaws shut at 200km/h; watch where you put your fingers! (JL)

All are fascinating and in many cases colonial creatures. Ant communities number millions of individuals that, like termites, are split into castes with distinct responsibilities. They have radiated to develop different niches; in Brazil alone, there are 2,500 species. Leafcutter ants (*Atta* or *Acromyrmex* spp.) denude vegetation around their colony, lines of ants scurrying nestwards waving squares of leaves – fodder for a fungus, which produces a spongy secretion that nourishes the ants.

A mud-dauber wasp rolling a ball of mud, construction material for its lair. (JL)

The army ant *Eciton burchelli* (Ecitoninae) makes swarming raids across the forest floor, thousands devouring arthropods unfortunate enough to lie in their path. Another voracious predator is the trap-jaw ant (*Odontomachus* sp.), which opens its long mandibles 180 degrees and snaps them shut at 200km/h. Fire ants (*Solenopsis saevissima*) escape flooding by 'congealing' into floating rafts or aggregating on grass stems reaching above the water.

With perhaps a fifth of Brazil's 2,000 species of bee, the Pantanal has plenty of pollinator potential. Stingless bees (Meliponini) are inexactly named; they have stings, albeit too rudimentary for defence. Highly social bees, meliponines produce honey – although seldom enough of it to make them worth cultivating. Orchid bees (Euglossini) are visually and ecologically distinctive; metallic green or blue, they are the only solitary pollen-carrying bees. Sweat bees (Halicitidae), meanwhile, are attracted to the salty skin of perspiring humans.

Wasps are less popular than bees, probably because their ecological contribution is less visible. Yet virtually every insect pest has a wasp that predates or parasitises it, and agriculturalists capitalise on these relationships. Spider wasps (Pompilidae) such as *Auplopus* are solitary species that sting a spider, then drag its paralysed form back to a nest burrow – no mean feat given that victim is larger than hunter. The wasp removes the spider's legs to prevent escape, then lays an egg on its abdomen, seals the burrow and departs. The larva hatches and feeds on the spider that – gruesomely – remains alive. Mud-daubers (*Sceliphron* spp.; Sphecidae) roll up balls of mud to create a lair in which they store paralysed spiders. In one of nature's bittersweet ironies, mud-daubers are themselves often parasitised by cuckoo wasps (*Chrysis*). Glossy blue-black warrior wasps (*Synoeca* spp.) construct papery nests that look like an armadillo: when threatened, they simultaneously beat their wings by way of warning.

Other wasps have a close relationship with plants – but in these instances the bond is two-way. Pollinating fig wasps (Agaoinidae) and their host fig trees (*Ficus* spp.) are a striking illustration of symbiosis. The tree allows wasps to use its fruit as egg chambers in exchange for pollination. Upon hatching, males have just two functions: first, to mate with females; second, to dig an escape tunnel so that females may escape to pollinate other trees.

ARACHNIDS

Arachnophobes have a fear of spiders (order Aranae), but the class Arachnida also includes other orders such as scorpions (Scorpiones), and ticks and mites (Acari). All have two body segments and four pairs of legs, differentiating them from insects, which have three of each.

Keep an eye out for Bolivian salmon-pink tarantula in the Pantanal, particularly on night walks. (UB/SS)

SPIDERS

The Pantanal has at least 200 spiders, spread across 105 genera in 25 families. Two-thirds are in just three families: orb-web spiders (Araneidae), tangle-web spiders (Theridiidae) and jumping spiders (Salticidae). Orb-web spiders are master engineers, building circular, spiral-patterned webs of silk that serve as both home and snare. An insect lurching into the web is subdued by a bite then cocooned in silk. Some, such as the bolas spiders *Mastophora*, have an alternative approach: they are anglers. These spiders secrete sticky globules infused with a pheromone and dangled on a single thread. The chemical entices male moths of particular species to approach – and get stuck, whereupon the spider reels in the line and feasts on its victim.

Three Pantanal tangle-web spider genera have contributed much to our understanding of arachnid life. Studies of widow spiders (*Latrodectus* spp.) have examined their venom, silk and sexual biology (which includes cannibalism). *Anelosimus* spiders cover the spectrum from solitary to permanently social. *A. eximius* lives in colonies of a thousand individuals that occupy a basket-like web 3m in diameter and supported by threads extending 8m towards the canopy. Each spider builds, defends and feeds from its own section of the communal web. *Parawixia* spiders have a different take on this 'social yet solitary' approach to life, feeding alone except where prey is scarce or a large prey item is trapped, at which point they attack en masse.

The long-limbed pantropical huntsman spider keeps lodges free of cockroaches. (JL)

Worldwide, one arachnid in seven is a jumping spider. Pantanal genera include *Chira*, *Cotinusa* and *Thiodina*. All are capable of amazing jumping feats; by altering blood pressure and flow, jumping spiders extend their hind limbs to leap 50 times their body length, equivalent to a human bound of 75m. Rather like human BASE jumpers, they leap while attached by a safety line – in this case a silk thread.

Such tiny creatures are less worthy sources of fear than the 13cm-long pantropical huntsman spider (*Heteropoda venatoria*), which often startles visitors as it ambushes cockroaches (Blattodea) around lodge buildings. Scarier still in many people's eyes are tarantulas (Theraphosidae), giants of the spider world that crush victims with huge fangs then drool digestive juices over them. The best way to see a hairy-legged giant, such as Brazilian salmon-pink tarantula (*Acanthoscurria chacoana*), is to go out at night and shine a torch into crevices in trees.

SCORPIONS

The oldest of all arachnids and infamous for surviving long periods without food or water, scorpions have a literal 'sting in their tail'. When hunting or threatened,

The scorpion *Tityus bahiensis* frequents agricultural areas. (RHJP/SS)

116

scorpions arch their tail forward over their body and prepare to strike with the venom-infused tip. The long, claw-like pincers are primarily for show, but prospective mates also use them to grapple one another in their twirling courtship dance. Although the sting of all scorpions is painful, only a low proportion of the world's almost 2,000 species are venomous to humans. The venomous few include several in the genus *Tityus*, which are famous for reproducing by parthenogenesis, a process whereby unfertilised eggs become living embryos. The Pantanal scorpion fauna forms a subset of the 25 species identified in west-central Brazil. Despite their notoriety, scorpions remain poorly known: in the year 2000, arachnologists described an entirely new genus (*Brazilobothriurus*), which occurs exclusively in the Pantanal.

TICKS AND MITES

Ticks are one tiny arthropod that most visitors hope not to encounter while wandering Pantanal grasslands. They and other mites (order Acari) survive by gorging on the blood of mammals and birds. Ticks (Ixodidae) wait on grass stems until they detect heat from a passing host, whereupon they hitch a ride and imbed jaws in the victim. Beneath rigid dorsal plates, their soft, flexible abdomens expand as they imbibe. Ticks are vectors for several diseases, including Lyme disease.

CENTIPEDES, SNAILS AND CRUSTACEANS

The remaining noteworthy Pantanal invertebrates fall into three evolutionarily separate groups. Centipedes and millipedes (subphylum Myriapoda) and crustaceans (superclass Crustacea) are all arthropods in the phylum Arthropoda, but snails (class Gastropoda) are members of a separate phylum, the molluscs (Mollusca).

CENTIPEDES AND MILLIPEDES

Centipedes (class Chilopoda) and millipedes (Diplopoda) have more appendages than insects by an order or two of magnitude. Millipedes have hundreds of legs (but never thousands, as their name suggests) and chunter slowly through leaf litter, munching decomposing

Millipedes curl up to reduce their vulnerability to predators. (JL)

plant matter. The Pantanal's 30 species are adapted to its aquatic idiosyncracies, breeding before the wet season and climbing trees to escape floods. Compared with millipedes, centipedes have a single pair (rather than two) of longer legs on each body segment. This enables them to move quickly, as befits an aggressive carnivore with venomous claws that pack a killer punch.

In the dry season, red freshwater crabs move across arid terrain in search of wetlands. (JL)

CRUSTACEANS

The size spectrum of crustaceans (superclass Crustacea) ranges from water fleas (Clacodera) to lobsters (Nephropidae). Almost all are aquatic. In the Pantanal, the most notable are shrimps (Palaemonidae, Sergestidae) and crabs (Trichodactylidae). Typical inhabitants of lowland rivers and wetlands, they play important roles at different trophic levels, being herbivores, predators, decomposers and prey for other groups. Shrimps are important fodder for carnivorous fish; the Pantanal hosts three members of the genus *Macrobrachium*, the most common being the Amazon river prawn *M. amazonicum*, a candidate for commercial farming. Of the seven crabs, visitors are most likely to encounter the red freshwater crab (*Dilocarcinus pagei*) as it wanders roads between dwindling water bodies. Such manoeuvres are risky, and many end up in the gullet of a snail kite.

SNAILS

Snails play an important role in the Pantanal ecosystem. These and other 'zoobenthos' that feed on algae and microorganisms serve as important prey for fish, mammals such as the South American coati, and birds such as the limpkin. The most common snail is *Pomacea lineata*, an aquatic apple snail; empty shells are a frequent sight beneath perches used by snail kites.

A shell is all that remains of this aquatic apple snail, its former occupant eaten by a snail kite or limpkin. (UB/SS)

WHERE TO GO

Fancy a wildlife-packed road trip along the Transpantaneira of Mato Grosso, Brazil? (PISS)

From a visitor's perspective, the Pantanal falls into four areas. This chapter considers each in terms of where to look for wildlife, offering a selection of accommodation options (based on where wildlife-watchers typically stay). Whichever area you choose, the Pantanal merits at least three nights, with a week advisable – or more, if you have journeyed from a far-flung continent!

The two main areas are in Brazil, which snaffles almost all tourism – and thus forms the vast majority of this chapter. In the north, the Transpantaneira highway of Mato Grosso state, southwest of Cuiabá city, provides access to varied habitat and a

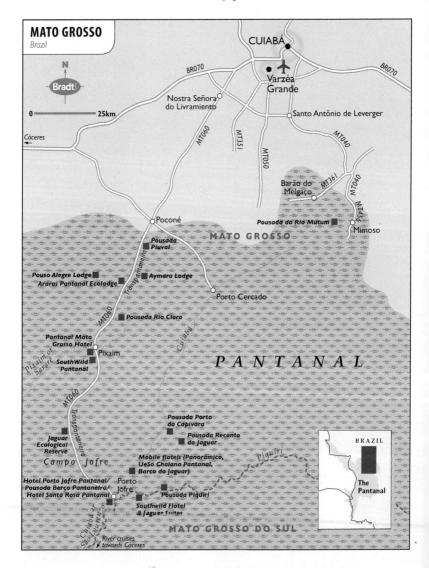

MATO GROSSO
Brazil

N

Bradt

0 ———— 25km

Cáceres

CUIABÁ

BR070

Varzéa Grande

BR070

Nostra Señora do Livramiento

Santo Antônio de Leverger

MT060

MT351

MT050

MT040

Barão do Melgaço

MT361

MT040

MT456

Poconé

Pousada do Rio Mutum

Mimoso

MATO GROSSO

Pousada Piuval

Pouso Alegre Lodge
Araras Pantanal Ecolodge

Aymara Lodge

Transpantaneira

Porto Cercado

MT060

Pousada Rio Claro

Cuiabá

Pantanal Mato Grosso Hotel

Pixaim

SouthWild Pantanal

Pixaim or Sarâre

PANTANAL

MT060

Transpantaneira

Pousada Porto da Capivara

Pousada Recanto do Jaguar

Jaguar Ecological Reserve

Campo Jofre

Mobile flotels (Panorâmico, UeSo Chalana Pantanal, Barco do Jaguar)

Piquiri

BRAZIL

The Pantanal

Hotel Porto Jofre Pantanal/
Pousada Berço Pantaneiro/
Hotel Santa Rosa Pantanal

Porto Jofre

Pousada Piquiri

Southwild Flotel & Jaguar Suites

Cuiabá

Cuiabá or São Lourenço

River cruises towards Cáceres

MATO GROSSO DO SUL

decent number of lodges; it is ideal for a multi-venue trip of one to two weeks and is the default option for many visitors. To the south, the cities of Campo Grande, Aquidauana and Miranda in Mato Grosso do Sul state are departure points for several lodges that are widely separated so need careful planning if they are to be combined. (Corumbá used to be a departure point for backpackers seeking cheap Pantanal trips, but has largely fallen by the wayside and will only be mentioned briefly here.) At its southern limit, the Pantanal scrapes into the Alto Paraguay department of Paraguay, where the adventurous traveller has potential for an exciting visit. Alternatively, to the west, the intrepid visitor could try the little-disturbed Bolivian Pantanal of Santa Cruz province, although access is currently complicated.

Independent travel – hiring a vehicle (typically from Cuiabá or Campo Grande airports) and driving yourself between lodges which you have booked directly – is possible in the Brazilian Pantanal, but most keen wildlife-watchers now prefer one of three options: reserving rooms directly with a lodge (communications by WhatsApp sometimes work more efficiently than by email) and taking advantage of transfers they offer or can organise; booking a bespoke trip via a domestic tour operator that provides a full package of transport, accommodation and guiding; or travelling in a group with an international company specialising in wildlife tours, using a local company as their ground agent. There are advantages in each approach, of course, but there is something to be said for the peace of mind in contracting a company to organise travel and accommodation, and guides familiar with the area will ultimately likely result in more and/or better wildlife sightings. If this appeals, some companies worth considering are namechecked on page 122 (some of whom advertise on this book's inside covers or from page 180 onwards).

Generally, Brazil's Pantanal lodges (and, in Mato Grosso, houseboats) are comfortable but simple: with the odd exception, do not expect the luxury of East African safari destinations, for example. Plentiful food is typically served buffet style, with a variety of meat, fish, bean and rice dishes, plus plenty of fresh fruit and rich desserts. Most lodges offer a variety of activities focused on seeing wildlife, from boat trips or cycle rides to walking safaris and night drives. They may bundle an in-house guide (either a naturalist, most of whom speak English, or a local *pantaneiro*, who probably does not) with the package you buy – unless, for example, your tour operator already provides one.

Given that this book is about Pantanal wildlife, the lodges covered here prioritise those regularly used by nature enthusiasts, and the accounts offered focus on the natural highlights each accommodation option offers. Note, however, that this is a snapshot in time, and that the experience will doubtless evolve during the lifetime of this edition. Species can come and go, so a particular animal that might be a 'dead cert' one year may be gone the next – and the same may apply to accommodation! If you have particular target species in mind, it pays to check with your chosen lodge that your chances of seeing them remain high before confirming a booking. The same applies to cost, which can change in quick time. I give approximate costs in US$ equivalent for sample packages for 2024/25. Finally, if you have no need of a proper bed, a couple of lodges have campsites, and wild camping is possible but not particularly recommended: you are in the realm of jaguars and crocodilians, after all…

TOUR COMPANIES

It is beyond the scope of this guide to provide a detailed and comprehensive assessment of tour operators but Brazilian companies with well-established reputations who are regularly used by wildlife-watchers include: Brazil Birding Experts (w *brazilbirdingexperts.com; advert, inside front cover*); Agami Nature Tours (w *agaminature.com; advert, page 186*); Biodiverse Brazil Tours (w *biodiversebraziltours.com; advert, page 184*); Birding Pantanal (w *birdingpantanal. com; advert, page 188*); Pantanal Phototours (w *pantanalphototours.com; advert, page 183*); Boute Expeditions (w *boute-expeditions.com*); and Pantanal Trackers (w *pantanaltrackers.com.br*). In Paraguay, your best bet is Fauna Paraguay (w *faunaparaguay.com*); in Bolivia, currently, Amboro Tours (w *amborotours.com*).

International companies offering Pantanal tours are too numerous to list here, but some small, wildlife-focused firms whose operations I personally admire include: Limosa Holidays and Wildwings (w *limosaholidays.co.uk* and w *wildwings. co.uk; advert, inside back cover*); Wildlife Travel (w *wildlife-travel.co.uk; advert, page 182*); Birding Ecotours (w *birdingecotours.com; advert, page 180*); Oriole Birding (w *oriolebirding.com; advert, page 186*); Wise Birding (w *wisebirding.co.uk; advert, page 185*); Tropical Birding Tours (w *tropicalbirding.com; advert, page 185*); Royle Safaris (w *royle-safaris.co.uk*); and Wild Images (w *wildimages-phototours. com*). Larger companies come here too, so if you regularly travel with firms such as Abercrombie & Kent (w *abercrombiekent.co.uk*), Naturetrek (w *naturetrek. co.uk; advert, page 187*), Pura Aventura (w *pura-aventura.com*), Reef & Rainforest (w *reefandrainforest.co.uk; advert, page 187*) Rockjumper (w *rockjumperbirding.com*) or Wildlife Worldwide (w *wildlifeworldwide.com*), you might wish to check out their Pantanal tours.

MATO GROSSO, BRAZIL

The only road to penetrate deep into the northern Pantanal, the Estrada Transpantaneira (road number MT060), provides excellent access for wildlife-watchers. Constructed in 1976 with the intention of linking the cities of Cuiabá in Mato Grosso and Corumbá in Mato Grosso do Sul, the dirt road extends south of the small town of Poconé only as far as Porto Jofre on the River Cuiabá, about 145km and 120 bridges later, and thus ends hundreds of kilometres short of its intended destination. Lodges identify their location in terms of distance along the road. Most are typical ranch-like buildings on working *fazendas*. All those mentioned have en-suite bathrooms.

The Transpantaneira provides more than just convenient access and accommodation: it is an outstanding wildlife-watching destination in its own right. During the dry season, roadside ditches created when building the highway often retain water so become a magnet for waterbirds, fish, reptiles, amphibians and mammals. Moreover, the Transpantaneira traverses a range of landscapes: dry grasslands and open scrub in the north gradually give way to large semi-deciduous forests and extensive swamps. This habitat gradient typically means that each lodge has its own distinctive wildlife offering: there is less point looking for jaguar in the north than the south, while the reverse is true for giant anteater. A good plan is thus to stay at three or more widely separated lodges: there is easily enough excitement for a fortnight!

Access is southwest from the state capital of Cuiabá. If kicking your heels for a few hours, a good option is to visit the heavily wooded **Parque Mãe Bonifácia**. Black-tailed marmoset can be seen here easily during the day, including drinking near the toilet blocks (✤ *15°34'43.0"S 56°06'05.7"W*). Many visitors make a pit stop in Poconé, where information, internet facilities and last-minute bookings may be sought. Indeed, for those on a tight budget, a reasonable approach involves staying in Poconé then making day trips along the Transpantaneira (perhaps entering lodges where they grant day-visitor access for a fee), although it will involve a lot of driving. Inexpensive accommodation options in Poconé include **Hotel e Churrascaria Pantaneira** (*18 rooms;* ☎ *+ 55 65 99979 4041*) and **Hotel Skala** (*22 rooms;* ☎ *+55 65 3345 1407, + 55 99985 9516;* e *reservas@skalahotel.com.br*), which both have simple, clean rooms with Wi-Fi from around US$40/double.

If travelling independently, be aware that there is no public transport south of Poconé and hitching will involve long waits (and lack flexibility). If you choose to self-drive, a saloon car is usually sufficient during the dry season provided that it does not rain. Should it do so, the Transpantaneira (particularly south of the RIver Pixaim) turns into slithery porridge, caking wheels with mud and impeding driving. For peace of mind, a 4x4 is probably best. Either way, drive cautiously and make provision for delays. Distances are short, but the average speed of 30km/h and frequent wildlife stops lead to low fuel efficiency. Moreover, petrol is a prized commodity along the Transpantaneira, so fill up in Poconé. In an emergency, be prepared to pay over the

The official entrance to the Transpantaneira highway. (RR/SS)

WATER UNDER THE BRIDGE?

Famously, all the bridges along the Transpantaneira used to be wooden. In some cases, these were rickety: indeed, in the early days of Pantanal ecotourism, travellers were advised to carry spare planks in their vehicle and 'loan' them to particularly fragile bridges to avoid unexpectedly plummeting into the waters below. As well as widening the road, a programme of infrastructural modernisation has been replacing the crossing points with concrete-and-steel structures. During the lifetime of this edition, the substitution is likely to become wholesale – and wooden bridges consigned to the past. Although this may remove an element of the character of the Pantanal experience, it will reduce the number

of heart-in-mouth episodes when vehicle takes on crossing point. That said, if climate change reduces rainfall permanently, and drought comes to permanently characterise parts of the Pantanal, a convenient but unsettling recent feature of Transpantaneira road trips – droughts that make it possible to drive around bridges rather than over them – may become disconcertingly common practice.

odds to persuade a lodge to relinquish some of its supply. Alternatively, a couple of accommodation offerings have private airstrips at which charter flights ('air taxis') may land. These are expensive, but the cost can be defrayed among a group.

It is worth noting that there have been instances of visitors being accosted on the Transpantaneira and robustly informed that travelling without an official local guide is illegal – and even that they will be arrested should they proceed without a guide. At the time of writing, there is no such law forbidding travelling without a local guide.

WILDLIFE HOTSPOTS AND ACCOMMODATION

The season – and its associated water levels – decrees how soon along the Transpantaneira you start seeing the throngs of waterbirds that characterise the Pantanal. Roadside ditches can teem with egrets (cattle, great and snowy), herons (cocoi, black-crowned night-, striated and rufescent tiger), ibises (plumbeous, green and buff-necked) and storks (wood, jabiru and the odd maguari). In the air, kites (snail and plumbeous) sail over marshy terrain replete with prey. Kingfishers (ringed, amazon and green, in descending order of size) use telegraph wires as a vantage point for their piscatorial activities. Below them, greater capybara families graze while hawks (roadside, black-collared and savanna) search for invertebrates from posts. Careful perusal of the shallows should reveal the eyes and nostrils of your first yacaré caiman – and then another, and another…

Freshly arrived visitors may find it hard to drag themselves away from this initial spectacle. The first impressions of tour guide Howard Vaughan speak volumes: "What followed between the gate to the Transpantaneira and our lodge was an emotional tidal wave of wildlife," he said. "Birds were everywhere. I am rarely lost for words but the sheer number of big birds of so many new shapes and forms was overwhelming."

The best news is that many more such opportunities await, whether along the highway or off-road in *fazendas* (ranches) that offer lodging, wildlife-watching facilities such as trails, hides (blinds), observation towers (particularly useful in the flat terrain!), vehicular and walking safaris, and boat rides. In suitable habitat, common Transpantaneira wildlife encounters include Argentine black-and-white tegu, black-and-gold howler, crab-

Capybara family may avoid caimans by relocating to the Transpantaneira – but put themselves in the path of vehicles. (KD)

eating fox, Azara's agouti, chaco chachalaca, capped heron, grey-cowled wood-rail and southern screamer. Marsh deer is most readily seen early morning on the margin of damp habitats; common brown brocket is a fixture in grasslands. Various common parrots, including yellow-collared macaw, occur in landscapes with decent coverage of trees, particularly palms. Inside forests, look for great rufous woodcreeper, black-fronted nunbird and rufous-tailed jacamar. Search along rivers for green iguana,

The Transpantaneira from the air. (BZG/SS)

Two Pantanal icons juxtaposed: the *lapacho* tree and the yacaré caiman. (RTO/SS)

sunbittern and piping-guans. Check under bridges for yellow anaconda and roosting bats, and also in abandoned buildings for the latter. Moreover, most Transpantaneira lodges are good for several key species that can be hard to see elsewhere in the Pantanal, including hooded capuchin, black-tailed marmoset, chestnut-bellied guan and bare-faced curassow.

The spectrum of habitats traversed by the Transpantaneira offers particular interest to birders, as it means that the avifauna changes gradually along the highway. Greater rhea and red-legged seriema, for example, are best seen along the first 40km of the road, and long-tailed ground-dove in the first 70km. Subtropical doradito, however, mainly occurs well south of there. To see the greatest variety of birds, it makes sense to stay at three places at intervals along the road. The following summary of lodges runs from north to south.

Lying 3km east of the Transpantaneira at km10, the first *fazenda* you come to is **Pousada Piuval** (✥ *16°22'43.6"S 56°37'17.7"W; 32 rooms;* ✆ *+55 65 4042 0460, +55 65 9983 7425;* e *reservas@pousadapiuval.com.br;* w *pousadapiuval.com.br;* ◷ *all year except Christmas. From US$750 pp sharing for a 2-night stay, inc transfers from Cuiabá, FB, English-speaking guide & selected activities).* This 7,000ha cattle ranch has been in the Eubank family for 150 years and, in 2024, celebrated 35 years of ecotourism. Eduardo Eubank is proud of the lodge's low environmental-impact management systems, which have won an industry sustainability award: showers are solar-heated, grey water is reused, rainwater irrigates gardens, batteries and other waste are recycled, and lighting is motion-activated.

This is a lodge where comfort and nature meet – a favourite of individual wildlife-watchers and tour groups alike. Contemporary décor with warm colours creates an inviting atmosphere, and the well-designed outside space includes fireside seating, a children's play area and an attractive swimming pool with great views. There is Wi-Fi, air conditioning and a games room, while the master bedroom boasts a jacuzzi. Post-2020 investment has seen refurbishments of the restaurant, swimming pool (and poolside kiosk), kitchen, all standard rooms and communal areas; in 2023, four new safari vehicles were introduced.

The word *piuval* means 'place with many *piuva*', the *lapacho* tree that splashes vivid pink across the spring forest: flowering peaks in August. Surrounded by seasonal wetlands, fine grassland and cerrado with abundant termite mounds standing tall like gravestones in a cemetery, Piuval offers an impressive array of fauna and flora. Six vehicular safaris per day transport visitors around a mosaic of grassland and woodlots interspersed with permanent water bodies. A sunrise safari offers the best prospects of giant anteater of anywhere along the Transpantaneira, often with a 'side order' of southern tamandua. Unusually so far north, jaguar is regular (including close to the lodge). In the dry season, 4x4 vehicles may venture off-track, enabling photographers to sidle up to grassland specialities such as greater rhea and red-legged seriema (the latter may even visit the lodge garden!). At night, particularly along the entrance track, look for lowland tapir, nine-banded armadillo, common red brocket, forest rabbit, great horned owl, various nightjars and common potoo. Some people strike lucky with black-banded owl, boat-billed heron, Azara's night monkey (in palm forests), ocelot or puma.

Alternatively, walk along four nature trails of 1.5–5km length, taking 1–3 hours. These are good for primates and for birding, which is probably best as the wet season dries out: nearly 400 species have been recorded on the property. Forest islands hold sought-after creatures such as black-tailed marmoset, chestnut-bellied guan, bare-faced curassow, the localised cinnamon-throated hermit and buff-bellied hermit, white-fronted and white woodpeckers, white-lored spinetail, dull-capped attila, helmeted manakin, black-bellied and large-billed antwrens, planalto slaty-antshrike and Mato Grosso antbird. It is hard not to see hyacinth macaw, as several breeding pairs munch on *buriti* palm nuts; blue-and-yellow macaw also occurs.

Close encounters with wildlife including lowland tapir epitomise the thrilling Pantanal experience. (UB/SS)

Horse-riding is available, while an observation tower gives panoramic views over an egret and stork colony. Wetlands around the *baía* (large bay) and elsewhere host yellow anaconda, aggregations of yacaré caiman and waterbirds including southern screamer, black skimmer, Pantanal snipe and grey-breasted crake. You can even view from a floating platform! Secluded pools may host sunbittern. At dusk, nacunda nighthawks emerge en masse and bulldog bats fly over the lodge-side lake.

Returning to the Transpantaneira, head south, passing through a decent wetland known as As Torda, before turning off at km25. Head 3km southeast to reach **Aymara Lodge** (⊕ *16°30'16.7"S 56°40'30.9"W; 18 rooms;* ☎+ *55 65 99612 0058, + 55 65 99922 4073;* e *reservas@aymaralodge.com;* w *aymaralodge.com.br;* ⊕ *Apr–Feb. US$250 pppn, including FB, guide & activities. See advert, page 188*). Aymara differs from competitors both by being based deep in the forest, with the streamside setting reflecting its ethos of integrating with nature, and by being a purpose-built wildlife lodge rather than a converted cattle ranch. Purchasing the lodge was a dream come true for top birder and experienced naturalist guide Giuliano Bernardon and wife Lisa Canavarros, who also run the tour company Birding Pantanal. "During my Pantanal expeditions with clients," Giu explained, "this resort became my favourite place, not because of the comfort or services offered, but because of where it was inserted, a place where we really experienced the idea of immersion and contact with nature". Unexpectedly, Aymara became available to purchase in 2019, and the couple snapped it up. Following complete renovation, the resulting accommodation is rustic yet well-appointed and cosy, the atmosphere relaxed and informal. There are mod cons too: air conditioning, Wi-Fi, a pool in which to escape the heat of the day and even the option of massages.

Aymara has a strong following among wildlife-watchers. Around 220ha of land encompasses deciduous forest, gallery forest, wetlands and savannah grasslands. Activities include guided walks along four nature trails (0.7–5km), daytime or nocturnal safaris in open-topped vehicles, a bicycle safari (no bad idea for covering ground quietly and efficiently), an observation tower new for 2025

Typical lodges (here, Aymara) are open, wooden structures. (AL)

and, normally during December–August, canoeing (which allows silent, close approach to animals) and 2h-long boat trips along the River Novo. Waterhole hides (blinds) are a real boon, offering decent prospects of photographing ocelot, lowland tapir and marsh deer: patience should bring rewards. Jaguar-watching day trips from Porto Jofre can be arranged. English-speaking guides are young biologists or naturalists, proudly trained by Giu himself.

In quick time, Giu and colleagues have already racked up an impressive 335 species of bird, 37 mammals, and 48 reptiles and amphibians. Black-and-gold howler is often seen from bedroom verandas, while hyacinth macaw nests beside the buildings and a sunbittern may even pick insects from the surface of the swimming pool, in which the odd capybara takes a dip. Chestnut-bellied guan, blue-throated piping-guan and

Aymara Lodge is unusual in sitting under a forest canopy (AI)

bare-faced curassow strut fearlessly around the feeding station and lodge buildings (perfect for photographers); look around here also for Azara's agouti, undulated tinamou, yellow-collared macaw, turquoise-fronted and orange-winged amazons, chestnut-eared aracari and crimson-crested woodpecker. Search the river for both otters, sungrebe (sometimes also visible from the restaurant!), sunbittern, and agami and zigzag herons. In the grasslands, look for greater rhea and red-legged seriema, and potentially both anteaters and three species of armadillo. Lowland tapir is reliable. Classy mammals such as giant armadillo, jaguar and maned wolf are also on the lodge list – but don't expect to see them.

Birding is really good. The forest holds avian specialities including black-banded owl, pale-crested and cream-coloured woodpeckers, rusty-backed and white-lored spinetails, planalto slaty-antshrike, Mato Grosso antbird, large-billed antwren and band-tailed manakin. The trees also harbour black-tailed marmoset. The entrance track is good for capped heron, cinnamon-throated and buff-bellied hermits, green-and-rufous kingfisher, red-billed scythebill, dull-capped attila and helmeted manakin. At night, the same stretch might produce boat-billed heron, both potoos, forest rabbit, various nightjars, crab-eating fox and possibly puma.

Travelling through rafts water hyacinths is a typical waterborne experience. (GG/SS)

Back on the Transpantaneira, turn southwest at km32 for **Araras Pantanal EcoLodge** (⊕ *16°30'43.4"S 56°42'42.3"W; 20 rooms;* ☎ *+55 65 3682 2800;* e *reservas@araraslodge.com.br;* w *araraslodge.com.br;* ⊕ *end Dec to end Nov. US$1,900 pp sharing for 5 day/4 night package in peak season, inc FB, transfers, bilingual wildlife guide, river canoeing, horse-riding, walking & vehicular safaris, plus US$600 pp for full-day jaguar excursion from Porto Jofre*). Charismatic owner André Von Thuronyi, son of a Hungarian nobleman, and team provide a warm welcome to this attractive lodge. This lodge is a member of the Roteiros de Charme Hotel Association, which comprises characterful accommodation offerings that adopt a sustainability policy established in co-operation with the United Nations Environment Programme. Attractive use of local materials creates a homely and intimate feel, and the food is good and varied. The lodge was substantially refurbished in 2020, with developments including a new swimming pool (cleaned by UV light and ozone), three new premium suites, a new metal observation tower (plus improvements to two wooden towers), 2km of upgraded boardwalks and new safari vehicles. Bedrooms have air-con, and there is Wi-Fi.

In Portuguese, *arara* means 'macaw', and hyacinth macaw nests near the breakfast veranda, sometimes sharing a tree with great horned owl plus roosting lesser bulldog and velvety mastiff bats. Habituated greater capybara wander around the gardens, which are frequented by hummingbirds and fruit-eating birds. Knowledgeable guides (who, between them, speak six languages) escort visitors around the 2,760ha ranch. More than 20km of road provide good access for vehicular safaris. Trails, including one with an elevated boardwalk, traverse good-quality forest holding avian specialities such as white-lored spinetail, band-tailed antbird, Mato Grosso antbird and helmeted manakin, plus black-and-gold howler, black-tailed marmoset and Azara's agouti. A trail through sandy scrub can be good for nine-banded armadillo, South American coati, hooded capuchin and bare-faced curassow. You can also explore on horseback.

Several waterholes (including right around the lodge) and two hides offer potential for seeing lowland tapir, brockets and other mammals. Three observation towers (11–25m tall) offer fabulous panoramic views, including over seasonally flooded wetland and drier grassland: one overlooks a jabiru nest, but also look for black-and-gold howler and marsh deer, plus capped heron among plentiful waterbirds. Night drives usually produce both brocket deer, forest rabbit and crab-eating raccoon. Trails lead through dry forest harbouring tayra, black-and-gold howler and black-tailed marmoset. Canoeing along the River Clarinho or River Corixo can be good for giant otter and sungrebe.

As well as Araras, André Von Thuronyi runs Pantanal Explorer (**w** *pantanalexplorer. com.br*), which offers river cruises (page 141) and packages to **Baiazinha Lodge** (⊕ *16°34'00.4"S 57°50'11.9"W. From US$2,145 pp, based on 2 sharing, for 3 nights, inc FB & activities*). This is a remote hotel on the River Paraguay, in the northwest Pantanal, southsouthwest of Cáceres. Jaguar can be seen with relative ease during July–October.

But back to the Transpantaneira… Heading south from Araras, you immediately pass a small café, **BarAra** (⊕ *16°30'57.2"S 56°42'39.4"W*), that provides a shady retreat with revitalising drinks and snacks. Keep an ear out for hyacinth macaw and white woodpecker, or wander southeast across the road to see white-lored spinetail or northwest along the path towards Pousada Araras for Mato Grosso antbird.

At km33, turn northwest and drive 7km to reach **Pouso Alegre Lodge** (⊕ *16°30'11.4"S 56°44'42.8"W; 22 rooms;* \+55 65 99981 7911; **e** *pousoalegrelodge@ gmail.com;* **w** *pousoalegrepantanal.com;* ⊕ *all year except 20 Dec to 5 Jan. US$275 pn based on 2 sharing, inc FB & free self-guided access throughout the property. Local guide, guided activities inc vehicle & walking safaris, & transfers extra*). This cattle ranch, whose name means 'happy watering hole', boasts a mix of habitats that excel for wildlife – and is consequently much-loved by keen wildlife-watchers who revel in the freedom to explore 7,500 ha of varied habitat along a recently expanded road and trail network. Lodge manager Luiz Vicente da Silva Campos Filho, a herpetologist, has compiled a mouth-watering catalogue of fauna and flora. He has also trained ranch farmhands to show visitors wildlife on foot or horseback along trails that cover forest, wetlands, cerrado and savannah; footbridges traverse damper areas. A 24-m-tall metal observation tower 0.5km west of the lodge offers commanding views.

Large trees provide this charmingly rustic and authentic lodge with respite from the searing sun. Large, simple, air-conditioned rooms have up to four beds, and have been recently refurbished. Wi-Fi is available. Good *pantaneiro* food is served in a large farmhouse-style restaurant with brightly coloured walls and polished wood ceilings. Even while shuffling from bedroom to breakfast, you can't avoid wildlife. The feeding station thrums with bare-faced curassow, Chaco chachalaca, chestnut-eared aracari, toco toucan, caciques and ground-doves – all at point-blank range. Hooded capuchin and South American coati sometimes join the throng, both brocket deer often loiter near

Watching wetland wildlife from an elevated boardwalk at Pouso Alegre. (AS/OB)

the buildings, lowland tapir may munch fallen mangoes, and leopard keelback (a colubrid snake) has been spotted sunbathing on the patio. Hyacinth macaw breeds, roosting within earshot; red-billed scythebill, ferruginous pygmy-owl and great horned owl occur nearby. A shed northeast of the lodge can hold roosting fringe-lipped, common vampire, Seba's short-tailed and velvety mastiff bats. Giant ameiva lizards rustle in adjacent leaf litter nearby.

Nearly 40 species of large mammal have been recorded, including giant armadillo and bush dog: both are so rare as to be near-mythical – yet the last-named was even filmed here by day in September 2024. The armadillo is occasionally seen while spotlighting along the entrance road, and diggings in forest c.3km southwest of the lodge, towards Capão das Araras, suggest that nocturnal stake-outs might pay dividends. Black-tailed marmoset, hooded capuchin and black-and-gold howler inhabit forests 0.5km northeast of the lodge and gallery forests along the River Bento Gomes (where giant otter occurs and good birding includes blue-crowned parakeet, dull-capped attila and band-tailed antbird). Permanent wetlands are the best place to see marsh deer. Six species of cat are known, with ocelot the most reliable. The lodge is probably the best on the Transpantaneira for lowland tapir and on the podium for both anteaters and tayra (the latter being regularly seen from hides). It is one of few Pantanal locations where Guianan squirrel has been recorded.

Nearly 100 species of amphibian and reptile (more than any other Pantanal lodge) include two-coloured oval frog, southern orange-legged leaf frog, Mato Grosso lancehead and yellow anaconda – all often seen by keen 'herpers'. The first state record

of mud snake was from Alegre, which also harbours the rare colubrid serpent *Helicops boitata*, a Mato Grosso exclusive. More than 350 bird species include 14 herons, 13 parrots, seven owls and 16 hummingbirds. The 550 species of plant identified include members of 100 families: seeds from around 70 species have been collected on the ranch for planting out and jumpstarting new habitat, notably the *manduvi* trees favoured by hyacinth macaws (page 67).

The recently improved entrance track is used by common brown brocket, crab-eating fox, South American coati, chestnut-bellied guan, bare-faced curassow and long-tailed ground dove. About 1km before the lodge, an elevated embankment crosses open grassland.

Although rare and incredibly elusive, bush dog does occur in the Pantanal, including at Pouso Alegre. (DH/D)

Scan from here, particularly at dawn and dusk: lowland tapir is regular, and greater rhea and red-legged seriema stroll around. Scissor-tailed nightjar and both potoos might be seen at night. From late afternoon onwards, watch waterholes from simple hides (blinds), including at Capão das Araras and Donato, for Argentine black-and-white tegu, piping-guans, undulated tinamou, capped hereon, green ibis, sunbittern, red-footed tortoise, lowland tapir, tayra, collared peccary, both brockets and South American coati.

Greater rhea is easily seen, particularly along the northern Transpantaneira. (KD)

As you head onwards along the Transpantaneira, stay alert for wildlife. At night, the area either side of the Alegre turn-off is good for ocelot (southern oncilla has been seen), both anteaters, three species of deer, crab-eating raccoon, crab-eating fox, brown four-eyed opossum and lowland tapir, plus boat-billed heron among black-crowned night-herons crowding out roadside ditches. During the day, South American coati, marsh deer and tayra may cross the Estrada at any time, while roadside trees hold peach-fronted parakeet and crimson-crested woodpecker.

This may be of particular value if you are staying at **UeSo Pantanal Lodge** (⊕ *16°33'05.4"S 56°43'13.1"W; 21 rooms;* ✆ *+55 65 9918 3358, + 55 65 99964 1701;* **e** *info@pantanal.ch;* **w** *pantanal.ch;* ⊕ *all year. US$1,158 pp sharing, for 5 day/4 night package inc transfers, FB, bilingual guide, excursions, bilingual guide & full-day jaguar trip from Porto Jofre).* Leave the Transpantaneira eastwards at km38 to access this cosy, rustic lodge run by a Swiss-Brazilian family. Ground and wall mosaics depict colourful Pantanal animals; simple but attractive rooms have air conditioning powered by locally generated solar energy. Guests can relax in hammocks or wooden rocking chairs – or cool off in the small swimming pool. Food comes partly from the on-site vegetable garden; waste is composted. Wi-Fi is available for a modest charge. Camping facilities are also available: camper-vans may hook up to electricity; and two-person tents may be hired. UeSo also operates the Chalana houseboat near Porto Jofre (page 141).

The 500ha *fazenda* (which is contiguous with UeSo Aventura's 850ha property) harbours forests, gallery forest, wetlands, grasslands and lakes. Well-marked trails are available for walking, bicycle and horse-riding safaris. Other facilities include canoe excursions and three observation towers. Argentine black-and-white tegu and greater rhea trundle across the grounds. Both anteaters are relatively frequently seen, attracted by the density of termite mounds. Jabiru and hyacinth macaw breed. Lowland tapir, Azara's agouti and primates are regular.

Continuing south, turn off the Transpantaneira at km42 then head 3km southeast to access **Pousada Rio Claro** (⊕ *16°37'15.2"S 56°44'06.6"W; 28 rooms;* ✆ *+55 65 3345 2449;* **e** *contato@pousadarioclaro.com.br;* **w** *pousadarioclaro.com.br;* ⊕ *all year. US$140 pppn sharing, inc FB, local guide, 1 activity per day and access to trails. Other activities & transfers extra).* External wooden décor belies 18 clean-cut, comfortable, air-conditioned 'standard' rooms with up to four beds, Wi-Fi and impressive, hotel-standard bathrooms. The ten 'premium' rooms are even better, with plush fabrics and a private patio complete with hammock and outdoors chairs. Guests may relax on sun-loungers beside a nice swimming pool; meals are taken in an airy and convivial dining hall. A good range of wildlife-watching options are available, comprising diurnal and nocturnal vehicular safaris, horse-riding, a choice of four trails to enjoy on foot and waterborne exploration along the eponymous River Claro (or River Sararé) by canoe or motorboat. Day visits are possible.

Pousada Rio Claro is the best place on the Transpantaneira for nanday parakeet. (JL)

Birdwatchers often visit expressly to see nanday parakeet, which frequents fruit-laden trees around the lodge but is otherwise rare in the northern Pantanal. Feeders attract chestnut-eared aracari and purplish jay. Chestnut-bellied guan and bare-faced curassow are common in the grounds. The surrounding forest and scrub hosts rufous-tailed jacamar, great rufous woodcreeper and Mato Grosso antbird, while hyacinth macaw often flies overhead. The same area holds good mammals: hooded capuchin, Azara's agouti, crab-eating fox and South American coati. The lodge's riverside location means that short walks can produce sungrebe, sun-bittern, helmeted manakin and Neotropical otter. On the short trail through gallery forest, look for Mato Grosso and band-tailed antbirds, and dull-capped attila.

Two avian stars are exclusively seen in dense riverside vegetation, particularly as dusk starts whispering its imminence: the shimmering agami heron and the tiny, reclusive zigzag heron. If you do not see them, consolation should be provided by blue-throated piping-guan, yellow-collared macaw, and various raptors and kingfishers (both often feeding on fishy treats proffered by the boatman). A particular joy here is that you are likely to have the river to yourself, which makes it easier to locate giant otter. Keep an eye out for proboscis bat, which typically roosts in single file down a tree trunk, and sparkling dragonflies. By night, look for both potoos.

At km48, the Transpantaneira crosses the River Pixaim (marked on some maps as the River Sararé), which signals a distinct change in soil and vegetation. Southwards, red earth predominates and the hitherto fairly stony road is replaced by a sometimes slippery or claggy surface. Forests become larger and denser, and wetlands more frequent and extensive. Immediately southwest of the bridge at km48 is **Pantanal Mato Grosso Hotel** (⊕ *16°44'53.4"S 56°51'26.0"W; 33 rooms;* ☎ *+ 55 65 2018 0444, +55 65 99981 3525;* e *pantanal@hotelmt.com.br;* w *hotelmt.com.br/pantanal-mato-grosso-hotel;* ⊕ *Apr–Nov. US$95 pppn sharing, inc FB, boat trip & access to trails: other activities extra; US$50 pp for day use, including lunch, walking trails & boat trip*). Although this riverside chain hotel essentially targets Brazilian clientele, some tour companies use it as a pleasant base or lunch stop. Relatively comfortable air-conditioned rooms have

Wi-Fi. The excellent swimming pool – complete with mini-waterfall – is a boon on hot days. Horse-riding, an observation tower and boat trips are available. Non-residents may make inexpensive day visits (09h–17h), which may be worth it for the River Pixaim boat trip and access to a riverside trail through gallery forest.

White-lined broad-nosed bats roost seasonally under lodge roofs; if absent there, it is worth checking for them under the road bridge. Lowland tapir sometimes feeds on fallen mangoes around the lodge, but may otherwise be seen along the river. Feeders attract purplish jay and the usual cardinals, cowbirds, doves and finches; various hummingbirds nectar on bougainvillea and other flowers, while giant ameiva lizards scurry around. Gallery forest holds hooded capuchin and a fine selection of birds, including buff-bellied hermit, white-wedged piculet, Mato Grosso and band-tailed antbirds, large-billed antwren, pale-bellied tyrant-manakin, helmeted manakin and buff-breasted wren. Dragonflies and butterflies sometimes provide riots of colour. Night drives along the road may produce lowland tapir and marsh deer; the rare Pantanal cat has been spotted.

Boat trips on the River Pixaim can be fun. Boatmen throw fish to raptors, herons, kingfishers and even an habituated caiman, granting excellent photographic opportunities. On quiet stretches, you might encounter a giant otter family or a Neotropical otter, while the shadiest sections with the densest vegetation are the places to look for agami, boat-billed and zigzag herons. Red- and blue-throated piping-guans rattle across the river in display, sunbittern lopes along the shoreline, sungrebe often skulks in water hyacinths, green iguana adorns overhanging branches and the odd rusty-backed spinetail flits across the water. At dusk, band-tailed and nacunda nighthawks wing through the riverine air alongside bulldog bats.

The other place to stay that offers boat trips along the River Pixaim (including on silent, electric vessels, a boon for photographers) is nearby **SouthWild Pantanal Lodge** (⊕ *16°45'28.7"S 56°52'35.5"W; 15 rooms;* ☏ *+1 443 660 6303, +55 11 5196*

Quiet stretches of the River Pixaim are great for giant otter, agami heron and zigzag heron (RMM/SS)

0168; **e** *info@southwild.com;* **w** *southwild.com/southwild-pantanal-lodge;* ⏲ *May–Nov. US$265 pppn sharing, inc FB, daily boat ride & access to trails, blinds/hides and towers – & a day and night safari drive for those staying 3+ nights. Bilingual wildlife guide, other activities & transfers extra. Non-residents can pay US$60 pp for ocelot viewing).* Also enduringly referred to by its original name of Fazenda Santa Tereza, the lodge is reached by turning west off the Transpantaneira 0.8km south of Pantanal Mato Grosso Hotel, then continuing for 2.5km.

Owned by wildlife conservationist and entrepreneur Charles Munn, whose Pantanal activities are not without local controversy, SouthWild Pantanal has a typical ranch-like appearance, with the smart dining room refurbished in 2024 to offer a panoramic view through its all-glass, bird-safe windows. Nicely decorated, comfortable rooms have air conditioning and Wi-Fi, and there is a plunge pool in which to cool off. A thermal roof reduces room temperatures, and a water-filtration system provides drinking water. SouthWild's Pantanal operations also include two 'flotels' (page 141).

Hooded capuchins can become habituated to human presence. (JL)

Wildlife-watching facilities on the 1,540ha property include three observation towers: one promises close, eye-level views of black-and-gold howlers; a second offers intimate insights into the life of nesting jabirus; and the third, in gallery forest, is good for birding and for observing both black-tailed marmoset and hooded capuchin. The riverine forest can also be explored at ground level, via 4km of trails either side of the lodge. Horses and *pantaneiro* guides can be hired. Vehicle safaris can be rented by night and day, aiding exploration of grasslands and wetlands.

The star (and unique) attraction comes at dusk, when guests and paying non-guests walk 500m from the lodge, through gallery forest, to gather on arena-like seating. This is positioned a few metres from trees where habituated ocelots feast on fishy or meaty morsels placed on tangled lianas. The 'hit rate' is roughly four nights in five, and artificial lighting pleases photographers; that said, provisioning wild carnivores is not to everyone's taste or moral compass.

There is plenty of other wildlife to see. Jaguar is spotted along the riverbank occasionally during the dry season: if you hear greater capybara barking, start scanning. Marsh deer occurs in damper parts. Lowland tapir feeds seasonally on fallen mangoes, including along the trail beyond the ocelot hide. Chestnut-bellied guan, bare-faced curassow and blue-throated piping-guan offer decent photographic opportunities. Scrubby areas, including along the entrance track, harbour laughing falcon, long-tailed ground dove, buff-breasted wren and rusty-backed antwren. Southern tamandua and crab-eating fox are possible. You might bump into the localised green kentropyx (a teiid lizard) on bare ground. Gallery forest holds white-wedged piculet, helmeted manakin and Mato Grosso antbird. For boat trip fauna, see page 135.

The lodge gardens are packed with wildlife. Amazon lava lizards skitter through the grounds, and two-coloured oval frog, Chaco and veined tree-frogs can be found at night. Flowering trees attract orange-backed troupial, chestnut-eared araçari and fabulously named hummingbirds such as blue-tufted starthroat, fork-tailed woodnymph, glittering-throated emerald and white-tailed goldenthroat. Toco toucan, purplish jay and orange-backed troupial attend the feeding station, and red-billed scythebill probes fence-posts for insects. Great horned owl and crab-eating fox are regular nocturnal visitors.

Beyond Southwild, there is no accommodation until km110. Wildlife interest along this stretch is limited, although roadside ditches hold waterbirds, caiman and capybara, and various mammals and lizards could cross the road at any moment. Birders examining roadside scrub and woodland should find insectivores such as buff-breasted and moustached wrens, rusty-fronted tody-flycatcher and ashy-headed greenlet.

West of the Transpantaneira at km110 is **Jaguar Ecological Reserve** (✪ *17°06'10.2"S 56°56'36.0"W; 13 rooms;* 📞 *+55 65 9958 4306, +55 65 9211 6733;* e *jaguar_lodge@ hotmail.com;* w *jaguarreserve.com;* ⊕ *Mar–Dec. US$380 pppn sharing, inc FB, transfers, jaguar boat trip, night safari, local guide & access to trails, all shared with other guests).* Owned by a *pantaneiro* family, the lodge celebrated its 25th anniversary in 2024. Set up by Eduardo Falcão and Juscineide C. Macedo, the lodge is now managed by the couple's son João Paulo and his wife Eduarda Fernandes, who also run the tour company Wild Jaguar Photographic Safaris (w *wildjaguarphotosafaris.com).* Created with the help of non-profit organisation the Focus Conservation Fund, the 1,200ha estate is legally protected as a *Reserva Particular do Patrimônio Natural* (private natural heritage reserve), a designation lauded by Brazilian scientists for contributing significantly to conservation.

Renovated in 2024, accommodation is modern and minimalist; rooms have stylish bathrooms, air conditioning and Wi-Fi. There is also a new swimming pool and a pleasing dining area. Food includes fruit and vegetables from the garden, and locally caught fish. Vehicular safaris are available by day and night: the three diurnal primates, crab-eating raccoon, nine-banded armadillo

The female bare-faced curassow is arguably even more striking than the male (page 65). (JL)

Jaguar gimmickry: should one laugh or cry? (UB/SS)

and Neotropical otter are often seen, with lowland tapir, marsh deer and ocelot reasonably regular. You can explore forest behind the lodge along walking trails or on horseback. Hyacinth macaw is common around *acuri* palms, including in the lodge garden; several pairs breed. Toco toucan visits the feeders. Regular reptiles include Paraguay caiman lizard and yellow-tailed cribo. White-lined broad-nosed bat and velvety mastiff bat may roost around the lodge. Jaguar is sometimes seen around the reserve or on the road nearby. In any case, jaguar-watching boat trips from Porto Jofre are part of the daily rate; non-stop, the 37-km journey to the River Cuiabá takes 50 minutes.

The first bridge south of the Jaguar Ecological Reserve can be good for giant otter, boat-billed heron and all five kingfishers. Derelict research centre buildings 300m along the Santa Isabel road (at km112), are good for wildlife. Great potoo and ferruginous pygmy-owl occur. Yellow-collared and hyacinth macaws gather in late afternoons. Lowland tapir and common red brocket are regular, and Seba's short-tailed bats roost in an abandoned hut. Black-tailed marmoset and lowland paca occur farther along the Santa Isabel road. Fawn-breasted wren occurs from km115 southwards.

The remaining 35km of the Transpantaneira offers great potential for memorable wildlife encounters: mammals and reptiles sometimes treat the road as their own, particularly if surrounding vegetation is wet. Roadside woodland and scrub are good for birding. A key area is **Campo Jofre**, a wetland that extends for several kilometres after km127. The area heaves with herons, egrets, limpkins, ibises and storks: the star waterbird is maguari stork, common here but rare farther north. Also present are southern screamer, great horned owl, Mato Grosso antbird, cinereous-breasted spinetail, white-naped xenopsaris, yellowish pipit and subtropical doradito (as currently identified; it may yet prove to be a species new to science). Large trees around an abandoned research station offer shade and shelter, notably for yellow-collared macaw, white-wedged piculet and white-lored spinetail, while fringe-lipped and common vampire bats have roosted inside; however, the building is best avoided if bees are present. After a hot day, the sun-warmed road is a good place to search carefully for yellow anaconda, false water cobra and Mato Grosso lancehead. Leaving Campo Jofre, you enter the final 10km of the Transpantaneira. From bridges, scan for marsh deer, Neotropical otter (which might also undulate across the road) and sungrebe. Jaguar and ocelot are often seen on night drives.

After passing Fazenda Jofre Velho (local base of the non-profit organisation Panthera, which sadly no longer offers tourist accommodation), your journey culminates at the riverside settlement of **Porto Jofre** (km145), which essentially serves sport fishermen and ecotourists bent on seeing jaguar. There are a few accommodation possibilities (including some under new ownership, which it will be interesting to see develop over the lifetime of this edition). The following – mostly fronting the River Cuiabá (marked on some maps as the São Lourenço, although this is strictly speaking a tributary of the Cuiabá) – are some current options.

At the fork in the road, heading straight brings you to **Pousada Berço Pantaneiro – Ninho do Jaguar** (⊕ *17°21'22.1"S 56°46'02.9"W; 11 rooms;* \ *+ 55 65 9990 81861;* e *contato@pousadabercopantaneiro.com.br;* w *pousadabercopantaneiro.com. br;* ⊕ *Mar–Dec. US$590 pp sharing for 3 days/2 nights, inc FB, local guide and full-day boat trip; transfers extra*) on the left (northeast). Air-conditioned rooms are simple but pleasant, with jaguar-print throws and monogrammed towels. The attractive dining room has long, hand-carved wooden benches. It is a short stroll from the neat garden to the riverside.

Alternatively, bear right (southwest) at the fork to reach the largest and best-known lodge, **Hotel Porto Jofre Pantanal Norte**, established in 1984 and also referred to as Hotel do Jamil (⊕ *17°21'51.8"S 56°46'28.6"W; 32 rooms;* \ *+55 65 3637 1593/1263;* e *reservas@portojofre.com.br, contato@portojofre.com.br;* w *portojofre.com.br;* ⊕ *Mar–Dec. US$190 pppn sharing inc FB. Boat hire & transfers extra*). The hotel has a private airstrip: some high-end tour companies and fishing groups charter an air taxi from Cuiabá. Spacious air-conditioned rooms are simple but comfortable, and have Wi-Fi. Breakfast is served from 05h: perfect for early-morning jaguar trips or going birding at dawn. In the grounds, hyacinth macaw is easily seen; habituated jabiru, wood stork and buff-necked ibis allow close approach; great horned owl roosts in trees and a greater capybara may bimble past lumbering caiman. For a while a semi-tame Neotropical otter even took dips in the pool. If not hit by drought, the nearby lake should boast giant waterlilies (native to the western Pantanal and presumably introduced here), plus waterbirds including southern screamer and Pantanal snipe.

Jaguar-watching on the River Cuiabá is done by motorboat. (JL)

Along the same road, then off to the right (bearing farther west), is **Hotel Santa Rosa Pantanal** (⊕ *17°21'59.8"S 56°47'09.3"W; 23 rooms;* ☏ *+55 65 9925 4595;* e *info@ santarosapantanal.com.br;* w *santarosapantanal.com.br;* ⊕ *Mar–Dec. From US$145 pppn, based on 2 sharing, inc FB, rising to US$200 pppn in Aug–Sep. Boat hire and night safari drives extra).* Air-conditioned rooms have Wi-Fi: the deluxe option is spacious, attractive and comfortable. The dining room is airy yet intimate, the swimming pool large and pleasant, and other communal spaces agreeably modern, and there is an explicit emphasis on family travel. Bare-faced curassow wanders through the grounds, and you should see hyacinth macaw and habituated jabiru (which even use vehicles as a vantage point). Ocelot, lowland tapir and hooded capuchin are sometimes seen.

Wherever you stay, it is worth exploring the wider Porto Jofre area. By day, forest may hold cream-coloured woodpecker, cinnamon-throated hermit and large-billed antwren. Fawn-breasted wren and gangs of white woodpecker favour scrubbier areas. Pied lapwing loves the riverside strand, where Marcellina sulphur butterflies blizzard yellow and royal firetip (a glam, multicoloured skipper) sups minerals. Amazonian long-tailed porcupine sometimes slumbers in riverside trees. At night, one tactic is to drive slowly up and down the roads. Brazilian guinea pig is common. Lowland tapir and common red brocket are frequent, and some lucky souls encounter ocelot or puma. Jaguar tracks are regularly found, and the animal sometimes seen – but for this pinnacle of the Pantanal experience, you really need to take to the river.

Motorboats and boatmen can be hired from the three accommodation options mentioned or from riverside fishermen. Expect to pay at least US$350 for a full-day tour for up to six people, rising to US$700 for a 12-seat boat. The main jaguar-watching area (sometimes rather tritely referred to as 'Jaguarland') is 1 hour northeast, so an early start is advisable.

Should you not want the palaver of a fast river journey twice a day (or four times if you return for lunch), an alternative accommodation approach involves overnighting in a houseboat or floating hotel ('flotel') on the river, closer to the area frequented by jaguars and with motorboats on hand. Catering principally for fishermen but also accommodating ecotourists, **Barco Hotel Jaguar do Pantanal** (*10 cabins;* ☏ *+ 55 65*

Houseboats (here the Panorâmico) offer the opportunity to explore deep into the Pantanal. (ME)

3053 0372, + 65 55 9236 6279; e *ricardo@ jaguardopantanal.com;* w *jaguardopantanal. com.br. US$1,150 pp sharing, for 4 days/3 nights, inc breakfast, local guide, transfers, motorboat excursions; other meals extra)* has comfortable cabins; its sister houseboat, **Barco Jacaré,** is available for exclusive hire. **Panorâmico** (*12 cabins;* \ *+ 55 65 99662 5456, +55 65 3345 2343;* w *transpantanal.com.br/en/Barco/4/ boat-panoramico*) is sometimes chartered by international tour operators such as Naturetrek to cruise west into remote parts of the Pantanal adjacent to the Bolivian border, a little-visited region where giant waterlily is native.

The River Cuiabá offers the world's best chances of watching intimate aspects of jaguar life, from safeguarding offspring to predating caiman. (*Above*, CT/WB; *below*, SU/SS)

UeSo Chalana Pantanal (*10 cabins;* \ *+55 65 9918 3358, + 55 65 99964 1701;* e *info@ pantanal.ch;* w *pantanal.ch/en/tour14_en.html*) is run by operators with a lodge on the Transpantaneira (page 133) – as is **SouthWild Flotel & Jaguar Suites** (⊕ *17°19'13.4"S 56°42'21.2"W; 22 cabins across two boats;* \ *+1 443 660 6303, +55 11 5196 0168;* e *info@ southwild.com;* w *tinyurl.com/SouthWild-river;* ⊕ *May–Nov. Flotel US$530 pppn & Jaguar Suites US$795 pppn, both based on 2 sharing,*

inc FB, 8–9 hours of boat trips daily and onboard lectures. Guide & transfers extra). Anchored together on the River Piquiri, both boats have air conditioning and Wi-Fi: as the name suggests, Jaguar Suites has larger, grander cabins with huge beds and floor-to-ceiling windows, and the layout is designed with photographers in mind. Both provide a photographer-focused motorboat with rotating seats and in-built gimbal tripod heads for large lenses, have exclusive land-based access to their own property, and are confident of also showing clients maned wolf (which is otherwise very rarely seen in the Mato Grosso Pantanal).

Another intriguing waterborne option – offered by Pantanal Explorers, the company behind Araras Pantanal Ecolodge (page 130) – is a 5-night **cruise between Cáceres and Porto Jofre**, (\ *+ 55 65 3682 2800, + 55 65 99983 1277;* e *reservas@pantanalexplorer.com. br;* w *tinyurl.com/Pantanal-Explorer-cruise;* ⊕ *select dates only, Jul–Oct. From US$3,600 pp, based on 2 sharing, for 6 days/5 nights, inc FB, bilingual guide and daily boat safaris*). This travels through remote and little-disturbed reserves and other areas along the Paraguay and Cuiabá rivers, with great potential for exciting wildlife encounters.

Finally, three remote lodges in prime jaguar country merit consideration. **Pousada Piquiri** (⊕ *17°19'51.8"S 56°35'41.3"W; 4 rooms;* \ *+ 55 65 9957 0570;* e *contato@ pousadapiquiri.com.br;* w *pousadapiquiri.com.br. US$260 pppn including FB & boat rides; transfers extra. Day visit US$35*) lies on the River Piquiri and can accommodate

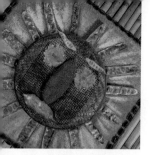

Lodges, as here at Araras, are often decorated with local artwork. (JL)

20 guests in simple but attractive rooms with stylish bathrooms. Communal areas have comfy sofas. Although focused on fishing, it caters for ecotourists too. The grounds have good numbers of chestnut-bellied guan plus bare-faced curassow, hyacinth macaw, nine-banded armadillo and Azara's agouti.

Named after the world's largest rodent, **Pousada Porto da Capivara** (⊕ *17°08'29.6"S 56°35'54.7"W; 7 rooms;* ☎ *+55 31 98483 4006;* e *reservas@pousadaportodacapivara.com;* w *pousadaportodacapivara.com. US$2,885 pp, based on 2 sharing for 4 days/3 nights, inc FB, bilingual guide & 2 full-day boat trips. Transfers extra)* is even farther north, on the River São Lourenço. Air-conditioned, individually designed rooms are comfortable, their walls decorated with large photographs of Pantanal wildlife, and have Wi-Fi. Charter flights can land at the private airstrip.

Four km southeast, on a neighbouring river, **Pousada Recanto do Jaguar** (⊕ *17°10'03.3"S 56°34'38.2"W; 10 rooms;* ☎ *+ 55 65 99635 1833, +55 65 99236 6279;* e *ricardo@jaguardopantanal.com.br. US$1,150 pp sharing, for 4 days/3 nights, inc breakfast, local guide, transfers & motorboat excursions; other meals extra)* is run by Grupo Jaguar Tour, which also owns the Jacaré and Jaguar do Pantanal houseboats (page 140–1). Catering primarily to sport-fishing tourism, it has pleasant, air-conditioned rooms, a large communal dining area and a games room. Its all-inclusive approach includes alcoholic drinks, so expect a convivial atmosphere.

Wherever you stay, the 100km worth of rivers upstream (northeast) of Porto Jofre – a complex comprising the São Lourenço, Cuiabá, Tres Irmãos ('Three Brothers'), Corixo Negro, Piquiri and São Pedrinho, all part of Encontro das Aguas State Park – is the best place to watch jaguar anywhere in its range. Sharp-eyed boat drivers know the area well and share sightings by radio. Such mutually supportive communication strengthens prospects of seeing this magnificent feline (page 166). Indeed, from May to November, you are likely to see multiple individuals per day: the ideal months to visit are now thought to be June, July and November. The downside, however, is that up to 20 boats may gather when a jaguar is spotted; fortunately, boat drivers tend to be respectful to both one another and the cat, and do not jostle for position. Nevertheless, after a few spectacular encounters, some visitors prefer to resist the knee-jerk reaction to chase other boats' finds and instead search for their own.

Or, indeed, look for other wildlife. On large sandbanks in the open river, pied lapwing and collared plover scuttle past terns and black skimmer. Black-and-gold howler, hooded capuchin, lowland tapir and hyacinth macaw forage along riverbanks. Chances of both otters, sunbittern, sungrebe, bare-faced curassow, piping-guans and green iguana are high on quieter stretches of narrow rivers. Greater capybara numbers seem to have dipped in recent years, but small groups are still seen. All five kingfishers and rufous-tailed jacamar perch on overhanging branches, boisterous pairs of black-capped donacobius scold from dense aquatic vegetation while a long-winged harrier may float past or a little cuckoo peer demurely from a horizontal branch. Keen eyes may pick out Amazonian long-tailed porcupine or Azara's night monkey high in a tree, proboscis bats roosting on a trunk, a marsh deer browsing or a yellow anaconda wrapped around a branch. As dusk falls, the air fills with band-tailed nighthawks and bulldog bats.

East of the Transpantaneira, but still in Mato Grosso, is the **Barão de Melgaço**. This area caters primarily to Brazilians, particularly fishermen, with less emphasis on wildlife-watching. One well-known lodge, however, may merit consideration as a complement (or even alternative) to a Transpantaneira trip. **Pousada do Rio Mutum** (⊕ *16°20'44.6"S 55°51'49.2"W; 22 rooms;* \+55 65 3052 7022, + 55 65 99671 7022; e *info.reservas@pousadamutum.com.br;* w *pousadamutum.com.br;* ⊕ *all year. US$1,820 pp sharing, for 4 days/3 nights, inc FB, activities, bilingual guide & transfers*) has a beautiful setting in the Baía de Siá Mariana. The most wildlife-focused of the area's establishments – although perhaps less so than Transpantaneira lodges – Rio Mutum is a 3-hour drive from Cuiabá along the MT040 and MT456, with the final 18km after the village of Mimoso being on a dirt road. Chalet-based accommodation is stylish, with smart bathrooms and air-conditioning. The large circular restaurant feels surprisingly intimate. A nice swimming pool with panoramic bar sits amid attractive gardens with bird feeders. Visitors can arrange vehicle safaris, horse-rides, walks along several trails, and a boat or canoe trip into Siá Mariana or Chacororé bays for giant otter and black-and-gold howler. Other mammals include giant anteater, lowland tapir, Amazonian long-tailed porcupine and Azara's night monkey – but jaguar is absent. Some Pantanal bird specialities occur in the vicinity, including chestnut-bellied guan, agami and zigzag herons, sungrebe, sunbittern, hyacinth macaw and planalto slaty-antshrike.

MATO GROSSO DO SUL, BRAZIL

The southern Brazilian Pantanal lies in Mato Grosso do Sul state. The best wildlife-watching experiences here are on a handful of well-run but relatively widely separated *fazendas*. Campo Grande provides the main initial access point; visitors arrive at the state capital by domestic flight or long-distance bus. From there, head west along the BR262 to Aquidauana (140km; 2h drive) or Miranda (210km; 2h45). As

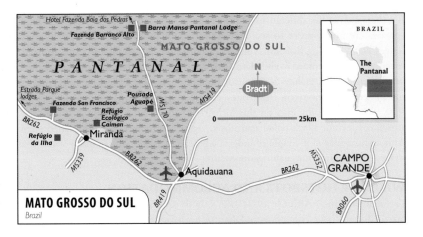

Many lodges (here, Pousada Aguapé) offer horse-riding as a way to see wildlife. (PA)

there is no direct equivalent of Mato Grosso's Transpantaneira highway that connects a number of lodges (although there is the Estrada Parque: page 153), it is less straightforward to execute a multi-venue trip. Moreover, the wildlife at each lodge tends to be more similar than in Mato Grosso so there is less compulsion to book a multi-venue visit.

Nevertheless, each lodge tends to have one or more species for which it is particularly good, and, perhaps for that reason, most visitors spend several days at a single lodge then move to another (or to the Mato Grosso Pantanal). Most independent travellers organise transfers through their lodge(s), some reducing costs by taking a bus from Cuiabá to Aquidauana or Miranda: check options online (w *buscaonibus. com.br*). Alternatively, book a taxi from those towns: a 4x4 will be essential outside the dry season of April to October (and, for most destinations, sensible during it too). Self-driving a 4x4 is feasible for most lodges but, unlike the Transpantaneira, offers little advantage, as lodges typically do not permit visitors to drive themselves around the property. Several lodges have private airstrips, which offer charter flights ('air taxis') year-round access; splitting the somewhat eye-watering cost between a group is advisable.

Wildlife is similar to Mato Grosso: the same core elements – storks, ibises, egrets, yacaré caiman and greater capybara – are present, albeit in less staggering abundance. But there are notable differences. On the plus side, peccaries, pampas deer and giant anteater are much easier to see. Macaws are more evident: as in the north, most lodges host breeding hyacinths, but blue-and-yellow, red-shouldered and red-and-green macaws are more likely. Mato Grosso do Sul is also better for six- and nine-banded armadillos, yellow-faced parrot and blaze-winged parakeet, but less good for marsh deer and sunbittern. The greatest chance of giant armadillo is at a lodge in this state (though clapping eyes on this formerly mythical mammal remains unlikely). Absentees include black-tailed marmoset, zigzag heron and chestnut-bellied guan. Although regular at a couple of lodges, jaguar is generally more elusive – but that makes any encounter arguably more exciting.

WILDLIFE HOTSPOTS AND ACCOMMODATION

Fazenda Barranco Alto (⊕ *19°34'41.2"S 56°09'02.3"W; 6 rooms;* e reservations@ fazendabarrancoalto.com; w *fazendabarrancoalto.com.br;* ⏰ *Feb–Nov. US$290 pppn*

*[Feb–May, Nov] or US$370 pppn [Jun–Oct] sharing, inc FB, 2 activities per day &
English-speaking guide*) flanks the black-water River Negro, 120km northwest of
Aquidauana, partly along the MS170. Although most of the 11,000ha, family-run
property is a working cattle ranch, a third forms a private protected area. This
safeguards forest, gallery forest, rivers, wetlands, wax-palm savannah and Barranco
Alto's special landscape – *salinas* (salty lakes) and *baías* (rounded freshwater lagoons),
separated by cerrado forest on raised areas (*capões* or, if large, *cordilheiras*) – which
characterises the area known as Nhecolândia.

The ambience at this much-loved lodge is intimate, relaxed and friendly: meals
are taken communally at a long dining table. Bare brick and dark wood lend a
refreshingly modern feel to the cosy living room and well-stocked library. There
is also a shady, hammock-filled terrace, Wi-Fi and a bar. Air-conditioned rooms
are relaxed and informal, redecorated in local *fazenda* style in 2021. Meals include
homegrown vegetables and homemade cheese, jams and breads. With so few clients
able to spread out over a large area, Barranco Alto provides a tranquil immersion
in nature and feels exclusive. Open-top safari vehicles head out by day and night.
Guests can explore the River Negro by canoe, electric boat or small motorboat – and
typically have the river to themselves. You can walk along numerous trails or traverse
larger areas on horseback. There are opportunities to accompany on-site wildlife
researchers and conservationists during fieldwork or even join *peão* farmhands as
they supervise cattle.

In total, 49 species of mammal have been recorded. Lowland tapir is regularly
seen. Giant anteater is fairly common during the cooler months of May–October,
and southern tamandua sometimes seen. Giant otter and Neotropical otter are not
uncommon along the river, while both peccaries are common in forests (and white-
lipped sometimes investigates fallen mangoes in the lodge garden). All four deer are
present (pampas is common) as are black-and-gold howler and hooded capuchin.
Jaguar is occasionally seen; puma is more regular. Due to a genetic quirk, some

Aerial view of Fazenda Barranco Alto Ecolodge. (AB/FBA)

A landscape mosaic at Fazenda Barranco Alto Ecolodge. (LL/SS)

greater capybara are blond variants. At night, look for three opossums, southern tamandua and crab-eating fox. Six-banded armadillo is common; giant and southern naked-tailed armadillos have been recorded but are very unlikely to be seen. Crab-eating raccoon visits the lodge garden, while scores of common vampire bat and Pallas's long-tongued bat roost in a disused building.

Among 23 species of reptile, Brazilian redtail boa, yacaré caiman (particularly along the river), both anacondas and Paraguay caiman lizard occur. Twenty species of amphibian, 94 fish and 415 bird species have been recorded. Greater rhea and red-legged seriema patrol grasslands. Pied lapwing favours sandy beaches. *Salinas* such as Lindoya retain water during the dry season; full of insect larvae, they are a magnet for egrets, stilts and ducks. Search the river for sungrebe and capped heron. A quintet of macaws includes hyacinth, red-shouldered and blue-and-yellow; these are complemented by three species of parrot (including yellow-faced) and six parakeets (including nanday). Some visit the lodge garden, as do bare-faced curassow, toco toucan and purplish jay. Seven species of owl occur, likewise eight nightjars and 15 woodpeckers. A good suite of Pantanal forest birds is present, including rusty-backed spinetail and pale-bellied tyrant-manakin. Butterflies include Marcellina and statira sulphurs, and gulf fritillary, particularly on river beaches.

Getting to the lodge involves planning. In the wet season (November–May), arriving by small plane, for example with ATT (e *comandantemadeu@hotmail.com*), is essential: flights take 1h from Campo Grande or 30 minutes from Aquidauana. During the dry season (June–October), you can usually travel by 4x4, although the GPS route can be hard to follow, may vary with conditions and involves opening and closing numerous gates; the lodge recommends booking a transfer with Vavatours (e *vavatour@bol.com.br*) rather than driving yourself. You should see plenty of wildlife overland, however, potentially including six-banded armadillo, pampas deer, greater rhea, hyacinth macaw, Argentine black-and-white tegu and false water cobra.

For a migratory shorebird, it may be a mere 50km flight northeast from Barranco Alto to another highly rated lodge, **Hotel Fazenda Baia das Pedras** (19°15'26.1"S 55°47'11.0"W; 7 rooms; + 55 67 99999 8323 ; e *baiadaspedras@baiadaspedras.com. br*; w *baiadaspedras.com.br*; Apr–Dec. US$2,400 pp for 4 days/3 nights, FB, guide,

2 activities per day & 4x4 transfers – or US$4,345 pp with air transfers), but humans take fully five hours to drive the route. It is worth it, though – for the quality of wildlife-watching both on the way (with species much as the previous paragraph, plus giant anteater) and once you reach the hotel. Like Barranco Alto, a pleasing conservation ethos permeates the 13,000ha of this family-run *fazenda*, where dedicated mammalogists have been fathoming the secrets of lowland tapir and giant armadillo. This also provides a direct and unique attraction for visitors: although it is not possible to join the researchers in the field, if one of the mammals under study is caught, guests are invited to observe as it is measured, tagged and released.

Upmarket, rustic-chic rooms make for a comfortable stay; four were upgraded in 2022 and are particularly stylish – even complete with cow-hide rugs and jaguar-print throws, plus a designer bathroom and a private terrace. Communal spaces are smart and convivial. The atmosphere is welcoming: meals are taken together, at a long table. English-speaking guides are available July–September (at other times, guides speak Portuguese only). Vehicular safaris are available night and day, and you can explore *vazante* watercourses by silent canoe, investigate scrub on foot and peruse grasslands on horseback. There are neither observation towers nor motorboat trips, however. To relax, sling a hammock under a mango tree and nab a book from the library. Although the hotel offers transfers in the price, these are delivered by a third party. You can fly in from Campo Grande (1h) or, during May–December, travel overland in a 4x4 (7 hours from Campo Grande).

This is the best place *anywhere* to see giant armadillo (and your only hope of southern naked-tailed armadillo, a rarely seen fossorial creature that emerges above ground only for a few minutes each day) – so if none is caught during your stay, a patient vigil beside these armoured creatures' fresh diggings at least offers hope. Bumping into one out and about is very unlikely: tracking studies here have revealed

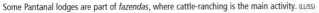

Some Pantanal lodges are part of *fazendas*, where cattle-ranching is the main activity. (LL/SS)

that females have a territory size of around 25km², with those of males almost three times larger! In better news, you should see several giant anteater and lowland tapir, plus southern tamandua, nine- and six-banded armadillos (both much easier to see than in Mato Grosso), white-lipped peccary, pampas and marsh deer, black-and-gold howler, South American coati, crab-eating raccoon and forest rabbit. Tayra is seen fairly regularly. At night, there is a chance of ocelot and perhaps puma (but not jaguar). Lesser bulldog bats roost in one of the lodge sheds.

Although the focus is rightly on mammals, birding is also good. Several pairs of hyacinth macaw breed. Red-shouldered macaws may fly by; toco toucan visits the garden; sunbittern (rare this far south) occurs; and greater rhea, red-legged seriema and black-throated saltator inhabit the grasslands. During a boat trip on the lake, you should see the usual long-legged waterbirds, stilts and black-collared hawk.

Open-sided 'safari' vehicles, here at Fazenda Barranco Alto Ecolodge, help visitors view wildlife. (SG/FBA)

Fazenda San Francisco (⊕ *20°05'10.5"S 56°36'54.5"W; 18 rooms;* \+55 67 3242 3333, + 55 67 99832 0304; e *reservas@fazendasanfrancisco. tur.br;* w *fazendasanfrancisco.tur.br;* ⏁ *all year. US$130 pppn sharing, inc FB, Portuguese-speaking guide & 3 activities. Day visit US$65 inc vehicular safari, boat trip, lunch & guide)* lies on the west bank of the River Miranda, an easy 25-minute (36km) drive northwest of Miranda; the final 6km are a long a gravel track. Occupying 14,800ha, this ranch runs a thriving ecotourism business alongside cattle ranching and rice cultivation, and has also supported researchers and conservationists working on species as diverse as ocelot and hyacinth macaw. Air-conditioned rooms are simple; amenities include a swimming pool.

Unlike other lodges, San Francisco is a regular, rather commercialised destination for Brazilian day trippers, which can reduce its attractiveness to keen wildlife-watchers seeking tranquillity. If, however, you can put up with noisy visitors on a vehicular safari in a large, shared vehicle with tiered seating, packages are relatively inexpensive – and there is stuff to see. The rice fields, interspersed with drainage channels and lightly wooded savannah, attract numerous rodents. These support a strong population of ocelot: reliability is on a par with the provisioned animals at SouthWild Pantanal Lodge (page 135) and you could easily see multiple individuals in a night drive. San Francisco is also one of the best bets for encountering jaguar in Mato Grosso do Sul.

Several lodges, such as Pousada Aguapé, have swimming pools: perfect for cooling off after a day watching wildlife. (LFM/PA)

Crab-eating fox, giant anteater (particularly near the lodge) and southern tamandua are frequent. Puma is not irregular and maned wolf occasional; nowhere offers a better chance of Pantanal cat. Six- and nine-banded armadillos grant good views, pampas deer graze the grasslands and marsh deer is remarkably common. A splash in a drainage channel might be a lowland tapir; a coiled shape, a yellow anaconda.

Boat trips along the River Miranda or Corixo São Domingos may be more focused on piranha-fishing than wildlife-watching, but offer prospects of giant otter, yacaré caiman, hooded capuchin, fish-seeking raptors and kingfishers. Horse-riding, canoeing, an observation tower, boardwalks and walking trails are also on offer. White-lined broad-nosed bat, lesser dog-like bat and Pallas's long-tongued bat sometimes roost beneath lodge roofs. Birding can be good, with 330 species recorded. Feeders at the lodge attract toco toucan, turquoise-fronted amazon and nanday parakeet. Four macaws include hyacinth and blue-and-yellow; blaze-winged parakeet is a speciality. In forests, look for great rufous woodcreeper, red-billed scythebill and Mato Grosso antbird. Nightbirds include common potoo, striped owl and scissor-tailed nightjar.

Run by the same family for 150 years, Fazenda São José remains a working cattle ranch, but today derives more income from ecotourism and sport fishing. Both activities are based at its lodge, **Pousada Aguapé** (⊕ *20°05'45.1"S 55°57'55.1"W; 15 rooms;* \ *+55 67 99963 0181, + 55 67 3258 1146;* e *reservas@pousadaaguape.com.br;* w *pousadaaguape.com.br;* ⊕ *all year except Christmas. US$130 pppn sharing, inc FB, local guide & 2 activities per day. Bilingual/wildlife guides and additional activities extra*) which turned 35 in 2025. To get here, leave Aquidauana southwest on the BR419 then turn west at the roundabout along the BR262; after 3km, follow the signposts north for 54km along a dirt road to reach the lodge (looking out for giant anteater, southern tamandua and greater rhea as you go). Alternatively an airstrip is available for small planes: the lodge can arrange (outsource) transfers. Recently refurbished, air-conditioned rooms are stylish, colourful and powered by solar energy. Artwork liberally adorns intimate shared areas, where there is Wi-Fi. Visitors can work off excess energy on the volleyball court, cool down in the swimming pool, then doze away their exertions in hammocks.

The habitat mosaic across the 2,260ha at this good-value lodge includes cerrado, wetlands, lakes, river, grasslands and gallery forest. A long-standing favourite of wildlife-watchers, Aguapé makes the most of its bounteous biodiversity. You can traverse large areas of the *fazenda* atop new safari vehicles (day or night), on horseback or (rather memorably) in a horse-drawn carriage, and explore smaller areas along several trails (1.5–4h). Motorboat and canoe trips along the River Aquidauana are particularly productive during the rainy season, offering a strong chance of lowland tapir.

Among other mammals, giant anteater is genuinely easy to see, as is six-banded armadillo (habituated individuals have even learnt to visit the open-sided dining room upon hearing the lunch bell!). Ocelot often takes top billing on night drives, while jaguar and puma are fairly regular. Hooded capuchin and both otters favour the river. Pampas deer and greater capybara are relatively common. Most visitors see southern tamandua, black-and-gold howler, nine-banded armadillo and crab-eating raccoon. Greater capybara and crab-eating fox wander through the garden. Other attractions include both peccaries.

With 375 bird species recorded, most usual suspects are present – from greater rhea to Mato Grosso antbird, capped heron to white-lored spinetail. There are an amazing seven species each of macaw (including red-shouldered and nesting hyacinth), parakeet (including blaze-winged, nanday and peach-fronted) and owl, plus six nightjars. White-fronted woodpecker is a speciality, and a bold red-legged seriema sometimes stalks the garden. Plush-crested jay and bare-faced curassow join many parrots at the lodge feeders, where proximity and clean backgrounds means they are much appreciated by photographers. A pocket of cerrado harbours the rare white-rumped tanager. 'Herp' highlights include Miranda's white-lipped frog, cururu toad, yellow anaconda, banded cat-eyed snake, false fer-de-lance and red-footed tortoise.

It is harder to see jaguar in the southern Pantanal, but that makes encountering one all the more rewarding. (CT/WB)

Refúgio Ecológico Caiman (⊕ *19°57'12.0"S 56°18'18.0"W; 29 rooms;* ☏ *+ 55 11 3706 1800, +55 11 93752 3064;* e *caiman@caiman.com. br;* w *caiman.com.br;* ◷ *all year. From US$375 pppn, based on 2 sharing, inc FB, bilingual guide & activities – plus a one-off US$90 pp donation to conservation. Jun–Nov: bookings taken for 3–4 nights only, starting Thu and Sun*) combines low-impact cattle-ranching, ecotourism and wildlife conservation. A tenth of the 53,000ha ranch is safeguarded as a *Reserva Particular do Patrimônio Natural* (private natural heritage reserve) and the lodge works with Onçasafari, the Instituto Arara Azul and others to help study or protect jaguar, hyacinth macaw, lowland tapir and turquoise-fronted amazon. Caiman is a large, slick but well-intentioned operation, an understandable winner of sustainable-tourism awards. If your budget permits, you can barely go wrong here.

Pampas deer is typically easiest to see in Mato Grosso do Sul. (LL/SS)

Most visitors stay in the 18-suite Casa Caiman, but small groups can exclusively reserve one of two self-contained private villas with five/six suites. All are upmarket and attractive options, with large communal spaces, swimming pool, bar, gym, sauna, firepit, hammock area, restaurant and luxurious, air-conditioned bedrooms with private terrace and Wi Fi. Access is easy from Miranda: at the roundabout where the BR262 and MS446 meet, head north, take the first left (west; signposted to Caiman), then follow the dirt road northwards for 35km (1 hour). A private airstrip is also available.

Bilingual, university-educated naturalists ('Caimaners'), escorted by *pantaneiro* guides, help guests explore savannahs, gallery forests, wetlands and seasonal rivers. Safari vehicles transport visitors by day or night. Canoeing enables silent approach to caiman and capybara. You can hire a motorboat to reach remote areas; the half-day trip returns after dark, spotlighting for mammals. There are a dozen trails, mostly in forest. You can also ride the grasslands on horseback. Special jaguar-focused and birdwatching tours can be booked in advance.

Of 40 mammal species recorded, giant anteater and southern tamandua are regular, particularly in the dry season. Herbivores include lowland tapir, all four deer, both peccaries, Amazonian long-tailed porcupine and lowland paca. Both otters occur. Jaguar and ocelot are reasonably regular, and the latter often fish at Paizinho bridge – a great spot from which to photograph caiman.

Look for red-footed tortoise on land and big-headed Pantanal swamp turtle in the water. A score of serpents include yellow anaconda, Neotropical rattlesnake and giant parrot snake. Look to the trees for Brazilian monkey lizard and damp scrub for Paraguay caiman lizard. Amphibians recorded include cururu toad, twin-coloured oval frog and Uruguay harlequin frog. The range of habitats enables birders easily to rack up 180 species – half the site total – in three days. Grasslands hold greater rhea, red-legged seriema and nacunda nighthawk. Macaws include plentiful hyacinth. Blaze-winged parakeet is fairly common and 11 hummingbirds an excellent total. Helmeted and band-tailed manakins flash scarlet in the dingy forest undergrowth.

The southern Pantanal tends to offer better chances of seeing giant anteater (*above*) and nine-banded armadillo (*below*). (CT/WB)

The above quintet of Mato Grosso do Sul lodges represents serious players most favoured by natural-history fans. Several other lodges have attractions too; some may become mainstream options for keen wildlife-watchers during the lifetime of this edition. For now, I cover them only briefly and provide contact details.

The best-known is **Barra Mansa Pantanal Lodge** (✪ *19°35'19.4"S 56°05'17.1"W;* ☎ *+5567998014544, +5567 3325 6807;* e *reservas@hotelbarramansa. com.br;* w *barramansalodge.com. US$770 pp sharing for 4 days/3 nights inc FB, local guide & 2 activities per day. Transfers extra*). Established in 1996, this family-run lodge is located beside the River Negro on the southern edge of Nhecolândia, just east of the MS170 and 6km eastsoutheast of Barranco Alto. There is a three-night minimum stay in classy, air-conditioned rooms. Jeep safaris and boat tours could produce giant otter, giant anteater, lowland tapir, black-and-gold howler, hyacinth macaw and nanday parakeet plus the usual fare, and there is a chance of jaguar along the River Negro. Transfers by air or land are arranged through a third party: a 4x4 costs about US$850 return from Campo Grande airport for up to four passengers, and takes 5h30.

Another promising option is **Refúgio da Ilha** (✪ *20°13'29.7"S 56°34'31.2"W; 8 rooms;* ☎ *+ 55 67 99266 5652, + 55 67 99944 4014;* e *reservas@refugiodailha.com. br;* w *refugiodailha.com.br. US$640 pp sharing, for 4 days/3 nights outside of holidays & July, inc FB, local guide & 2 activities per day*). Sitting beside the River Salobra, southwest of Miranda, it is just 11km off the BR262 highway, along a cobbled road – and thus is readily accessible without a 4x4. Expect to see giant anteater, both otters and possibly maned wolf, puma and jaguar, in addition to the usual waterbirds, yacaré caiman and greater capybara. There is a three-night minimum stay. The lodge can arrange transfers with third parties: a typical return trip from Campo Grande airport costs from US$310 for up to four passengers.

The nearest Mato Grosso do Sul comes to the Transpantaneira is the **Estrada Parque**, an unpaved road that heads north (as the MS184) off the BR262 at Buraco das Piranhas, 100km northwest of Miranda, then reaches Mercedes after 45km; from here it continues as the MS228 for c.75km west to Corumbá. The road provides access to good wildlife-watching terrain. From the BR262, after 8km you reach the community of Passo do Lontra, on the River Miranda. A somewhat under-the-radar but potentially savvy choice here is **Passo do Lontra Parque Hotel** (⊕ *19°34'48.6"S 57°01'16.7"W;* ✆ *+ 55 67 99922 5482, +55 67 99800 7871;* e *atendamiento@ passodolontra.com.br;* w *passodolontra.com.br. US$330pp sharing, for 3 days/2 nights inc FB & 4 activities. Transfers extra: US$430 per vehicle to/from Campo Grande),* because boat trips along the river stand a good chance of encountering jaguar and giant otter, without the crowds of Mato Grosso. The same applies to **Pantanal Jungle Lodge** (⊕ *19°34'35.1"S 57°01'52.2"W;* ✆ *+ 55 67 2020 0927, + 55 67 99614 3603;* e *reserva@pantanaljunglelodge.com.br;* w *pantanaljunglelodge.com.br. US$320 pp sharing, for 3 days/2 nights, inc FB & 6 activities),* which is 1km nearer the Estrada Parque. Back on the Estrada, head 11km north, then turn east for 12km to reach **Pousada Xaraés** (⊕ *19°29'37.0"S 56°57'25.6"W;* ✆ *+ 67 99906 9272, + 55 67 99906 9272;* e *reservas@xaraes.com.br;* w *xaraes.com.br. US$320 pp sharing, for 3 days/2 nights, inc FB & 4 activities);* in the wet season, access is by river. About 8km farther north is **Pousada São João Ecotur** (⊕ *19°24'05.4"S 57°02'25.1"W;* ✆ *+ 55 67 99648 3730;* w *pousadasaojoao.com.br. US$295 pp sharing, for 3 days/2 nights, inc FB & 6 activities)* is also signposted off to the east: air-conditioned accommodation is adorned with local artwork and surrounded by water, while wildlife highlights include hyacinth macaw and both anteaters.

Southern tamandua occurs widely in the Pantanal. (JL)

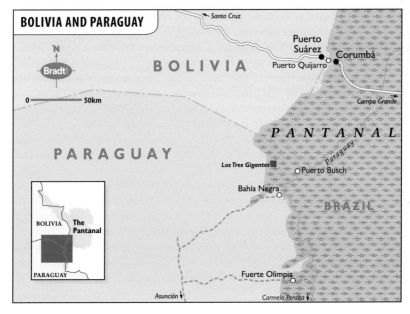

PARAGUAY

One-tenth of the Pantanal lies in Paraguay, part of which is ostensibly protected by the 123,000ha Río Negro National Park. Sited in the northeast of the Chaco, an otherwise predominantly arid region, this pristine wilderness is heaving with wildlife, but most is inaccessible: on average there is only one inhabitant for every 7km². For the adventurous, there are inexpensive opportunities for exploration from the gateway town of Bahía Negra, including to a research station run by the non-profit conservation organisation Guyra Paraguay (\+595 981 229097; e aviturismo@ guyra.org.py; w guyra.org.py). Nevertheless, you will need time – ideally a week or more – and patience because travel to this remote area is slow and arduous, and will also need to expect basic facilities.

The main entry point to the *Pantanal paraguayo* is Bahía Negra. An iconic ferry that formerly followed the River Paraguay from Concepción to both towns sadly ceased operation in 2023, so getting here now involves overland or air transport. One option is to hire a 4x4 and drive yourself, but this is not recommended: time-consuming at the best of times, the Chaco's poorly maintained dirt roads are usually impassable after rain. If you do this, allow 18 hours from the national capital of Asunción (only the first 400 of 1,000km road are paved), hire a guide and take emergency supplies. On the plus side, the section through the Chaco (particularly beyond Cruce Los Pioneros or Agua Dulce, depending which way you go) is great for mammals such as puma, jaguar, ocelot, jaguarundi and giant anteater.

If road conditions permit, the company San Juan runs buses weekly from Asunción to Bahía Negra (w plataforma10.com.py; out Thu, return Sat, 16–18h, US$25). Or, as long as there is no rain (which renders bare-earth airstrips unsafe), you can fly twice weekly from Asunción via Concepción and other towns, with Servicio de Transporte Aéreo Militar or SETAM (☏ +595 21 645885, +595 983 117964; *Wed, 3h, US$45*).

Given both the logistical difficulties and the wildlife-watching potential of the journey, perhaps the most convenient overall approach would be to book a bespoke nature tour through Paul Smith of Fauna Paraguay (e *faunaparaguay@gmail. com;* w *faunaparaguay.com. Rough prices are €300 pppn, based on 2 sharing, inc accommodation, FB, transport & guide; price pp decreases as group size increases*).

For comprehensive advice on travel around Paraguay, see Bradt's *Paraguay* guidebook.

WILDLIFE HOTSPOTS AND ACCOMMODATION

Core wildlife is broadly the same as in the Brazilian Pantanal. Among 340 bird species, herons, egrets, storks, ibises, screamers and skimmers ply the wetlands. Most Pantanal passerine specialities occur, examples being pale-legged hornero, cinereous-breasted and white-lored spinetail, rufous cacholote and Mato Grosso antbird. Marsh deer and common brown brocket are common. Both otters inhabit the rivers. Forty reptiles include snakes such as yellow anaconda, Neotropical rattlesnake and Neuwied's lancehead. Yacaré caiman are numerous; green iguana and Argentine black-and-white tegu frequently seen.

There are differences, however. The Paraguayan Pantanal offers opportunities for several species that are absent or less common farther north. The main mammal of difference is white-coated titi. Giant waterlily can be locally common. Among birds, white-barred piculet replaces white-wedged piculet, while Bolivian slaty-antshrike supplants planalto slaty-antshrike. On the downside, pampas deer is absent, greater capybara less numerous, and lowland tapir, Azara's night monkey, maned wolf and white-lipped peccary rare. Notable avian absentees (or effectively so) include agami and zigzag herons, bare-faced curassow, sunbittern, pied lapwing, hyacinth macaw,

Estación Los Tres Gigantes, Paraguay. (LM/GP)

long-tailed ground-dove, cream-coloured woodpecker and helmeted manakin. Other exciting birds – green ibis, great potoo, peach-fronted parakeet, American pygmy kingfisher and rusty-fronted tody-flycatcher – are harder to see.

The best base is the **Reserva Pantanal Paraguayo/Estación Los Tres Gigantes** (✪ *20°04'44.0"S 58°09'38.7"W; 3 rooms plus camping;* ☎ *+595 981 229097;* e *aviturismopy@guyra.org.py;* w *guyra.org.py/pantanal-paraguayo;* ⊕ *usually all year, but may be closed during dry-season fires, normally Aug–Sep. US$25 pppn for accommodation only; camping US$10 pppn.; day visitors US$8. Activities, local guides & transfers extra: canoeing US$12, guided walk US$25, boat trips US$55–75).* The 'Three Giants' lies 40km north of Bahía Negra, on the River Negro. Importantly, this is not a lodge, but the remote research station of a 14,600ha reserve managed by the country's leading conservation NGO, Guyra Paraguay. Staying here thus directly supports conservation – but also means you should not expect Transpantaneira-style facilities.

Hostel-like accommodation is in a rustic but pleasant two-storey wooden lodge, with capacity for nine people; the three rooms have fans and bathrooms. Mosquito screens are much appreciated, for the insects can be really bad here, particularly in December and January. Dark wood walls are decorated with local handicrafts made by the local Yshir indigenous community, and hammocks line shady terraces. Electricity is mainly solar powered. Substantial communal areas include a kitchen (you need to bring and prepare your own non-perishable food, and bring mineral water), dining room and library.

Access is either by motorboat (1h) from Bahía Negra (usually from around the naval base at the junction of Avenida J.J. Sánchez and Riachuelo). Alternatively, travel by 4x4 overland, firstly 12km north along *Linéa 1* then 19km east on a track newly fashioned by Guyra Paraguay (total 1h). In the latter case, contact Guyra Paraguay to make arrangements with park guards to ensure that gates are open. Transfers are provided by third parties, not Guyra Paraguay; for details of service providers, see under Bahía Negra (page 157).

Areas rich in water hyacinth can be good for yellow anaconda. (UB/SS)

The lodge name alludes to three gargantuan mammals ostensibly present: giant otter, giant anteater and giant armadillo. It can be easy to see the otter. There is also a good chance of the anteater, particularly from August–November. The chances of encountering the notoriously elusive armadillo, however, are zero. But even without the giants, there is plenty to see. Access to gallery forest, palm savannah and wetlands is by foot along short trails (*senderos*), or by a motorboat and canoe along the River Negro. There is also a new observation tower, from which marsh deer can be seen. Azara's night monkey occurs, and white-coated titi is best seen early morning after a cold night. An impressive 17 bat species have been recorded. The river is good for green iguana and, if water levels are low, potentially jaguar. Black-and-gold howler, common brown brocket and greater rhea are present.

In Pantanal terms, white-coated titi is a Paraguay speciality. (RJ/SS)

Around 30 species of amphibian and reptile have been recorded. Among them are snakes such as false water cobra and yellow anaconda, the latter particularly amid the riverine bloom of water hyacinths from September–November. Argentine black-and-white tegu and Paraguay caiman lizard are prominent in summer. Azara's agouti, nine-banded armadillo and white-lored spinetail are common along forest trails. During a three-night stay, keen birders can expect to see up to 150 bird species; the total reserve list is 315 species.

An alternative base is the town of **Bahía Negra**, from where visitors can make day trips along rivers and nocturnal forays along roads. Aiming to promote tourism here, WWF-Paraguay, Guyra Paraguay and the Asociacón Eco Pantanal Bahía Negra have produced an online travel guidebook to the town (**w** *tinyurl.com/Bahia_Negra-tourism*). Accommodation options (all basic, as is the norm in rural Paraguay) include: **Hotel El Dorado** (☏ *+591 948 129622. US$12*); **Hotel el Puertas del Pantanal o Nacho** (☏*+591 984 862609. US$12*) and **Hospedaje Hortencia** (☏*+591 982 944024. US$10*). All offer food, complementing the town's handful of eateries.

For boat trips, you need to negotiate with local boatmen. These include: Juan Ortiz, known as 'Don Gualí' (☏*+595 984 153484*); Jorge Matoso or 'Don Chito' (☏*+ 595 985 756822*); Agenor Da Silva or 'Nono' (☏*+595 986 691319*); Ramón Dutra (☏*+595 986 338871*); Errair Da Silva (☏*+595 984 255609*); Rubén Paredes (☏*+595 982 209197*); Carlos Matoso (☏ *+595 984 745233*) and Leonardo Matoso (☏ *+595 982 872097*). Average costs are at least US$3/km, plus the boatman's time. The further north of Bahía Negra you venture, the better the chance of giant otter and green iguana. In riverine forest, look for white-coated titi, Azara's night monkey and black-tailed marmoset.

Giant otter is one of the three large mammals captured in the name of Los Tres Gigantes. (KD)

Local taxi drivers with a 4x4 (essential) include: Basilio Peralta (☏ + 595 984 129622); Gustavo Arévalos (☏ + 595 983 838192); Claudio Dos Santos (☏ +595 984 467231); Damián de la Cueva (☏+595 984 172827), Derlis Arias (☏ +595 982 136683) and Nilsa Frutos (☏ +595 982 559789). Average costs are at least US$0.70/km, plus the driver's time. At night, drive slowly along roads surrounding Bahía Negra, searching for mammals such as lowland tapir, giant anteater, southern tamandua, common brown brocket, tayra, southern three-banded armadillo, crab-eating raccoon, South American coati, crab-eating and pampas foxes, and collared peccary. Mammal density can be impressively high.

South of Bahía Negra, **Fuerte Olimpo** makes a reasonable base. Given suitable weather, San Juan runs buses twice weekly from Asunción (15h, ostensibly) or you can fly from Asunción or Concepción with SETAM (page 154). In the dry season, roadside pools hum with activity: typical Pantanal waterbirds such as jabiru, plumbeous ibis, various herons and egrets, and black skimmer gather to harvest dying fish, while yacaré caiman and raptors, such as crane hawk and snail kite, also take advantage of easy pickings. Contact Blanca Vaccari (☏ +595 984 535859) for guided trips. **Carmelo Peralta** may be a viable base in future. Completion of the *Ruta Bioceánica* (*Ruta 15*), perhaps during 2030–35, coupled with a new international bridge across the River Paraguay to Brazil, may open up access and potential ecotourism opportunities, including around the Isla Margarita. Here the Organización Paraguaya de Conservación y Desarrollo Sostenible is actively investigating potential tourist circuits, including waterborne activities. It would be pleasing if these hatch into fully-fledged offerings in time to include in the next edition of this guide.

BOLIVIA

One-fifth of the Pantanal lies in Santa Cruz province, Bolivia, adjacent to the Brazilian and Paraguayan borders. Much is theoretically protected in two state-run reserves: the 2.9 million hectare San Matías Integrated Management Natural Area (w *globalnationalparks.com/bolivia/san-matias*) and the 1 million hectare Otuquis National Park and Integrated Management Natural Area (w *globalnationalparks.com/ bolivia/otuquis*). San Matías has Amazonian overtones to its flora and fauna, while Otuquis displays Chacoan and Chiquitano elements. Only one-eighth of San Matías and one-quarter of Otuquis comprise Pantanal. Unfortunately, both reserves face pressures, including San Matías from fire and Otuquis from mining.

In principle, this little-explored, relatively untouched area offers potential for exciting wildlife experiences and even discoveries: who knows what will be round the next river bend? In reality, there is little sense that ecotourism is encouraged. Tourism infrastructure is rudimentary, with little choice of accommodation and no reliable on-site service providers. Access is difficult, particularly for independent travellers.

What little tourism there exists is restricted to Otuquis. Moreover, the main access road in now suffers significant disturbance from mining operations. Indeed, the situation appears to have deteriorated since the first edition of this guide to the extent that, tellingly, a typical tour to the 'Bolivian' Pantanal actually spends a considerable part of its time in either Paraguay (at Estación Los Tres Gigantes: page 156) or Brazil!

From the few studies carried out, core wildlife should be similar to that in Brazil and Paraguay. If you can arrange a visit, you stand a fair chance of seeing giant otter, white-lipped peccary, pampas and marsh deer (the latter being particularly easy to see), black-and-gold howler, Paraguay caiman lizard, and potentially maned wolf and jaguar, plus the standard fare of yacaré caiman, greater capybara and numerous waterbirds. If you come across some gallery forest, you theoretically stand a chance of white-coated titi and Azara's night monkey.

WILDLIFE HOTSPOTS AND ACCOMMODATION

In extreme southeast Bolivia, the towns of **Puerto Suárez** (relatively pleasant) and **Puerto Quijarro** (unprepossessing), 12km apart, provide the starting point for trips to Otuquis. Both are accessed from Santa Cruz, either via comfortable train (taking 12–15h) or more regular (but less pleasant) bus (15–24h); you can buy tickets from w ticketsbolivia.com. There is no formal accommodation inside the Bolivian Pantanal (which is why guided tours overnight in the Pantanal in Brazil or Paraguay). Accordingly, if you are adamant that you wish to explore the Bolivian sector, stay in one of the two towns and make day trips.

Probably the most acceptable accommodation options are both in Quijarro. **Hotel Bibosi** (*Av. Luis Salazar 495;* \+ *591 3978 2290, +591 7315 8094;* e *jardinelbibosi@ hotmail.com;* w *hotelbibosi.com. US$65 dbl, inc breakfast*) has comfortable, if old-fashioned, 'executive' rooms with air conditioning, Wi-Fi and private bathroom. **El Pantanal Hotel Resort** (⊕ *19°01'11.1"S 57°43'07.9"W;* \+ *591 7210 3731;* e *hotelpantanal4@gmail.com. US$55 dbl, inc breakfast*) is southwest of town, just off the RN4. It has large rooms, a sizeable swimming pool and spacious grounds. In central Puerto Suárez, the less inspiring possibilities include **Hotel Casa Real** (*Calle Vanguardia 39,* \+591 3976 3335) and **Hotel Liloko** (*Avenida Naval 130;* \+ *591 3978 2088;* e *j.sanjines+1@hotmail.com. From US$25 dbl*).

Giant waterlilies are a feature of the Bolivian Pantanal. (JD/SS)

Egrets can gather in large numbers. (E/SS)

Puerto Suárez fronts the **Laguna Cáceres**, and the quickest way to get a feel for the Bolivian Pantanal is to pay a boatman to take you onto the lagoon, although water levels are increasingly low due to a nearby dam and intensifying drought. Nevertheless, here you could see jabiru, southern screamer, greater capybara and yacaré caiman. If you manage to explore channels (such as Sicurí, Tuyuyú and Tamengo) that connect the lagoon to the River Paraguay, you could encounter marsh deer, green iguana, giant waterlily and, conceivably, giant otter or jaguar.

By land, in a 4x4, the most practical option is to leave the RN4 on the south side of Puerto Suárez (⊕ *18°59'01.7"S 57°48'26.4"W*). From here, you follow a raised dirt road southsouthwest past the Mutún mine, sort any necessary permissions at the National Park checkpoint, then continue southeast towards **Puerto Busch** on the River Paraguay (⊕ *20°04'24.5"S 58°02'20.7"W*). Covering around 140km (4h plus stops) from Puerto Suárez, this is arguably Bolivia's answer to Mato Grosso's Transpantaneira – only without any infrastructure and with numerous mining lorries. If you reach Puerto Busch there may be possibilities to rough camp or hire boats – or you can just make a day trip and return to Puerto Suárez.

There should be wildlife to see throughout, although the 'species lists' are much less refined than in Brazil. Greater capybara, yacaré caiman and waterbirds frequent the *bañados* (wetlands), but yellow anaconda is now only rarely seen. Black-and-gold howler, marsh deer (common), toco toucan, red-and-green macaw (but not hyacinth) and Paraguay caiman lizard could be on the cards, plus ocelot at night. Azara's night monkey inhabits riparian forest. In grassland, look for greater rhea and giant anteater. Giant otter and maned wolf are plausible, but jaguar is hunted so is rarely seen: a river trip provides the best odds.

You are likely to have the smoothest experience by joining an organised wildlife-watching tour, but even this can be tricky to organise. Of four well-established operators based in Santa Cruz province, only one currently offers Pantanal trips: Amboro Tours (☏ *+591 7261 2515; e at.infotours@gmail.com; w amborotours. com. US$700 for 3 days/2 nights, based on 2 sharing (or US$470 for 3 people), inc camping, FB, transport, local guide & 2h boat trip)*. For completeness, and in case they again offer Pantanal tours should visiting become easier, the other three Santa Cruz operators are: Nick's Adventures Bolivia (☏ +591 784 58046, +595 773 13331; e *nicksadventuresbolivia@gmail.com; w nicksadventuresbolivia.com*); Ruta Verde Tours (☏ *+591 708 49871; e info@rutaverdebolivia.com; w rutaverdebolivia.com*); and Michael Blendinger Nature Tours (☏*+591 3944 6227, +591 7215 1115; e info@ discoveringbolivia.com; w discoveringbolivia.com*).

TOP TIPS

Canoeing can help you quietly approach wildlife on slow-moving rivers. (AL)

FINDING WILDLIFE

In many ways, finding wildlife is a cinch in the Pantanal. In season, roadside ponds teem with caiman and waterbirds, while spotting mammals is easier than anywhere bar African savannahs. Even a wildlife novice can readily enjoy spectacular sights. But there is more to Pantanal wildlife than immediately catches the untrained eye. The region's mosaic of habitats rewards visitors willing to rise earlier, look harder and stay out later. Whether you have a guide or travel independently, here are some thoughts on how to make the most of your trip. These include pointers on lodge facilities and managing your time, strategies for particular habitats and insights into identifying mammals without seeing them.

Mobile observation towers can be positioned to offer visitors great views of wildlife, here nesting jabiru. (JL)

LODGE FACILITIES

Lodges usually offer a variety of means to see wildlife. Walking along trails is an intimate way in which to appreciate nature. Cycling helps you cover considerable ground. Horse-riding enables you to enter otherwise inaccessible wetlands, but watching or photographing an animal can be tricky. Vehicular safaris help you approach animals. Boat trips are essential for good views of riparian wildlife (and canoeing can be an enchantingly tranquil experience). Observation towers are an

Pantanal lodges offer guides who may be trained biologists or local *pantaneiro* residents. (*Above*, AB/FBA; *left*, JL)

ideal place to gain height or see what wanders past. Most lodges offer guides for these activities. If you are keen to see a particular species, ask. Guides usually know the best trees for primates, a tamandua's foraging beat or a helmeted manakin's song perch. Some guides are trained biologists; others are *pantaneiros*. Both have their advantages. Biologists may speak different languages, carry voice-playback equipment to attract birds (which is used judiciously to avoid disturbing them), and offer background about what you see. Locals tend to know the area thoroughly and are often extremely sharp eyed.

YOUR PANTANAL DAY (AND NIGHT)

A typical Pantanal day capitalises on periods of greatest wildlife activity but allows you to recharge your batteries when things are quietest. Rising before dawn enables you to look for nocturnal mammals, such as anteaters, before they return to their dens. A cacophony of black-and-gold howlers and chaco chachalacas announces the lightening of the skies. Bird activity is greatest in the two hours following daybreak, but continues longer along the cooler river. As the air warms, reptiles emerge – but even they retreat to the shade during the heat of the day. As should you, taking a recuperative siesta.

When the sun abates, it's time to return to the fray. The last hour of daylight is good for large mammals, especially cats, deer and lowland tapir. At dusk, waterbirds, snail

Nocturnal safaris, by vehicle or on foot, are an essential part of any Pantanal visit. (AL)

kites and parrots flock to their roosts. As night falls, frogs vocalise, particularly after rain. If it is dry, nightjars hunt in the grasslands and forest edge. Night safaris are exciting: activity is greatest on warm, dark nights. Seeing animals at night is not as hard as you might think. A powerful torch (preferably fitted with a red filter) is essential. Most animals reveal their presence by two coloured pinpricks: this 'eyeshine' is the result of a structure behind the retina reflecting your torchlight. Thermal imagers or night-vision binoculars are useful complements and have no adverse impact on nocturnal creatures.

READING THE HABITAT

Each of the Pantanal's habitats poses particular challenges to the wildlife-watcher. A few simple strategies, helping you to look in the right places and at the right times, can enrich the experience and maximise the rewards.

Around the lodge

There's no reason to stop watching wildlife merely because you are lounging in a hammock. Lodge buildings and gardens hum with wildlife. By day, keep an eye on flowering plants for hummingbirds and orioles. Bird tables attract reams of yellow-billed cardinals, cowbirds and even greater capybara. Bats often roost in outbuildings, while lizards such as giant ameivas bask in sheltered suntraps. At night, crab-eating foxes may visit to feed on kitchen scraps. The post-prandial amble back to your room often reveals moths, bugs or beetles enticed by tungsten lights (and a portable, harmless moth trap can attract scores of 'night butterflies'). Insects attract predators such as cururu toads, tropical house geckos, bats and even giant anteaters. As you retire for the night, check your bathroom for a trio of tree-frogs.

An afternoon siesta is a good idea, but retaining an eye on wildlife (as here at Fazenda Barranco Alto Ecolodge) is worthwhile. (AB/FBA)

Mammals visiting lodge buildings can include giant anteater, crab-eating fox and – as here at Araras Pantanal Ecolodge – greater capybara. (JL)

Boat trips are an integral part of wildlife-watching in wetlands and rivers. (AL)

Wetlands

In lakes and swamps, it is impossible to miss seething masses of egrets, hordes of greater capybara and lines of yacaré caiman. But careful scrutiny should reveal much more. Bridges provide good viewpoints, so approach them quietly to avoid flushing birds. Look underneath for roosting bats or a slumbering yellow anaconda. Then scan the water, paying attention to well-vegetated edges for a skulking sungrebe or browsing marsh deer. If trees fringe the lake, check them for roosting black-crowned night-herons. If things look good, spend a tranquil hour or two, watching and waiting: who knows what might come to drink or bathe? In the meantime, look for dragonflies and damselflies flitting in waterside vegetation, check posts for

Catching fish to throw to giant otters, raptors and kingfishers. (JL)

kingfishers or examine temporary ponds for sleeping amphibians.

Visit the same wetlands at night for a different set of animals. A crab-eating racoon snuffling round the water's edge, boat-billed herons fishing, a lowland tapir grazing or – for the luckiest – a jaguar hunting capybara. Pinpoint individual frogs in the anuran chorus and illuminate them with a torch. Some species call from grass stems, others while semi-submerged in the water; serpents often hunt them. Drive slowly along roads traversing marshes; snakes, toads and crabs use these as thoroughfares – and it is better to see than to squash.

River trips enable you to look for aquatic creatures and denizens of gallery forest. Most are by motorboat. Encourage your driver to take bends slowly to avoid spooking wildlife around the corner. The quieter your boat, the more wildlife you will see and the closer you can approach. Noise-free electric catamarans – in operation at one lodge – are ideal. Canoes are good (and tranquil), although photography is difficult if you're paddling.

Trips along narrow, well-vegetated rivers are the best way to see otters. Gargling and whistling quietly often intrigues giant otters, which approach to investigate. Enjoy close views of kingfishers, caiman and fishing raptors such as black-collared hawk, particularly if you have caught fish to throw their way. Rivers provide natural vantage points for scanning the forest canopy; check flowering trees for black-and-gold howlers and guans. On larger rivers, visit sandbanks for terns, skimmers, pied lapwings and flocks of butterflies such as Marcellina sulphur. Yacarés, iguanas and jaguars bask here (see box below). Finally, stay out late. The closing of the day is best for agami and zigzag herons, as they emerge to feed. Towards dusk, tapirs and large birds such as bare-faced curassows come to drink. At dusk, river skies darken with band-tailed nighthawks and bulldog bats.

JAGUAR-WATCHING

There is no better place to see jaguar than the Mato Grosso Pantanal near Porto Jofre. In this guide's first edition, this box was entitled 'how to find a jaguar'. In the area that some guides nickname 'Jaguarland', *finding* a jaguar – from June to November, at least – is now unlikely to be an issue for anyone spending two days scanning the riverbanks where these immense cats bask. In suitable weather, it is more a matter of *how many* jaguars you see.

From 2005–2024, the Jaguar Identification Project has catalogued an incredible 369 jaguars, each individually identifiable from its markings. Scientists and local guides have developed a family tree for regularly encountered animals, which are named to facilitate tracking. The ease with which

The ecotourism industry follows a code of conduct for jaguar-watching. (KD)

jaguars are now seen is due to their peerless density (which derives from an abundance of prey) and their increasing tolerance of human observers (there were an astonishing 130 habituated jaguars in 2023, up from 29 in 2013).

Motorboat drivers maintain radio contact with one another, so once a jaguar is spotted, the shout goes up, and a score of boats may descend on the feline. Although not everyone's cup of tea, this approach offers great opportunities to see fabulous behaviours that would have been unthinkable to witness last century – from hunting to mating, scent-marking to a mother caring for cubs. But with such rich viewing comes responsibility. Before booking, please ensure that your guide adopts the jaguar-watching code of conduct developed by the local tourism industry, which prohibits disturbance and preserves a respectful distance between animal and admirers.

Away from Porto Jofre, jaguar-watching is a different story. Whether in the scrubby north of the Transpantaneira, on the River Miranda of Mato Grosso do Sul or in the wilds of southeasternmost Bolivia, encounters with this great cat are occasional and unexpected – and arguably all the more deeply appreciated as a result.

Use observation towers (here at Pouso Alegre) to get a panoramic view over savannahs. (RJ)

Savannahs and cerrados

One problem with wildlife-watching in open habitats such as grasslands, palm savannah and scrubby cerrado is that humans are highly visible – and animals perceive us as a potential threat. One solution is to use a vehicle as a mobile hide. When driving, stop and scan regularly, paying particular attention to shady areas where mammals may seek respite from the sun. On foot, use cover to conceal your movements. Another problem is the flatness of the terrain. Take opportunities to gain height, for example by climbing an observation tower. Scan for grazing marsh deer, peccaries, tapir and even the odd stalking cat. Check termite mounds for anteaters, armadillos and burrowing owls.

At ground level, look for reptiles warming up in the sun. Keep your ears open for the raucous calls of parrots as they fly between feeding areas. When approaching mammals, do so slowly and stay downwind. Drop to your knees to look for grasshoppers and dung beetles, or to enjoy termite activity. Visit grasslands by night as well as by day: on a nocturnal safari, you have a good chance of deer, lowland tapir, crab-eating fox, anteaters, ocelot and, in some areas, jaguar. And you should see nightjars sallying for insects.

Although the Pantanal is most famous for its wetlands, its forests (here at Aymara Lodge) offer great wildlife-watching too. (AL)

Forests

Whereas tropical evergreen forests, as in Amazonia, often seem devoid of animals, the Pantanal's semi-deciduous and deciduous forests usually hum with activity. The dawn roar of howlers is complemented by raucous chachalacas, repetitive forest-falcons and strident woodcreepers. Forest birds tend to be vocal, as dense vegetation means that it is easier to attract mates through sound than sight. Prepare by listening to recordings of bird vocalisations. Load cuts onto an mp3 player (or smartphone) and quietly play back the voice of a skulking bird. When it attracts the target into the open, this trick can feel like magic. (But avoid overuse, for the bird's sake.) Whistled imitations of bird

Forest are great at night: tracking down strange sounds might lead you to veined tree-frogs, here in a *Pseudobombax longiflorum* tree. (RJ)

calls also often help (with undulated tinamous, for example) as does squeaking with your lips ('pishing'). Whistling the repetitive notes of a ferruginous pygmy-owl can attract irate passerines.

Listen for movement. Rustling in the leaf litter could mean an agouti or paca. Louder crackling may be a deer or peccary. Scratching in the bushes betrays a tegu lizard. Snuffling in the undergrowth signifies an armadillo. Crashing in the trees could indicate hooded capuchin. A loud tapping usually emanates from a woodpecker; a softer version from a tiny piculet. Soft contact calls may be uttered by a group of South American coatis – and keep an ear open for the high-pitched whistle of the black-tailed marmoset. Sound is also the best way to locate invertebrates such as cicadas and crickets.

As you walk quietly through the forest, stepping over fallen branches and avoiding crunching leaves, look carefully at trees. Some lizards bask on sunny tree trunks. Common vampire bats gather in cavities, tarantulas in fissures. The large, mud ovals attached to the trunks of large trees are termite nests. Trogons perch serenely on horizontal branches. A flash of colour is often a butterfly such as a morpho flitting through the mid-storey. Check for frogs in any microhabitat with water, from a flooded tree cavity to a rain-filled depression. Snakes often sleep beneath logs and planks, so keen 'herpers' might wish to turn these over, albeit with care (and gloves!). After rain, rooting in the soil could even reveal a caecilian emerging from its subterranean lair.

Forests are great at night. Night-torching is best on foot, using a headtorch and powerful hand lamp. Use the headtorch to pick up eyeshine along the trail and watch the ground (you don't want to tread on a snake). Swing the lamp in a regular pattern; ahead of you along the trail (for terrestrial mammals, snakes, spiders and elephant beetles), into low shrubbery (for opossums, arboreal snakes and frogs), then up to the middle and upper strata (for night monkeys, owls and potoos).

MAMMAL TRACKS AND SIGNS

Whatever habitat you are in, looking down at your feet is also important. On sandy or muddy terrain, mammal hoof- and paw-prints are telltale signs of these animals' presence. If a set of prints is fresh, the individual that made them may still be around, so quietly following the trail sometimes produces dividends.

The size and shape of the impression enables you to distinguish between various groups of mammal, although beware that tracks of a species (even

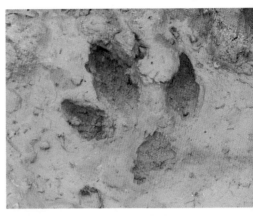

Lowland tapir tracks: a signal to look out for this impressively large mammal. (UB/SS)

an individual) vary with gait, slope and substrate. The cloven hooves of deer and peccaries leave pairs of oval tracks; in deer, these narrow towards the front. Tapir tracks are a trio of forward-pointing toes. Capybaras are similar, but toes are often joined by webbing – as they are on otters. The rear paws of anteaters resemble those of broad-footed humans, but the front paws leave an impression of their long claws; a southern tamandua also leaves a swishing mark where it drags its tail on the ground. Armadillos have three to five protruding toes. Coati prints have five toes, each with an obvious circular pad below long, slender claws. Canids such as crab-eating fox have four round toes, each with a short claw mark, leading forward from a broad central pad. Cats are similar, but their retracted claws leave no mark. The larger the cat, the bigger and broader the print.

Become Sherlock Holmes of wildlife by looking for other signs of mammals. Nibbled acuri palm nuts may indicate the presence of Azara's agouti. Droppings are distinctive. The scat of carnivores such as cats and crab-eating fox is long and slender. Deer and peccaries deposit piles of oval pellets. Tapir dung looks horse-like; that of giant anteaters is littered with termite casings. Diggings are another useful clue. A wrecked termite mound suggests the work of an armadillo; a mound with precise

Mammals betray their presence with faeces; this substantial pile 'belongs' to a lowland tapir. (JL)

incisions betrays an anteater. Mammal lairs are often obvious. A cleared area on a riverbank indicates you have found a giant otter holt. A strong odour suggests proximity to a fox den. A large hole may be an armadillo pad. A muddy wallow may be due to peccaries or tapir. And crushed grass maps out the body form of a deer.

PRACTICALITIES

A modicum of preparation will make your Pantanal trip easier and more enjoyable. This section offers advice on when to travel, what gear to pack and what health issues to bear in mind.

4x4 vehicles, here at Pousada Aguapé, help visitors explore the Pantanal. (LFM/PA)

WHEN TO TRAVEL

Cyclical water levels mean that wildlife-watching varies with the season. Tourism peaks during the dry period (typically July–October): wildlife throngs around scarce water resources, land-based transport is usually straightforward and temperatures relatively pleasant. During the rains (November–March), dry land becomes precious, so mammals congregate on raised areas, while visitors explore by canoe or horse. However, days become very hot and mosquitoes abound. Should price or the prospect of crowding deter you, visiting during the shoulder seasons (April–June, November–December) is an option. Although travel may be harder, your wildlife experience can be nearly as good, while tourists are fewer and prices slightly lower. Ultimately, as one experienced Pantanal guide says, "the best time to come here is whenever is convenient for you".

WHAT TO BRING

Wear lightweight clothing: cotton is good, as are new, breathable and fast-drying materials. Long-sleeved shirts and long trousers reduce the area of skin available to mosquitoes and other biting insects. Pale browns and greens are best, as they reduce your visibility to animals and enable you to spot biting insects quickly. Use insect repellent, be it DEET or citronella. Light hiking boots are adequate footwear, and walking sandals fine for boat trips and lodge buildings. Sunscreen, sunglasses and a wide brimmed hat ward off solar excesses. Bring swimwear if you envisage relaxing in lodge pools. A waterproof coat or poncho is an essential precaution (even if, hopefully, it remains unused), and both a windbreaker and jumper useful on cold winter nights.

Binoculars greatly enhance your appreciation of what you see and are essential for enjoying small birds. An mp3 player or smartphone loaded with bird recordings is useful for voice playback or to check what you heard in the dawn chorus (and sound-ID apps such as Merlin can even do the hard work for you). A decent camera (page 172) should be within most visitors' budget. For night safaris, bring a powerful headtorch, ideally fitted with a red filter to avoid disturbing animals. A thermal imager or night-vision binoculars are unintrusive. And pack any medication you need; it's a long way to the nearest pharmacy.

Cruising on quiet Pantanal waterways: the easiest and most pleasant way to photograph wildlife? (AL)

HEALTH AND SAFETY

Health problems in the Pantanal change frequently over time, so consult medical professionals for the current situation: for example, the UK Government bases its advice on that of w travelhealthpro.org.uk. Particularly outside the dry season, mosquitoes can be an irritant and potentially transmit diseases: long clothing and insect repellent reduce the chance of being bitten. The risk of malaria is currently very low in Brazil and Paraguay, and low in Bolivia. There is perhaps a small risk of dengue fever, yellow fever, chikungunya and zika in some areas. A yellow fever vaccination is advisable: inoculations need ten days to take effect and immigration authorities may ask to see your vaccination certificate. In the UK, a dengue vaccine is advised for people previously exposed.

Chigger mites are an irritation, causing itchy red skin that can blister; they congregate where clothes fit snugly against the skin, but can be deterred by applying sulphur powder in the morning and having a soapy shower at night. One species of parasitic botfly (*ura* in Spanish, *berne* in Portuguese) targets humans, the larva burrowing through the skin and producing a painful pink bump. Other diseases include Chaga's (transmitted by assassin bugs) and leishmaniasis (from sandflies). Checking yourself for ticks each day is worthwhile. Scorpion stings are rare. The Pantanal is a remote area with no medical facilities; the nearest hospital will be several hours away, at best.

Check your body each day for ticks. (LM/SS)

Safety issues vary across the three Pantanal countries and in time, so read the up-to-date travel advice provided by your government (such as the UK Foreign, Commonwealth and Development Office). In general, levels of crime and violence are high in Brazil, particularly in major cities –

but most tourist visits are trouble-free. Few problems are reported in Paraguay or Bolivia. Low population densities mean that, as a rule, there is very little crime in the Pantanal.

Sometimes Pantanal animals can come too close to be photographed... (UB/SS)

WILDLIFE PHOTOGRAPHY

With abundant wildlife at such proximity, the Pantanal is one of the world's top five nature-photography destinations. But the type of camera you bring, and the ways in which you use it, are key considerations should you wish to produce a visual record of your trip that is as vivid and vibrant as the experience itself.

The digital revolution has given birth to decent 'bridge' cameras with an inbuilt zoom lens that offers magnification up to 20x, which is similar to or greater than a telephoto lens. Select the 'action' setting (often depicted by a running person), and you should achieve some reasonable images from a comparatively compact, light and often inexpensive device.

For properly impressive results, however, it pays to invest in a DSLR or mirrorless camera and a long lens that enables you to 'get close' to an animal without disturbing it. Modern zoom lenses can be as sharp as 'prime' lenses (with a fixed vocal length) and offer compositional flexibility: on a full-frame camera body, a 200–400mm lens is probably ideal, perhaps complemented by a teleconverter when the subject is somewhat distant.

Whilst longer lenses (500–600mm) are a must for serious wildlife photography, they tend to be hefty. The heavier a lens, the harder it is to hold it still, so the greater the prospect of camera shake ruining an otherwise great shot. To get round this, consider several options. You could choose a lens with inbuilt image stabilisation, which particularly aids shooting in low light. If in a stationary vehicle, use the window frame as a support, buffered by a beanbag or homemade equivalent (even a bag of porridge oats or bunched-up clothing will do). When walking or on a boat, consider using a monopod. Ideally, also have a back-up camera body ready-mounted with a macro lens (useful for invertebrates) or a wide-angle lens for capturing scenery.

Equipment, of course, only gets you so far. Technique does the rest. Wait patiently for the animal to get used to your presence. Shoot a moving animal on a fast shutter speed to freeze the action. For a close creature, increase the depth of field to get all of its body parts in focus. Resist the temptation to shoot a terrestrial animal at close range while you are standing up; instead, get down low (if your knees allow it) for a more intimate portrait.

Finally, if photography is integral to your visit and you would benefit from having guidance on tap, you might consider joining a dedicated photographic tour, such as those offered by Pantanal Photo Tours (see advert, page 183).

FURTHER INFORMATION

There is much literature about the Pantanal in Portuguese, and a bit in Spanish. English-language information is harder to come by; Brazil travel guides contain only short sections on the Pantanal and no book (other than this one) covers the entire Pantanal across the three countries it spans. If visiting the Paraguayan Pantanal, Bradt's *Paraguay* guide is a must. Several of the following useful wildlife-related titles are sadly out of print, but may be found through online retailers.

NATURAL HISTORY
GENERAL
Field Guide to the Wildlife of the Pantanal: Illustrated Checklist with Geography. Riccardo Boschetti. Privately published (2023). Compact and wide ranging.

MAMMALS
A Field Guide to the Larger Mammals of South America. Richard Webb and Jeff Blincow. Princeton University Press, (2024). The best field guide around to the continent's mammals. (See advert, page 181.)
Jaguars of the Northern Pantanal. Paul Brooke and Paul Donahue. Academic Press (2020). Pricy but lovely celebration of the big cat.
Mamíferos: Não Voadores do Pantanal e Etorno. Wellington Hannibal *et al.* Natureza em Foco (2015). Succinct field guide to Pantanal mammals.
Mamíferos do Brasil. Nelio Roberto do Reis *et al.* (editors). Privately published (2011). Monograph of Brazilian mammals.
Mammals of the Neotropics, 3: The Central Neotropics. John Eisenberg and Kent Redford. University of Chicago Press (1999). Hefty academic tome.
Mammals of the Pantanal/Mamíferos do Pantanal. Fiona Reid. Privately published (2007). Chart with illustrations of 30 common large mammals.

BIRDS
A Photographic Guide to Birds of Southern Brazil including the Pantanal and Atlantic Forest. Clive Byers. New Holland (2008). Photographs and brief identification text for 300 common birds, including many Pantanal species.
Birds of Brazil: the Pantanal & Cerrado of Central Brazil. John A. Gwynne *et al.* Wildlife Conservation Society (2010). By far the best bird guide to the region.

REPTILES AND AMPHIBIANS
Serpentes do Pantanal. Otavio Marques, André Eterovic, Christine Strüssmann and André Sazima. Holos Editora (2005). Useful identification guide to snakes.
Field Guide to the Anurans of the Pantanal and Surrounding Cerrados. Masao Uetananbaro, Cynthia de Almeida Prado, Domingos de Jesus Rordigues and Zilca Campos. Editora UFMS (2008). Bilingual field guide to Pantanal frogs.

FLORA

Flora and Vegetation of the Pantanal Wetland. Gerardo Alves Damasceno-Junior and Arnildo Pott (editors). Springer (2020). Expensive but detailed.
Plantas Aquáticas do Pantanal Anildo Pott and Vali Pott. Embrapa (2001). Photographic field guide to 250 species of aquatic plant.

BACKGROUND READING

Pantanal: South America's Wetland Jewel. Theo Allofs. New Holland (2008). Sumptuous photographs and essays. One for the coffee table.
The Pantanal. Wolfgang Junk (editor). Pensoft Publishers (2011). Expensive but immense academic assessment of the region's ecology.
The Pantanal of Brazil, Bolivia and Paraguay. Frederick Swarts (ed.). Paragon House (2000). Inexpensive collection of essays derived from a conference on Pantanal ecology and conservation – although inevitably somewhat dated.

WEBSITES

w **faunaparaguay.com** An excellent community website covering much of Paraguay's wildlife, including many Pantanal species.
w **sbherpetologia.org.br** Website of the Brazilian Herpetological Society, including lists of the country's amphibians and reptiles.
w **wikiaves.com** Online, user-generated encyclopaedia of Brazilian birds.

GLOSSARY OF PORTUGUESE TERMS

baia	Permanent lake (also known as *corixo*)
caapõe	Small area of raised land that remains dry while lower-lying areas are flooded
camalote	Floating islands of vegetation, often very large
campo alagado	Wet savannah or seasonally flooded grassland
campo limpo	Open grassland without shrubs or trees (literally, 'clean field')
campo sujo	Grassland with occasional shrubs and trees (literally, 'dirty field')
cerradão	As *cerrado* (see below) but with denser, taller woodland
cerrado	Wooded savannah, typically comprising slim, twisted trees, herbaceous vegetation and grasses
cordilheira	Larger equivalent of a *caapõe*
pântano	Swamp
pantaneiro	Human inhabitant of the Pantanal
peão	Pantanal cattlehand or cowboy (*peón* in Bolivia and Paraguay)
planalto	Plateau
salina	Brackish lakes, typical of Nhecolândia, Mato Grosso do Sul, Brazil
vazante	Low-lying area; also used for the period when floodwaters retreat

Page numbers in *italics* refer to illustrations; those in **bold** to main entries.

Acanthochelys macrocephala, see turtle, big-headed Pantanal swamp
Acanthoscurria chacoana, see tarantula, Brazilian salmon-pink
Acestrorhynchus pantaneiro, see characin, pike
Acromyrmex sp. *see* ant, leafcutter
Agamia agami, see heron, agami
Agelaioides badius, see baywing, greyish
agouti
  Azara's 18, 47, *48*, 67, 125, 129–30, 133–4, 142, 157, 168–9
Alectrurus tricolor, see tyrant, cock-tailed
Alouatta caraya, see howler, black-and-gold
amazon,
  orange-winged 68, 129
  turquoise-fronted 68, 68, 129, 149, 151
Amazona
  aestiva, see amazon, turquoise-fronted
  amazonica, see amazon, orange-winged
Amblyramphus holosericeus, see blackbird, scarlet-headed
Ameerega picta, see frog, spot-legged poison
Ameiva ameiva, see ameiva, giant
ameiva, giant 94, 132, 135, 164
Amerotyphlops brongersmiana, see blindsnake, South American striped
Ammodramus humeralis, see sparrow, grassland
amphibians **99–102**
anaconda,
  yellow 2, 15, *95*, 96, 126, 127, 132, 138, 143, 146, 149–51, 155, 157, 160, 165
  green 96, 146
Anarhynchus collaris, see plover, collared
Andropogon, see grasses
anhinga 58
Anhinga anhinga, see anhinga
ani
  greater 70
  smooth-billed 70
Annona 16
Anodorhynchus hyacinthinus, see macaw, hyacinth
anole, Brazilian bush 93
ant **113–4**
  army 79, 113
  fire 114
  leafcutter 113
  red 17
  trap-jaw *113*, 114
antbird
  band-tailed 80, 130, 132, 134–5
  Mato Grosso 79, 80, 127, 129–31, 134–5, 137–8, 149, 150, 155
anteaters **20–2**, 123, 125, 112, 129, 132–3, 153, 163, 167,169
anteater, giant 16, *20*, 20, *21*, **21**, 123, 127, 144–5, 147–52, *152*, 154, 157, 158, 160, 164, 169

Anthracothorax nigricollis, see mango, black-throated
Anthus lutescens, see pipit, yellowish
Antilophia galeata, see manakin, helmeted
antlions 107–8
antshrike
  barred 80
  great 80
antwren
  black-bellied, 79, 80, 127
  large-billed 79, 127, 129, 135, 140
  rusty-backed 79, 136
Anumbius annumbi, see firewood-gatherer
anurans **100–1**
Aotus azarae, see monkey, Azara's night
Ara
  ararauna, see macaw, blue-and-yellow
  chloropterus, see macaw, red-and-green
aracari, chestnut-eared 75, *76*, 129, 131, 134, 137
arachnids **114–17**
Aramides cajanea, see wood-rail, grey-necked
Aramus guarauna, see limpkin
Araras Pantanal EcoLodge 130–1
Aratinga nenday, see parakeet, nanday
Ardea
  cocoi, see heron, cocoi
  alba, see egret, great
armadillos 20, **23–4**, 167–9
  giant *23*, 24, 129, 132, 144, 147, 157
  nine-banded 23, 127, 130, 137, 142, 144, 149–50, *152*, 157
  six-banded *23*, 23, 146, 148, 150
  southern naked-tailed 23, 146–7
  southern three-banded 24, 158
Arremon flavirostris, see sparrow, saffron-billed
Artibeus lituratus, see bat, great fruit-eating
Arundinicola leucocephala, see marsh tyrant, white-headed
Ascia monuste, see butterfly, great southern white
Astronium fraxinifolium 18
Athene cunicularia, see owl, burrowing
Atta sp, see ant, leafcutter
Aymara Lodge 128–9, *128–9*, *164*, 188

Bahía Negra 154, 156–8
Baiazinha Lodge 131
bananaquit 85
Barão de Melgaço 142
Barco Hotel Jaguar do Pantanal/Barco Jacaré 140–1
Barra Mansa Pantanal Lodge 152
Basileuterus flaveolus, see warbler, flavescent
bats **43–5**
  black myotis 45
  common vampire 43, *43*, 132, 138, 146, 168
  great fruit-eating 45
  greater bulldog 44
  greater round-eared 44

greater spear-nosed 44
  leaf-nosed 44–5
  lesser bulldog 44, 130, 148
  lesser dog-like 149
  Pallas's long-tongued 45, 146, 149
  proboscis 43, *44*, 131, 134, 142, 168
  Seba's short-tailed 45, 32, 138
  velvety mastiff 45, 132, 138
  white-lined broad-nosed 45, 135, 138, 149
baywing, greyish 88
beardless-tyrannulet, southern 81
bees **114**
beetle
  dung 108, 167
  rainbow scarab 108, *108*
  scarab 108
birds **51–88**
  ground **52–3**
  threatened 82
  trading 4, 68
blackbirds **88**
  scarlet-headed 88
Blastocerus dichotomus, see deer, marsh
blindsnake, South American striped 94
Boa constrictor, see boa, Brazilian redtail
boa, Brazilian redtail *96*, 97, 146
  rainbow 97
Bolivia 154, **158–60**
Bothrops
  mattogrossensis, see lancehead, Mato Grosso
  moojeni, see lancehead, Brazilian
brocket
  common brown (grey), 16 42, *42*, 125,132, 155, 157–8
  common red 42, 127, 138, 140
bromeliad 18
Brotogeris chiriri, see parakeet, yellow-chevroned
Bubo virginianus, see owl, great horned
Bubulcus ibis, see egret, cattle
bugs **109**
bulrush 15
burhead 15
Busarellus nigricollis, see hawk, black-collared
  albonotatus, see hawk, zone-tailed
Buteogallus
  meridionalis, see hawk, savanna
  urubitinga, see hawk, great black-
Butorides striata, see heron, striated
butterflies *105*, **110–12**
  banded orange heliconian 111
  Marcellina sulphur 111, *111*, 140, 146, 166
  eyemarks 112
  great southern white 111
  grey cracker *110*
  gulf fritillary 111
  Julia heliconian *111*
  morpho 111, 168
  owl-butterfly 2, 111
  swallowtails 111, *111*
buzzard-eagle, black-chested 62

cacholote, rufous 78, *155*
Cacicus
  cela, see cacique, yellow-rumped

chrysopterus, see cacique, golden-winged
  solitarius, see cacique, solitary black
cacique
  golden-winged 88
  solitary black 88
  yellow-rumped 88
caecilian, Boettger's 102, 168
caiman, yacaré 2, 3, 4, *89*, **91–2**, *91–2*, *95*, *121*, 124, *126*, 126–7, *141*, 144, 146, 149, 153, 155, 158–60, 165, 166
Caiman yacare, see caiman
Cairina moschata, see duck, muscovy
Calidris fuscicollis, see sandpiper, white-rumped
Callichthys callichthys, see cascarudo
Calliphlox amethystine, see woodstar, amethyst
Campephilus
  leucopogon, see woodpecker, cream-backed
  melanoleucus, see woodpecker, crimson-crested
Camptostoma obsoletum, see beardless tyrannulet, southern
Campylorhamphus trochilirostris, see scythebill, red-billed
Campylorhynchus turdinus, see wren, thrush-like
capuchin
  hooded (Azara's) 18, 24, *26*, 26, 126, 130–2, 134–6, *136*, 140, 142, 145, 149–50, 168
capybara, greater 2, 3, 15, 46–7, 47, 81, 124, 129–30, 136–7, 139, 142, 144, 146, 150–1, 153, 155, 159–60, *164*, 164–5, 169
caracara
  southern crested *64*, 64
  yellow-headed 64
cardinal
  red-crested 86
  yellow-billed 86, *86*, 164
Cariama cristata, see seriema, red-legged
Carmelo Peralta 158
carnivores **27–38**
Carollia perspicillata, see bat, Seba's short-tailed
Caryocar brasiliense, see trees, pequi
cascarudo 104
catfish
  callichthyid armoured 104
  long-whiskered 104
  spiny dwarf 104
Cathartes
  aura, see vulture, turkey
  burrovianus, see vulture, lesser yellow-headed
cats **29–33**
  Pantanal 32, 135, 149
cattle 10–11
Cavia aperea, see guinea pig, Brazilian
Celeus
  flavus, see woodpecker, cream-coloured
  lugubris, see woodpecker, pale-crested
centipedes 117
Cercomacra melanaria, see antbird, Mato Grosso
Cercosaura schreibersii, see lizard, Schreiber's spectacled

Cerdocyon thous, see fox, crab-eating
cerrado **16–17**
Ceratopteris pterioides, see fern, aquatic
chachalaca, Chaco 65, 65, 125, 131, 163, 167
characin, pike 104
Chauna torquata, see screamer, southern
Chelonodis carbonaria, see tortoise, red-footed
Chironectes minimus, see opossum, water
*Chloroceryle
aenea, see* kingfisher, American pygmy
amazona, see kingfisher, Amazon
americana, see kingfisher, green
inda, see kingfisher, green-and-rufous
Chlorostilbon aureoventris, see emerald, glittering-bellied
Chordeiles nacunda, see nighthawk, nacunda
Chrysocyon brachyurus, see wolf, maned
chytrid fungus 101
cicada 109, 168
Ciconia maguari, see stork, maguari
Circus buffoni, see harrier, long-winged
climate and seasonality 9
coati, South American 37–8, 38, 118, 130–4, 148, 158 169
cobra, false water 98, 98, 138, 146, 157
Coccycua minuta, see cuckoo, little
Cochlearius cochlearius, see heron, boat-billed
Coendou longicaudatus, see porcupine, Amazonian long-tailed
Coereba flaveola, see bananaquit
Colaptes campestris, see flicker, campo
Colaptes melanochloros, see woodpecker, green-barred
colubrids **98–9**
*Columbina
picui, see* ground dove, picui
squammata, see dove, scaled
talpacoti, see ground dove, ruddy
Comatogaster, see ants, red
Conepatus semistriatus, see skunk, striated hog-nosed
conservation **13**
*Copeoglossum
nigropunctatum, see* skink, black-spotted
Copernicia alba, see wax-palms
coralsnake, Argentinian 98
cormorant, Neotropic 58
Corygyps atrata, see vulture, black
cowbird
giant 88
screaming 88
shiny 88, 88
crab, red freshwater 118
crake, grey-breasted 59, 127
Crax fasciolata, see curassow, bare-faced
cribo, yellowtail 99, 138
crickets **107–8**, 168

Crotalus durissus, see rattlesnake, Neotropical
*Crotophaga
ani, see* ani, smooth-billed
major, see ani, greater
crustaceans 118
Crypturellus undulatus, see tinamou, undulated
cuckoo
guira 69, 70
little 70, 142
pheasant 70
squirrel 70
striped 70
Cuiabá 120–3
Cuniculus paca, see paca, lowland
curassow, bare-faced 18, 65, 66, 126–7, 129–32, 134, 136, 137, 140, 142, 146, 150, 156, 166
Curatella americana, see trees, sandpaper
*Cyanocorax
chrysops, see* jay, plush-crested
cyanomelas, see jay, purplish
Cyclarhis gujanensis, see peppershrike, rufous-browed
Cyperus giganteus 16

Dasyprocta azarae, see agouti, Azara's
Dasypus novemcinctus, see armadillo, nine-banded
deer **41–2**, 163, 165, 167–9
marsh 15, 41, 42, 125, 129–30, 132–3, 135, 136, 138, 142, 144, 148–9, 155, 157, 159–60, 165, 167
pampas 16, 42, 144, 146, 149–50, 151, 153
Desmodus rotundus, see bat, common vampire
Diastatops pullata 106, 107
Didelphis albiventris, see opossum, Brazilian white-eared
Dilocarcinus pagei, see crab, freshwater
Dione vanillae, see butterflies, gulf fritillary
Diospyros sp, *see* persimmon
Dicotyles tajacu, see collared peccary
dogs **27–8**
bush 28, 132, 132
donacobius, black-capped 84, 84, 142
dorado, golden 103, 103, 104
dove
eared 69
grey-fronted 69
scaled 69, 69
white-tipped 69
Dracaena paraguayensis, see lizard, Paraguay caiman
Dromococcyx phasianellus, see cuckoo, pheasant
Dryadula phaetusa, see butterflies, banded orange heliconian
Drymarchon corais, see cribo, yellowtail
Dryocopus lineatus, see woodpecker, lineated
duck, muscovy 58–9

Echinodorus paniculatus, see burhead
Eciton burchelli, see ant, army
egret 124, 127, 138, 144, 146, 156, 158, 160, 165

cattle 54, 124
great 54, 124
snowy 54, 124
*Egretta
caerula, see* heron, little blue
thula, see egret, snowy
Eira barbara, see tayra
Elachistocleis bicolor, see frog, twin-coloured oval
Elanoides forficatus, see kite, swallow-tailed
Elanus leucurus, see kite, white-tailed
emerald, glittering-bellied 73, 73
environment **5–18**
Epicrates cenchria, see boa, rainbow
Estación Los Tres Gigantes 156–7
Estrada Parque 144, 153
Eucometis penicillata, see tanager, grey-headed
Eumorpha fasciata, see moth, banded sphinx
*Eunectes
murinus, see* anaconda, green
notaeus, see anaconda, yellow
Eupemphix nattereri, see frog, Cuyaba dwarf
Eupetomena macroura, see hummingbird, swallow-tailed
euphonia, purple-throated 87
Euphonia chlorotica, see euphonia, purple-throated
Euphracteus sexcinctus, see armadillo, six-banded
Eurypyga helias, see sunbittern
Euroryzomys nitidus, see oryzomys, elegant

Falco rufigularis, see falcon, bat
Falco sparverius, see kestrel, American
falcon
bat 64
laughing 64, 98, 136
Fazenda Barranco Alto Ecolodge 144–6, 145–6, 148, 164
Fazenda San Francisco 148–9
Ficus sp., *see* trees, fig
firewood-gatherer 78
flicker, campo 77
flies **109**
Fluvicola albiventer, see water-tyrant, black-backed
flycatcher
bran-coloured 81
cliff 80
fork-tailed 80
piratic 81
vermilion 80, 81
yellow-olive 81
forest-falcon
barred 64
collared 64
forests **17–18**
Formicivora rufa, see antwren, rusty-backed
Formicivora melanogaster, see antwren, black-bellied
Forpus xanthopterygius, see parrotlet, cobalt-rumped
fox
crab-eating 27, 27, 28, 120, 132–4, 137, 146, 149–50, 164, 167, 169
pampas (Azara's) 28, 158
frogs **100–1**
Cuyaba dwarf 100, 101
paradoxical shrinking 100

two-coloured oval 101, 132, 137
weeping dwarf 101
yellow-bellied narrow-mouthed whistling grass 100, 101
Fuerte Olimpo 158
*Furnarius
leucopus, see* hornero, pale-legged
rufus, see hornero, rufous

Galbula ruficauda, see jacamar, rufous-tailed
*Galictis
cuja, see* grison, lesser
vittata, see grison, greater
gallinule, purple 59
Gampsonyx swainsonii, see kite, pearl
gecko, tropical house 94, 164
South American dwarf 94
geography and geology 8
Geothlypis aequinoctialis, see yellowthroat, masked
*Geranoaetus
melanoleucus, see* buzzard-eagle, black-chested
albicaudatus, see hawk, white-tailed
Geranopsiza caerulescens, see hawk, crane
Glaucidium brasilianum, see pygmy-owl, ferruginous
Glossophaga soricina, see bat, Pallas's long-tongued
gnatcatcher, masked 84
goldenthroat, white-tailed 73
Gracilinanus agilis, see opossum, gracile
grasshoppers **107–8**
greenlet, ashy-headed 83, 137
grison
lesser 36
greater 36
ground dove
long-tailed 16, 69, 126, 132, 136, 156
picui 69
ruddy 69
guans **65–6**
chestnut-bellied 3, 66, 82, 126–7, 129, 132, 134, 136, 142–4
guinea pig, Brazilian 47,48, 140
Guira guira, see cuckoo, guira

habitats **14–18**
Hamadryas februa, see butterflies, grey cracker
harrier, long-winged 62, 142
hawk
black-collared 63, 63, 124, 148, 166
crane 62,
great black 63, 63
roadside 63, 124
white-tailed 63
zone-tailed 63
health and safety **161**
*Helicops
leopardinus, see* keelback, leopard
Heliornis fulica, see sungrebe
Hemeroplanes triptolemus 112, 112
Hemidactylus mabouia, see gecko, tropical house
Hemitriccus striaticollis, see tody-tyrant, stripe-necked
Hercalides sp. *see* butterflies, swallowtails

hermit, cinnamon-throated 73, 127, 129, 140
herons 54, 132, 135, 138, 155
agami 54, 55, 134–5, 143, 155, 166
boat-billed 54, 54, 127, 129, 133, 138, 165, 169
capped 54, 54, 125, 129–30, 146, 150
cocoi 54, 124
little blue 54
striated 54, 124
whistling 54, 95
zigzag 54, 129, 134–5, 143–4, 155, 166
Herpetotheres cachinnans, see falcon, laughing
Herpailurus yaguarondi, see jaguarundi
Herpsilochmus longirostris, see antwren, large-billed
Heteropoda venatoria, see spider, pantropical huntsman
Himantopus mexicanus, see stilt, black-necked
Hirundinea ferruginea, see flycatcher, cliff
Holochilus sciureus, see marsh rat, Amazonian
Hoploxypterus cayanus, see lapwing, pied
hornero
pale-legged 78, 155
rufous 78
Hotel Fazenda Baía das Pedras 146–8
Hotel Porto Jofre Pantanal Norte 139
Hotel Santa Rosa Pantanal 140
hoverflies 19
howler, black-and-gold 18, 24, 25, 125, 129–132, 136, 142–3, 145, 148, 150, 152, 157, 159–60, 163, 166, 167
human impact 4, 10–12, 35, 68, 82, 92, 101
hummingbirds *72–3*
gilded 73, 73
swallow-tailed 73
hunting 92
hyacinth, common water 14–5, 92, 130, 135, 156, 157
Hydrochaeris hydrochaeris, see capybara, greater
Hydrodynastes gigas, see cobra, false water
Hydropsalis torquata, see nightjar, scissor-tailed
Hylocharis chrysura, see hummingbird, gilded
Hylophilus pectoralis, see greenlet, ashy-headed
Hypocnemoides maculicauda, see antbird, band-tailed

ibis 3, 15, 138, 144, 155
buff-necked 56, 124, 139
green 56, 56, 133, 156
plumbeous 56, 158
Icterus croconotus, see troupial, orange-backed
Ictinia plumbea, see kite, plumbeous
Iguana iguana, see iguana, green/common
iguana, green (common) 93, 93, 125, 135, 142, 155, 157, 160, 166
Inga vera, 17
insects **106–14**
invertebrates **105–18**

jabiru 5, 57, *57,* 68, 124, 130, 133, 136, 139–40, 162, 158, 160, *162*
Jabiru mycteria, see jabiru
jacamar, rufous-tailed 6, 6, 73–4, 125, 134, 142
jacana, wattled *15,* 59
jaguar *2–3,* 4, 13–5, *19,* 20, 27, 29, **29–31**, *29, 30,* 127, 129–31, 133, 136–145, 148, 150–4, 157, 159–60, 165–7
Jaguar Ecological Reserve 137–8
jaguarundi 33
jay
plush-crested 83
purplish *83,* 83, 134–7, 146

keelback, leopard 99, 131
kestrel, American 64
kingbird, white-throated 81
kingfishers **74–5,** 124, 134–5, 138, 149, 165
Amazon 75, 124
American pygmy 74, 156
green 75, 124
green-and-rufous 75, 129
ringed 74, *74, 124*
kiskadee, great 80, *80*
kites
pearl 62
plumbeous 62, 124
snail *62,* 118, 124, 158, 163
swallow-tailed 62
white-tailed 62

Laguna Cáceres 160
lancehead
Brazilian 97, *97*
Mato Grosso 6, 97, 132, 138
lapwing
pied 61, *61,* 140, 142, 146, 155, 166
southern 61
Laterallus exilis, see crake, grey-breasted
Latrodectus, see spider, widow
Legatus leucophaius, see flycatcher, piratic
Leopardus
braccatus, see cat, Pantanal
pardalis, see ocelot
tigrinus, see oncilla, southern
wiedii, see margay
Lepidocolaptes angustirostris, see woodcreeper, narrow-billed
Lepidosiren paradoxa, see lungfish, South American
Leptophis ahaetulla, see snake, giant parrot
Leptodeira annulata, see snake, banded cat-eyed
Leptotila
rufaxilla, see dove, grey-fronted
verreauxi, see dove, white-tipped
Lethocerus maximus, 109, *109*
limpkin 60, 118, 138
lizards **93–4**
Amazonian lava 93, 137
Paraguay caiman 94, 148, 146, 152, 157, 159–60
Schreiber's spectacled 94
Lontra longicaudis, see otter, Neotropical
lungfish, South American *103*
Lycalopex gymnocerca, see fox, pampas
Lygodactylus wetzeli, see gecko, South American dwarf

mabuya, Dunn's 94
macaws 142
blue-and-yellow 67, 67, 127, 144, 146, 149
hyacinth 4, *13,* 18, *51,* **66–7,** 76, 127, 129–34, 138–40, 142–4, 146, 148–53, 155
red-and-green 67, 160
yellow-collared 67, 125, 129, 138
Machetornis rixosa, see tyrant, cattle
Macrobrachium amazonicum, see prawn, Amazon river
manakin
band-tailed 82, 129,
helmeted 18, *82,* 82, 127, 129–30, 134–5, 137, 156, 163
Manciola guaporicola, see mabuya, Dunn's
mango, black-throated 72, *73*
mantids **107–8**
mantis, praying 107, *107*
margay 32
marmoset
black-tailed 6, 18, *24,* 24, 26, 123, 126–7, 129–32, 136, 138, 144, 157, 168
marsh rat, Amazonian 49
marsh tyrant, white-headed 81
marsupials **49–50**
Mato Grosso do Sul, Brazil **143–53**, *143*
Mato Grosso, Brazil *120,* **122–43**
Mazama
americana, see brocket, common red
gouazoubira, see brocket, common brown
Megaceryle torquata, see kingfisher, ringed
Megascops choliba, see screech-owl, tropical
Melanerpes
cactorum, see woodpecker, white-fronted
candidus, see woodpecker, white
Mesembrinibis cayennensis, see ibis, green
Mesomesia sp, *see* butterflies, eyemarks
Metachirus nudicaudatus, see opossum, brown four-eyed
Mico melanurus, see marmoset black-tailed
Micrastur
ruficollis, see forest-falcon, barred
semitorquatus, see forest-falcon, collared
Microbleptarus maximiliani, see microteiid, Maximilian's blue-tailed
microteiid, Maximilian's blue-tailed 94
Micrurus pyrrhocryptus, see coral snake, Argentinian
millipedes 117, *117*
Milvago chimachima, see caracara, yellow-headed
Mimus
saturninus, see mockingbird, chalk-browed
triurus, see mockingbird, white-banded
mites 117
mockingbird
chalk-browed 85, *85*
white-banded 85
Molossus molossus, see bat, Pallas's mastiff

Molothrus
bonariensis, see cowbird, shiny
oryzivorus, see cowbird, giant
rufoaxillarius, see cowbird, screaming
Momotus momota, see motmot, Amazonian
Monasa nigrifrons, see nunbird, black-fronted
monkey, Azara's night 6, 18, 25, 25, 26, 127, 142–3, 155, 157, 159–60, 168
monjita
grey 81
white 81
Morpho sp. *see* butterflies, morphos
mosquitoes 109
moth
banded sphinx 112
tiger 112
motmot, Amazonian 73, *73,* 74
Mycteria americana, see stork, wood
Myiophobus fasciatus, see flycatcher, bran-coloured
Myiopsitta monachus, see parakeet, monk
Myotis nigricans, see bat, black myotis
Myrmecophaga tridactyla, see anteater, giant
myths 12

Nandayus nenday, see parakeet, nanday
Nasua nasua, see coati, South American
near-passerines **69–77**
Neopelma pallescens, see tyrant-manakin, pale-bellied
nighthawks
band-tailed 72, 132, 135, 143, 152, 166
nacunda 72, 127, 135, 152
night-heron, black-crowned 54, 124, 133, 165
nightjars **71–2,** 127, 129, 146, 150, 164, *167*
scissor-tailed 72, 133, 149
Noctilio
albiventris, see bat, lesser bulldog
leporinus, see bat, greater bulldog
Nothura maculosa, see nothura, spotted
nothura, spotted 53
nunbird, black-fronted 76, 76, 125
Nyctibius
grandis, see potoo, great
griseus, see potoo, common
Nycticorax nycticorax, see night-heron, black-crowned
Nyctidromus albicollis, see pauraque, common
Nyctiprogne leucopyga, see nighthawk, band-tailed
Nystalus
chacaru, see puffbird, white-eared
maculates, see puffbird, spot-backed
ocelot 4, 29, 32, *32,* 38, 127, 129, 132–3, 136, 138, 140, 148, 150–1, 154, 160, 167
Odontomachus sp., *see* ant, trap-jaw
Oecomys roberti, see rice rat, Robert's arboreal

oncilla, southern 29, 32
opossums 49, 146, 168
  brown four-eyed 50, 133
  gracile 50
  grey four-eyed 50
  water 50
  Brazilian white-eared 50, 168
Opuntia stenarthra, see trees,
  prickly pear
oropendula, crested 88
Ortalis canicollis, see
  chachalaca, Chaco
oryzomys, elegant 49
osprey 62
otters 14, **34–6**, 129, 142,
  150–2, 155, 166, 169
  giant 20, 27, 34–5, *34, 35,*
  131–2, 134–5, 138, 143, 145,
  149, 152–3, 157–60, *158,*
  166, 169
  Neotropical 36, *36,* 134–5,
  138–9, 145
ovenbirds 78
owls 132, 168
  burrowing *70,* 98, 167
  great horned 71, *71,* 127, 130,
  132, 137–9
Oxyrhopus petolarius, see
  snake, forest flame
Ozotoceros bezoarticus, see
  deer, pampas

paca, lowland 18, 28, 47,
  48, 138, 151, 168
pacu 104
Pandion haliaetus, see osprey
Panorâmico 141
Pantanal Jungle Lodge 153
Pantanal Mato Grosso Hotel
  134–5
Panthera onca, see jaguar
Paraguay **154–7,** *154*
parakeet
  blaze-winged 68, 144,
  149–50, 152
  blue-crowned 68, 132
  monk 67, 67
  nanday 67, 134, *134,* 146,
  149–50, 152
  peach-fronted 67, 133, 150, 156
  white-eyed 68
  yellow-chevroned 68
Paroaria
  capitata, see cardinal, yellow-
  billed
  coronata, see cardinal, red-
  crested
Parque Mãe Bonifácia 123
parrot, scaly-headed 68
parrotlet, blue-winged 69
parula, tropical 87
Passer domesticus, see sparrow,
  house
passerines **78–88**
Passo do Lontra Parque
  Hotel 153
Patagioenas
  cayennensis, see pigeon, pale-
  vented
  picazuro, see pigeon, picazuro
pauraque, common 71, *71*
peccaries 40, 144–5, 150–
  1,167–9
  collared 40, 133, 158
  white-lipped 40, *40,* 41, 148,
  155, 159
Penelope ochrogaster, see guan,
  chestnut-bellied
peppershrike, rufous-browed 83
persimmon 18
Phacellodomus rufifrons, see
  thornbird, rufous-fronted

Phaethornis nattereri, see
  hermit, cinnamon-throated
Phaetusa simplex, see tern,
  large-billed
Phalacrocorax brasilianus, see
  cormorant, Neotropic
Phanaeus, see beetle, rainbow
  scarab
Philander opossum, see
  opossum, grey four-eyed
Phoebis marcellina, see
  butterflies, Marcellina
  sulphur
photography 172
Phyllostomus hastatus, see bat,
  greater spear-nosed
Physalaemus biligonigerus, see
  frog, weeping dwarf
*Piaractus mesopotamicus,
  see* pacu
Piaya cayana, see cuckoo,
  squirrel
Piculus chrysochloros, see
  woodpecker, golden-green
pigeon
  pale-vented 69
  picazuro 69
Pilherodius pileatus, see heron,
  capped
pintado 104
Pionus maximiliani, see parrot,
  scaly-headed
Pipile
  cujubi, see piping-guan,
  red-throated 65, 135
  cumanensis, see piping-guan,
  blue-throated 65, 129, 134–6
pipit, yellowish 85, 138
Pipra fasciicauda, see manakin,
  band-tailed
piranha
  red-bellied 104, *104*
  spotted 104
  red ruby 104
Pitangus sulphuratus, see
  kiskadee, great
Platalea ajaja, see spoonbill,
  roseate
Plecturocebus pallescens, see titi,
  white-coated
plover, collared 61, 142
poaching 23, 31, 35, 92
Poconé 123
Poecilotriccus latirostris, see
  tody-flycatcher, rusty-fronted
Polioptila dumicola, see
  gnatcatcher, masked
Polyborus plancus, see caracara,
  crested
Polychrus acutirostris, see
  anole, Brazilian bush
Polytmus guainumbi, see
  goldenthroat, white-tailed
Pomacea lineata, see snail,
  aquatic apple
Pontederia crassipes, see
  hyacinth, common water
porcupine, Amazonian
  long-tailed 46, *46,* 140,
  142–3, 151
Porphyrio martinica, see
  gallinule, purple
Porto Jofre 122, 139–41
Potamotrygon falkneri, see
  stingray, largespot river
potoos 129, 133–4
  common *72,* 127, 149
  great *72,* 138, 156,
Pousada Aguapé *144,* 149–50,
  170
Pousada Berço Pantaneiro –
  Ninho do Jaguar 139

Pousada do Rio Mutum 143
Pousada Piuval 126–7
Pousada Piquiri 141–2
Pousada Porto da Capivara 142
Pousada Recanto do Jaguar 142
Pousada Rio Claro 133–4
Pousada São João 153
Pousada Xaraés 153
Pouso Alegre 131–3, 136, *167*
Pouteria ramiflora 16
prawn, Amazon river 118
primates **24–6**
Primolius auricollis, see macaw,
  yellow-collared
Priodontes maximus, see
  armadillo, giant
Prochilodus lineatus, see
  prochilod, streaked
Procyon cancrivorus, see
  raccoon, crab-eating
Psarocolius decumanus, see
  oropendula, crested
Pseudalbizzia niopioides, see
  tree, silk
Pseudis paradoxas, see frog,
  paradoxical shrinking
Pseudobombax longiflorum 168
*Pseudoplatystoma
  corruscans, see* sorubim,
  spotted
  fasciatum, see sorubim,
  barred
Pseudoseisura unirufa, see
  cacholote, rufous
Psidium guineense, see guava
Psittacara aurea, see parakeet,
  white-eyed
Pteroglossus castanotis, see
  aracari, chestnut-eared
Pteronura brasiliensis, see otter,
  giant
Puerto Busch 160
Puerto Quijarro 159–160
Puerto Suárez 159
puffbird
  spot-backed 76
  white-eared 76
puma 29, 33, 33, 127, 129, 140,
  145, 148–50, 153–4
Puma concolor, see puma
pygmy-owl, ferruginous
  71, 132, 138, 168
Pygocentrus nattereri, see
  piranha, red-bellied
Pyrocephalus rubinus, see
  flycatcher, vermilion
Pyrrhura devillei, see parakeet,
  blaze-winged

Qualea grandiflora 16

rabbit, forest 49, *49,* 127,
  129–30, 148
raccoon, crab-eating 37, *37,*
  130, 133, 135, 146, 148–9,
  158, 165
Ramphastos toco, see toucan,
  toco
Ramphocelus carbo, see tanager,
  silver-beaked
raptors **62–5**
rat, roof (black) 49
rattlesnake, Neotropical *97,* 97,
  151, 155
Rattus rattus, see rat, roof/black
Refúgio da Ilha 152–3
Refúgio Ecológico
  Caiman 151–2
Reserva Pantanal Paraguayo
  156–7
reptiles **89–99**
Rhea americana, see rhea, greater

rhea, greater 16, 52–3, *52,*
  126–7, 129, *132,* 133–4,
  146, 148–50, 152, 157,
  160
Rhinella diptycha, see toad,
  cururu
Rhynchonycteris naso, see bat,
  proboscis
Rhynchotus rufescens, see
  tinamou, red-winged
rice rat, Robert's arboreal 49
rodents **46–9**
Rostrhamus sociabilis, see kite,
  snail
Rupornis magnirostris, see
  hawk, roadside
Rynchops niger, see skimmer,
  black

Sacoramphus papa, see vulture,
  king
salinas 15, 145–6
Salminus brasiliensis, see golden
  dorado
Salvator merianae, see
  Argentine black-and-white
  tegu
sandpiper
  solitary 61
  white-rumped 61
Sapajus cay, see capuchin,
  hooded
sapphire, gilded 73
savanna **16,** *16*
Sceliphron sp., *see* wasp, mud-
  dauber
*Schoeniophylax phryanophilus,
  see* spinetail, chotoy
Scinax spp. *see* tree-frog
Sciurus aestuans, see squirrel,
  Guianan
scorpions 116–17, *116*
screamer, southern 59, 59,
  125, 127, 138–9, 160
screech-owl, tropical 71
scythebill, red-billed *79,* 79,
  129, 137, 149
seedeater
  double-collared 86, 86
  rusty-collared 86
  white-bellied 86
seriema, red-legged *16,* 16, 53,
  53, 126–7, 129, 133, 146,
  148, 150, 152
Serrasalmus spp., *see* piranha
Siphonops paulensis, see
  caecilian, Boettger's
skimmer
  carmine *107*
  black 61, *61,* 127, 142, 158
skink
  black-spotted 94
skunk
  striated hog-nosed 37
snails 118
  aquatic apple 60, 116, *116*
snakes **95–8**
  banded cat-eyed 99, 150
  Brongersma's worm 94
  Chaco sepia 99
  forest flame 98, *98*
  giant parrot 99, 99, 151
  indigo 99
Solenopsis saevissima, see
  ant, fire
SouthWild Flotel & Jaguar
  Suites 141
Southwild Pantanal Lodge
  135–7
sparrow
  grassland 87
  house 87

rufous-collared 87, *87*
saffron-billed 87, *87*
Speothos venaticus, see dog, bush
spiders **115–16**
  pantropical huntsman 116, *116*
  tangle-web 115
  widow 115
spinetails 78
  chotoy 78
  cinereous-breasted 18, 78, 138, 155
  white-lored 78, 127, 129–31, 138, 150, 155, 157
spoonbill
  roseate 56, *57*
Sporophila
  caerulescens, see seedeater, double-collared
  collaris, see seedeater, rusty-collared
  leucoptera, see seedeater, white-bellied
squirrel, Guianan 46, 132
Stelgidopteryx ruficollis, see swallow, southern rough-winged
Sterculia
  apetala 18, 76
Sternula superciliaris, see tern, yellow-billed
stilt, black-necked 61, 146, 148
stingray, largespot river *102*, 103
storks 14, 57, 124, 138, 144, 155
  maguari 57, 124, 138
  wood 57, 124, 139
sunbittern 60, *60*, 126–7, 129, 133–5, 142–4, 148, 155
sungrebe 60, 129, 131, 134–5, 138, 142–3, 146, 165
sorubim
  spotted 104
  barred 104
swallow
  southern rough-winged 83
  white-rumped 83–4
  white-winged *83*, 84
Sylvilagus brasiliensis, see rabbit, forest
Synallaxis
  albilora, see spinetail, white-lored
  hypospodia, see spinetail, cinereous-breasted
Synoeca sp., *see* wasp, warrior
Syrigma sibilatrix, see heron, whistling

Tabebuia spp. 18
Tachycineta
  albiventer, see swallow, white-winged
  leucorrhoa, see swallow, white-rumped
Tamandua tetradactyla, see tamandua, southern
tamandua, southern 16, **21**, 22, *22*, 127, 136, 145–6, 148–51, *153*, 158, 163, 169
tanager
  grey-headed 85
  palm 85
  sayaca 85
  silver-beaked 85, *85*
Tapera naevia, see cuckoo, striped
tapir, lowland 38, 39, *39*, 83, 127, *127*, 129–33, 135–6, 138, 140, 142–3, 145, 147–52, 155, 158, 163, 165–7, 169, *169*

Tapirus terrestris, see tapir, lowland
Taraba major, see antshrike, great
tarantula, Brazilian salmon pink *115*, 116
Tayassu pecari, see peccary, white-lipped
tayra 33, 36, *37*, 131–3, 148, 158
tegu
  Argentine black-and-white 94, *94*, 125, 133, 146, 155, 157, 168
  gold 94
  Matipu 94
termites *12*, **112–13**, *112*, 127, 167, 168
tern 142, 166
  large-billed 61
  yellow-billed 61
Thalurania furcata, see woodnymph, fork-tailed
Thamnodynastes chaquensis, see snake, Chaco sepia
Thectocercus acuticaudata, see parakeet, blue-crowned
Theristictus
  caerulescens, see ibis, plumbeous
  caudatus, see ibis, buff-necked
thornbird, rufous-fronted 78
Thraupis
  palmarum, see tanager, palm
  sayaca, see tanager, sayaca
thrush
  creamy-bellied 85
  pale-breasted 85
  rufous-bellied 85
Thrythorus
  genibarbis, see wren, moustached
  guarayanus, see wren, fawn-breasted
  leucotis, see wren, buff-breasted
Tigrisoma lineatum, see tiger heron, rufescent 54, 124
tinamou
  red-winged 53
  undulated 18, *53*, 53, 129, 133, 168
titi, white-coated 25, 155, *157*, 157, 159
toad, cururu 101, *101*, 150, 152, 164
Todriostrum cinereum, see tody-flycatcher, common
tody-flycatcher
  common 80
  rusty-fronted 81, 137, 146
tody-tyrant, stripe necked 81
Tolmomyias sulphurescens, see flycatcher, yellow-olive
Tolypeutes matacus, see armadillo, southern three-banded
Tonatia bidens, see bat, greater round-eared
tortoise
  red-footed *90*, 91, 133, 150–1
toucans **75–6**
  toco 75–6, *75*, 131, 137–8, 146, 148–9, 160
tracks and signs 159
Transpantaneira highway *119*, 120–138, *123–5*
tree-frog
  fuscous-blotched snouted 100

lesser snouted *99*, 100
Mato Grosso snouted 100
veined 100, 137, *168*
trees
  fig/strangler fig 17, *18*, 114
  lapacho (ypê) 18, *126*, 127
  manduvi 18, 67, 76, 132
  palm 16–8, 67, 88
  pequi 16
  piúva 7
  sandpaper 16
  silk 18
  wax-palm 16
Tringa
  flavipes, see yellowlegs, lesser
  solitaria, see sandpiper, solitary
Triplaris americana 17
Troglodytes aedon, see wren, house
trogon, blue-crowned 73
Tropidurus spp., *see* lizards, spiny
troupial, orange-backed 18, 88, *88*, 137
Tupinambis
  matipu, see tegu, Matipu
  teguixin, see tegu, gold
Turdus
  amaurochalinus, see thrush, creamy-bellied
  leucomelas, see thrush, pale-breasted
  rufiventris, see thrush, rufous-bellied
turtle, big-headed Pantanal swamp 91, *151*
Tyrannus
  albogularis, see kingbird, white-throated
  savanna, see flycatcher, fork-tailed
tyrant
  cattle 81, *81*
  streamer-tailed 80
tyrant-manakin, pale-bellied 82, 135, 146

UeSo Chalana Pantanal 141
UeSo Pantanal Lodge 133
ungulates **39–42**
Uropelia campestris, see ground dove, long-tailed
Vanellus chilensis, see lapwing, southern
Veniliornis
  mixtus, see woodpecker, checkered
  passerinus, see woodpecker, little
Victoria cruziana, see waterlily, giant
vipers **97**
vireo
  red-eyed 83
  chivi 83
vultures 63
  black *64*, 65
  king 65
  lesser yellow-headed 65
  turkey 65

warbler, flavescent 87
wasps **114**
  cuckoo 114
  mud-dauber *114*
  warrior 114
waterlily, giant 15, *15*, 141, 155, 159, 160
water tyrant, black-backed 81
wetlands **14–15**
what to bring 170

when to travel 170
whistling-duck, black-bellied *58*
wolf, maned 17, 20, 28, *28*, 38, 129, 141, 149, 153, 155, 159–60
woodcreeper **78**
  great rufous 79, 125, 134, 149
  narrow-billed 79
woodnymph, fork-tailed 73, 137
woodpeckers **77**, 146
  checkered 77
  cream-backed 77
  cream-coloured 77, 129, 140
  crimson-crested 77, 129, 133
  golden-green 77
  green-barred 77
  lineated 77, 77
  little 77
  pale-crested 77, 129
  white *77*, 77, 127, 131, 140
  white-fronted 127, 150
wood-rail, grey-cowled *59*, 59, 125
woodstar, amethyst 72
worm lizard, red 94
wren
  buff-breasted 84, 135–7
  fawn-breasted 84, 138, 140
  house 84
  thrush-like 84

Xiphocolaptes major, see woodcreeper, great rufous
Xolmis
  cinereus, see monjita, grey
  irupero, see monjita, white

yellowlegs, lesser 61
yellowthroat, masked 87, *87*

Zebrilus undulatus, see heron, zigzag
Zenaida auriculata, see dove, eared
Zonotrichia capensis, see sparrow, rufous-collared

Small group birding tours worldwide
Superior **quality** and **conservation** donations set us apart

www.birdingecotours.com info@birdingecotours.com

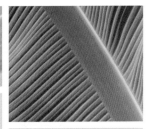

Hummingbirds
A Celebration of Nature's Jewels

Glenn Bartley
Andy Swash

Birds of the
Tropical
Andes

Owen Deutsch
Michael J. Parr

Wildlife of Ecuador
A Photographic Field Guide to Birds,
Mammals, Reptiles, and Amphibians

Andrés Vásquez Noboa
Photography by Pablo Cervantes Daza

Field Guide to the
Birds of
Chile

Daniel E. Martínez Piña
& Gonzalo E. González Cifuentes

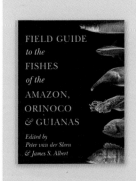

FIELD GUIDE
to the
FISHES
of the
AMAZON,
ORINOCO
& GUIANAS

Edited by
Peter van der Sleen
& James S. Albert

A field guide to the
Larger Mammals
of South America

Richard Webb and Jeff Blincow

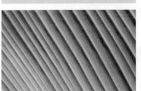

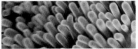

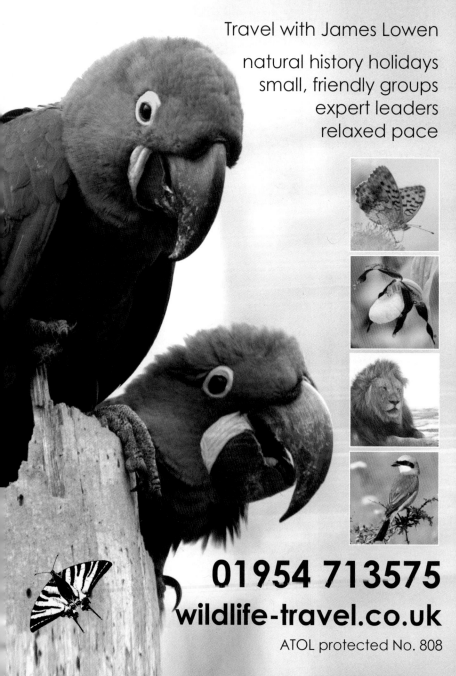

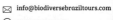

Life is out here.